AF228909

BATTLEGROUND BÉXAR

BATTLEGROUND

The 1835 Siege of San Antonio

Béxar

RICHARD L. CURILLA

State House Press

STATE HOUSE PRESS

At Schreiner University • Kerrville, TX • 325-660-1752 • www.mcwhiney.org

Cataloging-in-Publication Data

Names: Curilla, Richard L. author.
Title: Battleground Béxar: the 1835 siege of San Antonio / Richard L. Curilla.
Description: First edition. | Kerrville, TX: State House Press, 2022. | Includes bibliographical references, illustrations, and index.
Identifiers: ISBN 9781649670090 (cloth); ISBN 9781649670113 (e-book)
Subjects: LCSH: San Antonio (Tex.) – History – Siege, 1835. | Texas – History – Revolution, 1835-1836 – Campaigns.
Classification: LCC F390 (print) | DCC 976.4

First edition 2022

Cover and page design by Allen Griffith of Eye 4 Design

Printed in Canada by Friesens

Distributed by Texas A&M University Press Consortium
800-826-8911
www.tamupress.com

CONTENTS

INSPIRATION AND ACKNOWLEDGMENTS

The Birth of a Passion

If one were to label me, I am probably an "avocational historian." This is certainly foreign to my college degree from Penn State as a Bachelor of Arts with an emphasis on Theater and Film. The truth is that, in addition to filmmaking, I have a passion for history. Unlike professional historians, however, I am only into certain history.

Like so many other children growing up in the mid-1950's, I got hooked on the Disneyland TV presentation of "Davy Crockett at the Alamo." Fess Parker as Davy became my greatest television hero, even beating the Lone Ranger, Superman and Zorro. Within a few years, after the Davy Crockett "craze" had mostly died out, the flame was reignited by John Wayne with his monumental 1960 motion picture "The Alamo," a multi-million-dollar, giant-screen epic aimed at an older viewing audience. I was thrilled all over again.

At this point, family encouragement kicked in. On our summer vacation, Dad and Mother took me to San Antonio, Texas, to see the real Alamo. After four days of visits to the historic site and poking around the charming San Antonio River Walk, we drove 120 miles west to visit John Wayne's sets built for his movie. These were located on the Shahan Angus Ranch near Brackettville. Owner Happy Shahan treated us like "kinfolk," and I was instantly captured by the engaging replicas of the 1836 Alamo fort and the village of San Antonio.

Since Happy Shahan continued to promote his movie set for other Hollywood films as well as tourism, and I had just started college at Penn State in theater and film production, my summer job became working at Happy Shahan's "Alamo Village," albeit as a tourist entertainer. In 1967, Happy landed another major Hollywood production for the Fall, a western called "Bandolero!" I wanted to stay for the filming, but my mother insisted that my college education was more important. Then my advisor at Penn State, David H. Shepard (also head of the Film Department and a major film enthusiast and collector) went to bat for me. "Richard will get far more experience in filmmaking" he told Mother "by watching a major 20th Century Fox movie being made, than we could ever teach him in two courses at Penn State." She finally acquiesced—Dad was already on my side—and I spent the Fall on the set watching this major western go together. I even got to be in a scene with my long-time hero James Stewart! The director of photography, William H. Clothier (a hero of mine because he had been the chief cinematographer on John Wayne's "The Alamo"), took me under his wing, and I watched his every move.

After graduating from Penn State, I continued to work in the Film Department as motion picture equipment manager and instructor. Then in 1983, I moved to Texas and ultimately to Brackettville in 1988 to work full-time at Alamo Village as a tourist entertainer and guide.

So how did this Alamo passion turn into a deep interest in Spanish Colonial San Antonio of 1835-1836? Quite simply, while others were busy building models and drawing pictures of the historic Alamo, not even realizing there had been a town outside the walls, I fell in love with this quaint Spanish colonial village across the river. My passion for the town actually began as the result of seeing a drawing in a children's book titled *The Story of the Alamo—Told in Exciting Pictures* by Frederic Ray, purchased for me by my father in the Alamo's gift shop during our 1961 visit. It included a two-page drawing of San Fernando Church and Plaza de las Islas (also called Main Plaza).

This drawing, plus Chapter 1 of Lon Tinkle's wonderful 1958 book, *13 Days to Glory—The Siege of the Alamo,* introduced me to the town and its atmosphere. In his first chapter, he tells a very visual story of a young sentry watching for the enemy from the bell tower of San Fernando Church and observing life down below. He also describes the sentry's view of the Alamo, "the mission that rose out of the hard-stamped earth a scant half-mile east, its handful of buildings barely catching the morning sun inside the rectangular outer walls." This imaginative description instilled an image in my mind that fanned my imagination. I wanted to stand in that bell tower.

Contributors to the Passion

Many books have contributed to my passion over the years. Walter Lord wrote the quintessential Alamo book in 1961 entitled *A Time to Stand—The Epic of the Alamo Seen as a Great National Experience*. Highly accurate due to Lord's thorough research, it has never been equaled. In it, he clearly describes the town's "undeniable charm" composed of "flat-roofed adobe houses that lined the narrow streets." For me, this image stuck.

After learning much about this Spanish-Colonial town, I found myself disappointed with John Wayne's sets at Alamo Village. Wayne's art director Alfred Ybarra designed and built a passionate Alamo compound, but his town was nothing more than a typical western movie street with a Mexican look, and his San Fernando Church bore absolutely no resemblance to the historic structure. It was a wonderful place for tourism and moviemaking but clearly not for what it was built to represent. While I did spend some time in its bell tower staring at the Alamo (incorrectly placed 90 degrees off in relation to the town), I still longed for accuracy.

Ultimately, I became film liaison for motion pictures being shot at Alamo Village, and, in 2001, I hosted Hollywood production designer Michael Corenblith who was scouting locations for a new movie about the Alamo to be produced by Ron Howard. Spending the day together, Michael and I bonded, and I stayed in touch with him even though the decision was made to build their sets from scratch at another location near Austin. Michael was tasked with designing and building both the Alamo and San Antonio for the film, and from September 2001 to April 2002, I became, in his words, "the only human I was able to barrage with questions." He even started calling my "Richiepedia." I loved every minute of it. By the beginning of production in 2003, he had designed and constructed highly accurate sets for both the Alamo and the town with an excellent replica of San Fernando Church. My most exciting moment was when he first took me up into the bell tower, and I got to view the Alamo in the distance—from the right direction. Thanks to this imaginative and generous man, I was realizing a childhood dream. During the world premiere of "The Alamo" at the Majestic Theater in San Antonio on March 27, 2004, I was honored to have a seat with Michael and the main production team. After these exciting adventures, Michael and I stayed in touch, and, several years later, he introduced me to SketchUp, the architectural design computer program I ultimately used to create the virtual models I used for illustrations in this book.

Much appreciation also goes to John Lee Hancock, the writer-director of the 2004 movie "The Alamo," for allowing me to look over his shoulder during the filming and sharing his excitement over certain scenes that he would have his assistant re-run for me on the video-assist monitor. We also have remained good friends.

Many other friends and colleagues have contributed to the research and writing of this book through their friendship, guidance and publication over the years. I got to know Dr. Richard Bruce Winders, later to be historian and curator of the Alamo for 23 years, when he was participating in a living history reenactment at Alamo Village. His 2004 book, *Sacrificed at the Alamo—Tragedy and Triumph in the Texas Revolution* as well as a few great conversations have taught me how to write a book. In February 2004, Bruce presented me with a copy of this wonderfully informative book and included a handwritten 1836 toast: "As you travel through life, may you live well on the road." I have indeed, Bruce, as I'm sure you have. Thank you.

Another friend, whose books and personal encouragement have meant a lot over the years, is Dr. Stephen L. Hardin, the quintessential Texas historian and author. During a walking tour he gave in San Antonio, he kindly threw me "plums" if he thought I might know the answer to a specific question. We have also had some good talks at friend Joan Headley's wonderful annual gatherings. His book *Texian Illiad—A Military History of the Texas Revolution* is a must for every person interested in Texas history. Steve served as historian for John Lee Hancock, writer-director of Ron Howard's "The Alamo."

The military historian on "The Alamo" was Alan Huffines, another long-time buddy. Alan has always encouraged me in my endeavors and is often the first to applaud my on-line posts. His Osprey book, *The Texas War of Independence 1835-1836—From Outbreak to the Alamo to San Jacinto*, is careful to include Act 1 of the war: Gonzales through the Battle of Béxar. This important and exciting period is often ignored or minimized by writers and historians.

Dr. Alwyn Barr, in 1991, had written a succinct 94-page book titled *Texans in Revolt—The Battle for San Antonio, 1835*. This short but thorough book plus Dr. Barr's lectures have been major inspirations for my book.

Dr. James E. Crisp was kind enough to allow me to use portions of his new translation of German adventurer Herman Ehrenberg's account as a participant in the Battle of Béxar. This has added much insight and color to the story and balances well with other participants quoted.

Several letters had to be translated from Spanish. Help with these came from friends Gail Goth, Rick Range, Juan Soto, and Dr. Rocio Gil Martinez y Escobar of Mexico City. Archive translator John Wheat from the Dolph Briscoe Center for American History, University of Texas in Austin, who is more familiar with archaic Spanish and military terms, provided an excellent translation of a particularly difficult letter.

James Boddie of Canton, Georgia, generously created all the 3-D figures that populate my SketchUp models, thus adding life to my book illustrations. These include commanders, frontiersmen, townspeople, New Orleans Greys, Tejanos and Mexican soldiers according to my needs and descriptions. In addition, he also designed cottonwood trees and a versatile three-piece *jacal* (Mexican shack) used throughout my virtual model of the town. The intricate columns for the Alamo facade and the highly realistic saint icons for its four niches are his work as well.

Mark Lemon, of Acworth, Georgia, has provided much visual and in-formational stimuli for me in his book *The Illustrated Alamo, 1836: A Photographic Journey* (State House Press, 2008). With numerous photographs by Gary Foreman of Mark's very realistic and highly accurate scale model of the Alamo compound, Mark has presented details I had never noticed before. His physical model was also the basic inspiration for my virtual model of the Alamo, and his numerous well-researched illustrations over the years have provided me with additional visual understanding.

Gary Zaboly, a Yankee like me and just as fascinated with the Alamo and the Texas Revolution, is a top historical author and artist. His magnum opus, in my opinion, is another one-of-a-kind history book titled *An Altar for Their Sons: The Alamo and the Texas Revolution in Contemporary Newspaper Accounts* (State House Press, 2011). In the section of his book presenting articles on the Siege of Béxar, I was able to latch onto details not available in any other sources.

Clinton M. M. McKenzie, Historical Archaeologist at the Center for Archaeological Research at the University of Texas at San Antonio, provided much help, not the least of which was digging through records and pinpointing the location of the Cadena house on Acequia Street (now called Main Avenue), clearly making it the third goal originally planned for the Federalists' attack on December 5, 1835. Clint is a very generous colleague and friend.

Susan Snow, World Heritage Coordinator and Archaeologist for the San Antonio Missions National Historical Park, introduced me to a richly detailed 543-page dissertation by James E. Ivey titled Of Various Magnificence—The Architectural History of the San Antonio Missions in the Colonial Period and the Nineteenth Century. Mr. Ivey's thorough research enabled me to rework my virtual models of Missions Concepción and Espada into more accurate renditions of their condition in 1835. Susan also gave me and my group of three a very informative personal tour of Mission Concepción.

San Antonio folks who have helped in various ways are Kay Hindes, former San Antonio city archaeologist, Betty Bueché, Director of the Bexar

Heritage & Parks Department, David Carlson, Ph.D., the Béxar County Archivist, and Edward Aranda, who practically lives in the archives building gathering information on the location, ownership and history of many of San Antonio's Spanish Colonial buildings. Edward was my main source of information for the four houses on the north face of Plaza de las Islas (Main Plaza) that played a major part in the final breakthrough and battle.

A big debt of gratitude is owed to William R. Chemerka, William Groneman and Michael Boldt of *The Alamo Journal* for publishing my original two articles on the Siege and Battle of Béxar, and particularly to Bill Chemerka for giving me the first opportunity to deliver my Battle of Béxar slide presentation at the 2016 Alamo Society Symposium. These footholds encouraged me to climb the mountain and create this book.

Long-time friend John Farkis has developed into a wonderful author on moviemaking, and, while I encouraged him to do so when he was still unsure of himself, his triumph has encouraged me to research and write this book.

Friend and colleague Brad Ponder has come to my rescue numerous times during the preparation of my book, and now I must come to his and encourage him to get his book finished. It will be a worthy volume about some unexplored aspects related to San Antonio and the Battle of the Alamo.

A big thank you to the world-renowned Phil Collins for his continuing friendship and encouragement—and great music. An avid Alamo buff, Phil visited Alamo Village some years ago, and I gave him the grand tour. Later we reunited at another one of Joan Headley's gatherings and have stayed in touch ever since.

To my core group of emotional support goes special and undying gratitude. Rocco Fortunato, my close friend since High School in Pennsylvania, also came to Texas and stayed! He has been an award-winning music producer and drummer for professional rock and country groups all over the United States and many other countries. He has also collaborated with me on my own film and video projects over the years as actor, technical provider, film music score writer and producer, and over-all encourager. His guidance has always been appreciated, and most wonderful of all, he has cats!

Dear heart Kristi Hale lives in far-off Dallas but we stay in touch constantly, and she is always ready to cheer me on and share moods—a close confidant. My niece Connie Curilla spent many years as a missionary in Haiti and is now back home in State College, PA, where I spend the holidays. Her late father (my brother, and 20 years my senior) claimed we were both 13 years old and always would be, even though I was 13 when Connie was born. Connie and I are like brother and sister. Her adventures in Haiti, still nearly in its colonial state in some areas, have helped my understanding of early Spanish Colonial San Antonio de Béxar. Connie is always my greatest fan.

I owe a major debt of gratitude to my proofreaders for drawing my attention to errors that I continually missed in my own rereads. These patient and generous folks were Kristi Hale, Connie Curilla and my good friend Stacie Todino.

Dr. Donald S. Frazier, my publisher at State House Press and director at The Texas Center at Schreiner University in Kerrville, Texas, has performed wonders guiding this newcomer over the hurdles. My thanks to him and to his wonderful wife Susan, who is chief financial officer at

State House Press. My hat is off to their supremely capable team that has fielded my book through to completion. A big thank you!

Additional folks who have helped me in one way or another during my book incubation period include Carol Pirie, Leah Durden, Tom Copeland, Bill and Karen Beckwith, Tom Schobert, David Lee and Jana Murray, Wendy Fortunato Lieberman, Donna Pritzel, Windy Goodloe, Stephen Joseph Oleszek, Betty Jean Walker, Ela Ponder, Ned Huthmacher, Craig Covner, Tom Feeley, Mike Harris, Tony Pasqua, Ken Pruitt, Frank Thompson, Jack Edmondson, Wade Dillon, James V. Woodrick, Carla Curry, Daniel Orlandi, Patrick Saunders, Albert Seguín Gonzales, Dustin Klisz, George Nelson, Chris Nolen and Charles Martin Brazil.

A huge thank you to all who have helped over the years, and my apologies to anybody I might have missed.

—*Richard L. Curilla*
July 10, 2022

FOREWORD

Residents and visitors have long acknowledged that San Antonio de Béxar is a magical place. Moreover, it seems to have been so even before its founding in 1718 as a Franciscan mission and colonial outpost. For eons, a river flowed whose life-giving waters attracted animal and human life to its banks. Spanish explorers first encountered Payaya Indians inhabiting the area around San Pedro Springs. The original native dwellers called the vicinity *Yanaguana*, which meant "refreshing waters." On June 13,1691, Spanish soldiers and missionaries first set eyes on the river and the Payaya village. It happened to be the feast day of St. Anthony of Padua, and thus they named the spot and stream "San Antonio" in his honor. Even today, it is the river and the celebrated "River Walk" that charm tourists and fill them with such a wonderous sense of enchantment. It's just this simple: the river is life. Without those "refreshing waters," there would be no missions, no Alamo, no great and growing city.

As the adage tells it, "Every Texan has two hometowns, his own and San Antonio." That is certainly the case with Richard — his friends call him "Rich" — Curilla. Although he is a native of Pennsylvania, even as a youth the Alamo City seemed to beckon him, first on the silver screen and then by way of a job opportunity. As fate would have it, however, it would not be the real San Antonio that lured him but rather a cinematic version.

James Tullis "Happy" Shahan played a major role in Rich's story. He was a rancher, producer, full-time booster, and part-time mayor of Brackettville, a dusty, sun-bleached South Texas town in Kinney County. Shahan worked tirelessly to interest Hollywood in utilizing the Brackettville area as a movie location. In 1951, he hit pay dirt when he persuaded executives at Paramount Studios to film the western *Arrowhead* near the town. Other productions followed, including *The Last Command* in 1955. But Shahan's big "get" arrived when screen legend John Wayne agreed to shoot his historical epic *The Alamo* (1960) not only near Brackettville but actually on Happy's ranch.

As was common in the industry, Wayne intended to build his set as facades. Yet when he ran out of money and halted construction, Shahan agreed to continue the work while the Duke raised more funds. With an eye fixed firmly on the future, Shahan drove a hard bargain, shrewdly insisting that the set incorporate functional buildings, complete with four walls, floors, and roofs. Wayne agreed.

When filming wrapped, possession of the set reverted to the land owner — one James T. Shahan. He lost no time marketing "Alamo Village" as an Old West town, tourist attraction, and (of course) a movie set. In the years that followed, the site attracted numerous productions that greatly benefited the local economy. Shahan's wheeling and dealing did not go unnoticed. In 1995, Governor George W. Bush lauded him as the "Father of the Texas movie industry."

The paths of Curilla and Shahan intersected while Rich was pursuing his bachelor's degree in theater arts and film at Penn State. During summer vacations, he made the long journey to Texas to work part time at Alamo Village. Every summer from 1966 to 1970, Rich entertained visitors in comedic street performances. Shahan did not forget the enthusiastic

Pennsylvanian. In 1988, he offered Rich full-time employment as Alamo Village's director and tourist host. For all intents and purposes, Rich became Happy's right-hand man, supervising operations and putting out fires.

When Alamo Village hosted production companies, Rich served as Shahan's film liaison. Happy knew how to talk business; Rich knew how to talk filmmaking. It was an opportune partnership. Rich even acted in a few of the features shot at Alamo Village. He has fond memories — and several great stories — revolving around his time on set with Hollywood royalty James Stewart and Raquel Welch during the 1968 filming of *Bandolero!*

Rich assisted Shahan until his death in 1996. Then he continued in the same capacity for Virginia Shahan, who assumed management of Alamo Village after her husband's passing. Rich worked along side Mrs. Shahan until her demise in 2009. In 2010, the surviving Shahan children decided to discontinue operations.

Freed from his responsibilities at Alamo Village, Rich now pursued his own interests. Having spent years working in (and explaining the operations of) John Wayne's faux San Antonio, he wanted to learn more about the history of the real one. Since childhood, he had possessed a fascination for the Alamo and the Texas Revolution, a passion that had drawn him to Texas in the first place. He began an intense study of the 1835 siege and storming of Béxar, an episode that historians had largely ignored. Since it was an urban battle, it was essential that he gain an understanding of the configuration of the town as it then existed. This proved a challenging task, as a thriving, modern city had overgrown the site, obliterating most of the historic features.

The new millennium brought a new cinematic Alamo, this one helmed by director John Lee Hancock. Early on, while searching for an appropriate filming location, the production staff reached out to Rich. Although the producers ultimately opted not to shoot at Alamo Village, Rich remained closely associated with the project because of his deep knowledge and many Texas contacts. (It was through Rich's good graces that the team learned about some obscure history professor named Hardin, who eventually got a gig as the film's historical advisor.)

Under the watchful eye of production designer Michael Corenblith, an entirely new set underwent construction on the Eugene Reimers Ranch outside Dripping Springs, Texas. During pre-production, Corenblith and Curilla became close working associates. Indeed, it was Corenblith who introduced Rich to the software frequently employed in the industry, a program sold under the name SketchUp.

It was a steep learning curve, but Rich went to work, eventually mastering the program. It provided the keys to the kingdom. Rich understood that with this cutting-edge technology, he now had the tools he needed to recreate 1835 Béxar in three dimensions. He set about reconstructing the contours of a lost time and place — down to the millimeter. The illustrations herein provide ample evidence of his success.

The volume you hold is nothing less than a time machine. It transports readers back to San Antonio de Béxar during one of its most crucial periods. Over the years, I have conducted several tours of downtown San Antonio. It is always fascinating (and, frankly, more than a little humbling) to have Rich accompany me on these. No other living person knows as much about historic San Antonio as he does; he is nothing less than a walking encyclopedia. As absorbing as those tours were, we could only imagine the various structures Rich described. Now, thanks to all his hard work, we can actually *see* them. Not only that, we can view them at a level of detail that would have been impossible only a few years ago. As a longtime student of the Texas Revolution, I stand in awe of Curilla's achievement.

This book raises the bar for all historians. By skillfully combining a highly readable narrative with computer-generated images, Rich has contributed mightily to our collective knowledge of this critical event in Texas history. I should also recognize Dr. Donald S. Frazier and all the good people at State House Press. Not only is this an important book, but it is also a beautiful one — a work that will stand as a benchmark for years to come. Rich Curilla has provided a visual feast.

Chow down.

—*Stephen L. Hardin*
Abilene, Texas
June 2022

THE SIEGE OF BÉXAR, ORDER OF BATTLE

THE FEDERALIST ARMY OF TEXAS, OR THE ARMY OF THE PEOPLE

October 11 to November 24, 1835

Commanding General

Stephen F. Austin

General Staff

Colonel James Bowie, Aide de Camp

Colonel Warren D. C. Hall, Adjutant General

Colonel Francis W. Johnson, Adjutant General

Colonel David B. McComb, Assistant Adjutant General

Patrick C. Jack, Quartermaster General

Valentine Bennet, Assistant Quarter Master General

Noah Scott, Deputy Assistant Quartermaster

William H. Jack, Brigade Inspector

Peter W. Grayson, Aide de Camp

William T. Austin, Aide de Camp

Regimental Officers

Colonel John H. Moore

Lieutenant Colonel Edward Burleson

Lieutenant Colonel Philip A. Sublett

Major Alexander Somervell

Volunteer Companies

Captain Thomas Alley

Captain Plácido Benavides

Captain Andrew Briscoe

Captain Mathew Caldwell

Captain Robert W. Coleman

Captain Jacob Eberly

Captain James W. Fannin

Captain Michael R. Goheen

Captain William Hall

Captain Byrd Lockhart

Captain Albert Martin

Captain Robert C. Morris (Second Company, New Orleans Greys)

Captain J. Robinson

Captain James G. Swisher

Artillery

Captain James C. Neill

Captain Thomas L. F. Parrott

Scouting Companies

Colonel Benjamin R. Milam

Captain Juan Seguín

Captain William B. Travis

Scouts

Hendrick Arnold

Erastus "Deaf" Smith

John W. Smith

Surgeon General and Chaplain

William P. Smith

Medical Corps

Joseph E. Field

Thomas Kenney

Amos Pollard

THE FEDERALIST ARMY OF TEXAS

November 24 to December 11, 1835

Commanding General

Edward R. Burleson

General Staff

Colonel Francis W. Johnson, Adjutant and Inspector General

Colonel Philip A. Sublett, Assistant Adjutant and Inspector General

Colonel William T. Austin, Aide de Camp

Captain N. R. Brister, Adjutant

Colonel William H. Jack

Major Alexander Somervell

First Division

Colonel Benjamin R. Milam

Major Robert C. Morris

Volunteer Companies

Captain John Crain

Captain George English

Captain William Landrum

Captain Thomas Llewellyn

Captain William Patton

Captain John York

Artillery

Lieutenant Colonel Nidland Franks

Second Division

Colonel Francis W. Johnson

Colonel James Grant

Volunteer Companies

Captain Thomas Alley

Captain Plácido Benevides

Captain Thomas H. Breece (First Company, New Orleans Greys)

Captain William G. Cooke (Second Company, New Orleans Greys)

Captain Peter J. Duncan

Captain H. H. Edwards

Captain J. W. Peacock

Captain James W. Swisher

Reserves and Scouts

Colonel James Bowie

Captain Thomas W. Bordon

Captain John M. Bradley

Scouts

Hendrick Arnold

Erastus "Deaf" Smith

John W. Smith

Volunteer Companies

Captain James Cheshire

Captain Robert W. Coleman

Captain M. B. Lewis

Captain John S. Roberts

Nacogdoches Company

Captain Michael Ruth

Captain Juan Seguín

Captain Peyton Splane

Captain William Sutherland

Captain Henry Teal

Artillery

Captain James C. Neill

Medical Corps

Joseph E. Field

Thomas J. Gazely

Thomas Kenney

Albert M. Levy

Amos Pollard

EJERCITO MEXICANO

General Martín Perfecto de Cos

Infantry

Colonel Nicolás Condelle

Permanente Battalion Morelos

Additional Infantry Companies

First Nuevo León

Second Nuevo León

Pueblo

Río Grande

First Tamaulipas

Second Tamaulipas

Cavalry

Colonel Domingo de Ugartechea

Colonel Mariano Cos

Presidial Companies

Agua Verde

First Company, Álamo de Parras

Second Company, Álamo de Parras

La Bahia

Béxar

Lampazos

BATTLEGROUND BÉXAR

1

FLASHPOINT GONZALES

For Texas, 1835 would be a decisive year. The region now known as Texas was part of Mexico, and an awkward appendage of the Mexican state of Coahuila to the south in a blended political unit saddled with the unwieldy name Coahuila y Tejas. This hybrid entity mixed Mexican citizens with ancestral roots in La Frontera with a blend of newcomers from the United States and elsewhere who had, in most instances, not even been residents for half of a generation.

This marriage of strangers had other stresses, too. For the last few years, Mexico's politics had whiplashed between feuding factions. Some — the Centralists — favored a strong central government that would keep regional warlords and powerbrokers in check, while others — the Federalists — saw the country's widely differing regions as part of the national character as well as its strength. Bound together by a common nationality, these regions could play to their strengths and answer to local conditions rather than being tied to political solutions that might not suit the needs of their people. Settlers from the United States favored this view, believing they brought a unique character and ingenuity to the nation that complimented the gritty pragmatism of the local Tejanos but might find itself out of step with Mexicans in provinces father south in places like Oaxaca or Michoacán.

Some leaders tried having it both ways. In 1832, the president of Mexico, General António López de Santa Anna, championed the popular Federal Constitution of 1824. Texians, as the settlers from the United States called themselves, and their Tejano friends and neighbors were quite happy with this Federal document patterned after the U.S. Constitution; they believed Santa Anna to be the savior of the nation and a leader who would break the cycle of coup and countercoup, civil war and insurgency, that had destabilized the nation. Once settled in the president's chair, however, Santa Anna changed his position. He tore up the Federal constitution, disbanded the national congress, and established a Centralist despotism with the support of the clergy and wealthy landowners. He claimed that his benevolent authority was the best form of government for Mexico; the inhabitants needed a firm hand. "One hundred years from now," he wrote, "the Mexican people will not be ready for self-rule." This, of course, ran contrary to everything the American settlers believed true about human nature.

Santa Anna believed his distrust of the people north of the Rio Bravo del Norte (the Rio Grande) to be justified. Two years earlier, the most energetic organizer of American colonists, Stephen Fuller Austin, had made the 900-mile overland journey to Mexico City to plead the cause of Federalism. His specific purpose was to convince the president to give Texas full statehood rather than continue its connection — and subservience — to Coahuila. Santa Anna, quickly tiring of affairs of state, had temporarily installed his proxy, Valentín Gómez Farías, who as acting president turned a deaf ear to the Texian's pleading. The disgruntled Austin penned an angry letter back home complaining of the government's shortsightedness before starting the long return journey.

Austin's letter headed north ahead of him and arrived in San Antonio de Béxar in weeks. "I recommend," he wrote, "that the ayuntamientos of Texas place themselves in communication with each other without a moment's delay for the purpose of organizing a local government for Texas as a state of the Mexican federation according to the law of May 7, 1824." The normally cool-headed Austin was suggesting that the local governments in Texas organize themselves to defy Santa Anna's Centralism. "This step is indispensable as a preparatory measure for there is no doubt but that the fate of Texas depends upon itself and not upon this government; nor that that country is lost if its inhabitants do not take its affairs into their own hands," Austin lectured. "I am firmly persuaded that what I recommend is the only means of saving us from anarchy and total ruin."

In the eyes of the law-abiding Tejanos of the Béxar *ayuntamiento*, this was sedition, and more than they could bear. After discussion, they decided to forward the letter to the national government. In short, they betrayed Austin to buy themselves favor with the new political powers.

As Austin passed through Saltillo, he was detained. Vicente Filisola was an Italian-born general in the Mexican army and a fellow empresario — a settlement promoter — in Texas. He knew and liked Austin but found himself duty bound to follow orders. On January 3, 1834, Filisola showed Austin his arrest order. The Texian would be heading back to Mexico City "as a prisoner to answer charges that the government would bring against him," Filisola wrote, "without saying what they were."

Upon returning to Mexico City, Austin learned that he was being accused of trying to incite insurrection in Texas. "He was imprisoned incommunicado in the dungeons of the former Inquisition," Filisola wrote. Austin languished for nearly two years even though no formal charges were made against him and no court would accept jurisdiction of his case. After months in confinement, Austin was released under a general amnesty and finally gained an audience with President Santa Anna. After the encounter, Austin wrote to his friend Samuel May Williams: "He informed me yesterday that he should visit Texas and take me with him. . . He is very friendly to Texas [so said Santa Anna] and it would be an advantage to that country if he would pay it a visit." Austin returned to Texas via the Gulf of Mexico, and by the time he arrived in New Orleans, he had grown even more cynical. He wrote to Mary Austin Holley, a cousin in the United States, "Gen. Santa Anna told me he should like to visit Texas next month — as a friend. His visit is uncertain — his friendship more so." Thus, despite the president's show of warmth toward Austin, he returned to Texas fearing Santa Anna's veiled duplicity.

While in prison in Mexico, Austin had found clarity and focus and had contemplated retiring from public life. "I am happier than I have been for 14 years, for during all that period my mind has been laboring and worrying for the benefit of others and for the common good," he wrote to his friend Williams. "My thoughts are now confined, or I should say are beginning to confine themselves to a narrower space — myself, my family, my own individual affairs — it is a novelty, a new life to me, for heretofore I have thought more of other matters than of my own — but I shall soon get accustomed to it and be much happier — I want some money to travel next year — that at present is all my *cuidado* [all I care about]." The skirmish at Gonzales and the prospect of war had changed all of that.

Instead of retirement, Austin now planned a rebellion. Even so, he labored under fatigue and illness acquired from his time in Mexico. Upon his return, the people of Texas, according to nephew Moses Austin Bryan, had welcomed him home "as one risen from the dead." This resurrection carried with it a grave responsibility. "All eyes are turned towards you," wrote a young lawyer and political gadfly, William Barret Travis; "and the independent manly stand you have taken has given the Sovereigns confidence in themselves — Texas can be wielded by you and you alone; and her destiny is now completely in your hands. I have every confidence that you will guide us safe through all our perils."

Santa Anna's actions also played poorly elsewhere in Mexico. The strong, wealthy, and jealously independent state of Zacatecas immediately rebelled against what inhabitants considered tyranny and dictatorship. In May 1835, Santa Anna answered this defiance and marched north with a military force of 3,000 men to quell the revolt. In the battle that followed — and the two days of rape and pillage that Santa Anna allowed his army as a reward — he killed more than 2,500 of his fellow Mexicans in that city. Learning that there was also unrest in Texas resulting from his unpopular shift in government policy, Santa Anna determined to raise a large army and march farther north; he would put an end to this discontent in the American settlements as well. Such an army would take time to organize, however, so he sent his best general, Martín Perfecto de Cos, to garrison the key town of San Antonio de Béxar (now modern San Antonio) to better monitor the unrest.

When Centralist forces arrived on the coast of Texas, Austin drew a logical conclusion. On September 19, 1835, his friend Gail Borden published a circular presenting his evolving views of Texas' relationship with Mexico. The most peaceful intellect in Texas announced: "War is our only resource. There is no other remedy but to defend our rights, ourselves, & our country by force of arms."

The Mexican authorities understood this danger as well and moved to disarm the people of Texas. Colonel Domingo de Ugartechea, commandant of the presidial troops permanently stationed at Béxar, sent a detachment of 100 soldiers under Lieutenant. Francisco Castañeda to the town of Gonzales, sixty-seven miles east.[1] Castañeda was under orders to retrieve a bronze 6-pounder cannon that had been lent to the community in 1831 for protection against hostile Indians. The locals, having been incited by Austin's circular, decided that this was deliberate disarmament at a crucial moment. At the crossing of the Guadalupe River just south of town eighteen townsmen pulled the ferry to the east bank of and stalled Castañeda until other Texians could be rallied from neighboring communities.

OCTOBER 2, 1835

On October 2, this hastily formed militia — now numbering 160 colonists — confronted Castañeda's force camped on Ezekiel Williams' farm seven miles upstream from town. The Texians rolled forward two cannon and waved a homemade flag over them, challenging Castañeda: "Come and take it!" A few shots were fired, and Castañeda, a Federalist himself and somewhat sympathetic to the insurgents, found himself in an untenable situation. Ugartechea had ordered him to avoid engaging a superior force. "Today, at five in the morning, I was attacked . . . by 200 Americans, more or less, with an average piece and a small cannon, and because of the superiority of the enemy forces, as by the repeated orders of Your Excellency, I have begun my withdrawal for Bejar, "Castañeda reported. The Texians had "won" their first "battle."

OCTOBER 3

The day after the confrontation on the Williams farm, the Texians formed a committee to spread the word of the dustup near Gonzales and to call for help. William S. Fisher, the chairman of the Committee of Gonzales,

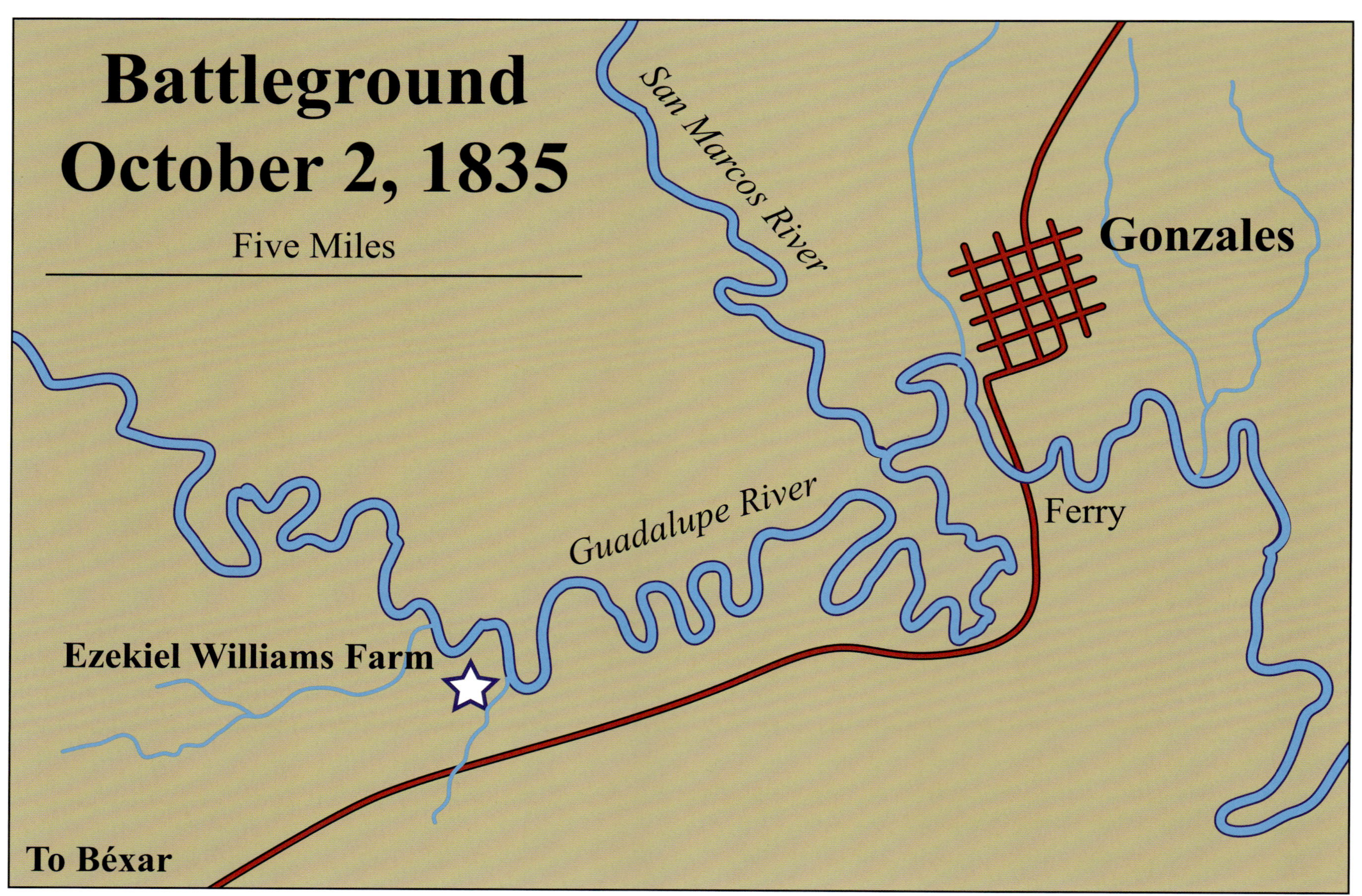

Battleground
October 2, 1835
Five Miles
San Marcos River
Gonzales
Guadalupe River
Ferry
Ezekiel Williams Farm
To Béxar

sent a report on the incident to Austin in San Felipe. Not only had a defiant band of fewer than two dozen men brushed back the Centralists as they tried to cross the Guadalupe, but Texian reinforcements had arrived and sent the Mexican *soldados* in retreat to Béxar. Even so, Fisher believed there would be consequences. "We expect a formidable attack from Ugartachie [sic]," he wrote. Barring that, the assembled Texian militia should seize the initiative and march on San Antonio "as soon as we can receive reinforcements, to prevent this country as far as possible from becoming the Battle ground. Better to fight the Centralists in their garrison at Béxar than to subject the farms and town of the settlements to the scourge of war."

The day that Austin had warned against had arrived. He responded by sending out another circular outlining the grievances that had led to open hostilities. "It is well known to all that the reforms . . . now being made in Mexico, contemplate the abolition of the whole federal system, the establishment of a central or consolidated government, which is to absorb and swallow up all the powers and authorities of the nation," the bulletin read. "Military commandancies will supply the place of the state governments, and the vested rights of Texas under the constitution and law of May 7, 1824, are to be disregarded and violated." He urged his fellow Texians to rally at Gonzales. "The head quarters of the Army of the People for the present is at Gonzales. It is already respectable in numbers, and invincible in spirit," the circular continued. "This Committee exhorts every citizen who is yet at home, to march as soon as possible to the assistance of his countrymen now in the field. The campaign was opened. Texas must be freed from military despots before it is closed."

Austin, despite his lingering fatigue and illness, was suddenly very busy in San Felipe. Gonzales had changed everything. Instead of retirement, Austin now planned a rebellion.

OCTOBER 4

The scaffolding for an insurrection had been in place since 1832. Committees of Safety and Correspondence had been increasing in number throughout the American settlements, in the same tradition as those assembled during the American Revolution. Ostensibly, their purpose was simply to secure the organization of the militia to coordinate defense against Indians, a constant threat throughout Texas. After the events at Gonzales, they suddenly had a new purpose. Austin was chairman of the committee in San Felipe de Austin, and, understanding the leadership role he must fill, he has just prepared another circular to send to committees in other communities from Nacogdoches to the Gulf Coast. "War is declared against military despotism," the document screamed. "Public opinion has proclaimed it with one united voice. The campaign has opened. The military at Bejar has advanced upon Gonzales. General Cos has arrived and threatens to overrun the country." The conflict that Austin had warned would come had arrived, yet the Texians would make the next move. "But one spirit, one common purpose, animates everyone in this department, which is to take Bejar, and drive all the military out of Texas before the campaign closes," the circular advised. "There are about three hundred volunteers at Gonzales at this time, and there will be upwards of five hundred in a few days. It is confidently believed in this quarter, that the people of the department of Nacogdoches will turn out, and join the ARMY OF THE PEOPLE, now in the field, and facing the enemy."

This insurgent army would need weapons and ammunition. "We have more men than guns," the bulletin explained, but urged those who could to gather the tools of war "from the other side of the Sabine." Not only wagonloads of muskets and cartridges but stout arms and patriot hearts would be welcomed. "Could not volunteers be had from the United

States?" the circular questioned. "Our cause is one that merits the moral and physical aid of a free and magnanimous people; and those who now step forward, may confidently expect that Texas will reward their services."

Austin had another purpose for his circular as well. He introduced a Mexican friend and colleague — a staunch Federalist — for those who did not already know him to make certain that this rebellion was not seen as a war against Mexicans. The fight was not a race war but a political contest against Centralism and military despotism, a view shared by a large percentage of local Tejanos in San Antonio de Béxar, Goliad, and elsewhere. "That distinguished and virtuous patriot, Don Lorenzo de Zavala, former governor of the State of Mexico, and late minister to France, has just arrived from his residence on the San Jacinto, and is now here," the circular continued. "He is a citizen of Texas and enters fully and warmly into the cause of the people. He also approves very much of the position they have taken against military despotism." The news spread quickly: On to Béxar!

OCTOBER 5

While Austin leaned into war, the Centralist forces under General Martín Perfecto de Cos had already landed at Copano on the Texas coast and established a base at Presidio La Bahia at the small village of Goliad. The Mexican commander trusted that the Austin of days past — the levelheaded diplomat — would help him diffuse the situation in Texas.[2] He hoped to renew that trust by sending greetings from the interim ruler of Mexico.[3] "The Most Excellent Señor President Don Miguel Barragán was pleased to recommend you to me in a most expressive way, so that I might attend you in all those matters in which you see fit to employ my insufficient talents" Cos wrote. "The Most Excellent Señor President himself tells me that, with regard to everything that is necessary to address with respect to Texas, I will find in you a man of wisdom and local knowledge, and at the same time a good citizen who looks upon his adopted country with appreciation, and who will be able to employ all of his influence on behalf of the well understood interests of the nation." Cos dismissed the Texian defiance at Gonzales and the call to arms as so many "ridiculous pretentions imposed by some men, who doubtless will be the ones who risk the least in turmoil. With their exaggerated notions, they are going to inflict great harm on honorable Texans." Surely Austin was one of these honorable Texans. As such, Cos reasoned, he should make himself useful to the government of Mexico as a law-abiding man and help to avoid a tragedy in Texas. "No man can think himself excused from contributing by all means at his disposal to prevent the misfortunes of a people worthy of a better fate," Cos wrote. The general asked Austin to meet him in Béxar. Shortly after sending this dispatch toward San Felipe, the Mexican Centralists formed their columns and marched up the San Antonio River. Austin would also be heading to Béxar, just not as a guest of Cos.

THE ARMY OF THE PEOPLE

OCTOBER 6

Austin understood his predicament. He needed either to strike fast, and decisively, or to prepare for a long, arduous fight and thus squander the initiative he believed his army held. Others were quick to point out the problem as well. Attorney Peter W. Grayson, a Virginia-born Kentuckian related to the former American President James Monroe, owned a league of land in Austin's Colony and was close to the Texian leader. He warned his friend that Mexican retribution was on its way and that time was of the essence. The Centralists still wanted that gun at Gonzales. "Col Ugartachea and probably Gen Cos are now on their march here," Grayson warned Austin, "with all their forces to take the Gun if it is not delivered." Grayson suggested stalling for time — by some sort of a ruse or diversion. "That will give us an opportunity to entertain him a little while," he wrote, "until we can get in more men."

OCTOBER 8

While Austin assembled his Army of the People, a detachment of Texian militia commanded by Captain George M. Collinsworth was heading toward Goliad. "We shall enter [Presidio La Báhia at Goliad] to Night or tomorrow, there is from 60 to 100 troops in that place," Collingsworth wrote Austin. "I have under My charge 47 Good and Effective men which I think all Sufficient to take that place." After securing that post, Collingworth would pursue the Centralists toward Béxar. This offensive move made sense. General Cos left supplies behind at La Bahía, including food and ammunition. Fearing little from the Texian insurgents, the Mexican general had left a garrison of only two dozen men to guard the depot. Collingsworth figured to make short work of such a small force.

Ninety-five miles upriver from Goliad, San Antonio de Béxar prepared for the arrival of Cos and his 500 soldiers. Colonel Domingo de Ugartechea, commanding the two companies of presidial troops in town, ordered José Ángel Navarro, the *jefe politico* (chief magistrate) of Béxar to arrange quarters for Cos and his officers. But several prominent Béxareños, including Navarro himself, refused to turn over their homes to the incoming troops. Instead, many residents, both wealthy and poor, simply locked up their homes and left town.

They had good reason for their reluctance. A generation before, in 1813, General Juaquín de Arredondo and his Spanish royalist army imprisoned or shot several hundred Béxareños after they captured the city from American insurgents, Mexicans, and Indians during Mexico's War of Independence. In addition, the Spanish general ordered the town women brutalized and locked in a building known as *"la quinta"* (the cottage), forcing them "to grind corn for his soldiers." Local memory remained fresh regarding the brutality of invading armies. That revolution — and a devastating flood in 1819 — practically finished Béxar, and the town had barely gotten back on its feet by the time this new storm burst upon it. For most Béxarenos, it was easier to flee than to cooperate and take their chances.

San Antonio de Béxar as it appeared in October 1835, looking west. San Fernando Church stands between the Plaza de las Islas in front and Plaza de Armas behind. The San Antonio River meanders in a horseshoe bend around the eastern side of the town called El Potrero (the pasture). Early locals grazed their horses in the open areas.

As columns of frightened townspeople left Béxar, some unwitting travelers happened to come into town at the same time, bewildered by the chaos they encountered. One, Samuel Augustus Maverick, was a 32-year-old American who had come to Texas to advance his fortunes. A graduate of Yale, Maverick had studied law before running for the state legislature from his hometown of Pendleton, South Carolina. He lost that race and left for Georgia to rebuild his career and reputation. There he decided that Texas beckoned, and he had crossed the Sabine in March in search of his destiny. His explorations landed him in Béxar just as the Mexican Centralist forces arrived. Colonel Ugartechea put the gregarious, well-educated, well-traveled American under arrest until he could determine his intentions.

The Nixon house (with gable roof in foreground) where Sam Maverick was held prisoner on Potrero Street.

When Maverick arrived at his new quarters, he discovered fellow American John W. Smith, a local civil engineer and surveyor, and A. H. Holms also held without charges. Despite the turn of events, the Americans occupied decent quarters. The stone house that they occupied stood on the north side of Calle del Potrero (Potrero Street) about 200 feet east of the Plaza de las Islas, the easternmost of the two main squares of Béxar. Gable-roofed, it also had a fenced back yard that backed up to the San Antonio River. Ever the observer, Maverick settled in to await his fate by pulling out a notebook to record any interesting events. He did not have to wait long. He heard that Gonzales still refused to give up its cannon. Then he noted, "This day (8th) arrived Genl Perfecto de Cos and also Ugartechea's family from Monterey." Tensions between the American colonists and the Centralist authorities seemed to be building, and the Mexican troops seemed to be planning to stay for a while.

Back in San Felipe, Austin prepared to leave for Gonzales. He had no idea how long he would be gone. He penned a quick personal note to Gail Borden in their Committee of Safety. "Send me some sugar, coffee and 4 quires paper and three or four sticks of sealing wax and some wafers — it is uncertain when I shall be back." [1]

In Nacogdoches, 150 miles to the northeast, another leading figure in the growing insurgency issued directives of his own. The newly formed provisional government of Texas had recently appointed General Sam Houston to the Department of Nacogdoches, and he wasted no time in issuing orders. He started with a history lesson and some current events. "The time has arrived when the revolutions in the interior of Mexico have resulted in the creation of a dictator, and Texas is compelled to assume an attitude defensive of her rights, and the property of her citizens," he wrote. "Our oaths and pledges to the Constitution [of 1824] have been preserved inviolate. Our hopes of promised benefits have been deferred. Our constitutions have been declared at an end, while all that is sacred is menaced by arbitrary power! The priesthood and the army are to mete out the measure of our wretchedness." The American colonists, he claimed, were innocent of any agitation. But now that the new regime in Mexico had changed the rules, Americans would defend their rights as they always had. "War is our only alternative!" Houston wrote. "War, in defense of our rights must be our motto!"

The coming conflict should not be feared, he argued. "The morning of glory is dawning upon us," Houston declared. "The work of liberty has begun. Our actions are to become a part of the history of mankind. Patriotic millions will sympathize in our struggles, while nations will admire our achievements. We must be united — subordinate to the laws and authorities which we avow, and freedom will not withhold the seal of approbation. Rally around the standard of the Constitution, entrench your rights with noble resolution, and defend them with heroic manliness. Let your valor proclaim to the world that liberty is your birthright. We cannot be conquered by all the arts of anarchy and despotism combined. In heaven and in valorous hearts we repose our confidence."

Houston believed that taking a stand against the Centralists was the duty of anyone who believed in the foundational principles of their home country — the United States. "Our only ambition is the attainment of rational liberty — the freedom of religious opinion, and just laws," he declared. "To acquire these blessings, we solemnly pledge our persons, our property, and our lives. Union and courage can achieve everything while reason combined with intelligence, can regulate all things necessary to human happiness." This was not merely a quarrel over political opinions that had been tearing at the fabric of Mexico for the last decade — it was also a contest over how the two neighboring republics in North America viewed the world.

OCTOBER 10

While Houston issued rhetorical flourishes in Nacogdoches and Austin packed his bags for Gonzales, Captain Collingsworth moved against the Centralist depot at Presidio La Bahía. His small command of about fifty men had grown to more than twice that many as Plácido Benavides, the *alcalde* (mayor) of Victoria, brought in Tejano and Texian volunteers from Victoria and the surrounding region. Collinsworth dispatched a small advance party in to scout the town just outside the walls of the fort. Suddenly, a stranger loomed up out of the darkness and almost got shot. He turned out to be the popular 47-year-old Kentucky-Texian, Benjamin Rush Milam, who had been imprisoned in Monterrey by Santa Anna's government along with the federal governor of Coahuila-y-Tejas, Augustín Viesca. Both had recently escaped and then separated, and Milam was just arriving at Goliad wondering what was going on. They filled him in and took him along on the assault.

The insurgents attacked in the early morning hours. They forced open the doors to the presidio's church and overran the post, but not before Centralist couriers had ridden away, heading toward Béxar to spread the alarm. The insurgents killed one Mexican *soldado*, wounded three others, and captured three officers and twenty-one men at the price of one man wounded. Collingsworth knew he wouldn't remain that lucky. "They have dispatched couriers for troops to several points," he wrote another Texian captain, Ben Smith, "and expect I shall need your aid . . . Come on as speedily as possible."[2] The position was important. The capture of Presídio La Bahía blocked General Cos' only supply route from the coast, and the confiscation of his munitions and provisions would severely handicap him and his army during their occupation of Béxar.

OCTOBER 11

San Antonio took on a festive atmosphere, as though the troubles in Texas were of little concern. Maverick, in his comfortable confinement, took the opportunity that Sunday to attend Mass with a large congregation of recently arrived Centralist *soldados*. The military band provided the music and filled the simple San Fernando Church and the Plaza de las Islas outside with tunes both sacred and martial. The parish priest, Padre Refúgio de la Garza, lived on the north side of this town square; as was common in the far-flung and barely governed northern *frontera* of Mexico,

he was a prominent and wealthy landowner and a father of three children. Before long, his church would become much less festive.

While Béxar prayed, Gonzales roiled with the rhythms of war. Amazingly, the Texian "Army of the People" had been assembled in a matter of days from militia companies arriving in Gonzales from all over East Texas. They had rushed to meet the emergency, spurred on by the words of Austin and Houston. All they lacked was a commander-in-chief. Whomever they chose, though, would have to be one of them — someone with the common touch. Unlike regular armies of the time, these would-be soldiers jealously held to their rights and believed the rules and regulations of the regular army impinged upon their liberties. Instead, the Army of the People would be led by a candidate who shared this view. It would be war by committee.

San Fernando Church being fortified by the Centralist soldiers under General Cos.

The American colonists in Texas had little military experience. Bearing arms and conducting military training was not permitted under Mexican law. The national government would provide military protection when needed. Unfortunately for the colonists in East Texas, local occurrences such as sudden Indian raids could not wait for the Mexican garrison at San Antonio to be mustered and sent hundreds of miles to their aid. Thus, Mexico permitted communities to form small militia companies for their own protection. These were made up of locals who elected their own officers and voted on certain orders. They were active only in a crisis. When the crisis was over, they disbanded and went home, back to their farms, stores, cattle, and crops.[3]

This process might work at the local level, but it was difficult to scale to the needs of a growing army. Strangers from faraway communities would have to be accepted as the legitimate leadership. This meant politics would whittle away at the passions and cohesion that had assembled the army in the first place. Whoever commanded would have to command the highest degree of popularity and recognition from the widest number of settlements.

P. W. Grayson, the president of an impromptu governing body dubbed the Council of War, gave Austin the news. "It appears that you have been chosen without opposition commander-in-chief of the volunteer army of Texas now in the field," he wrote. "The members of this board take this occasion to congratulate you on the high office to which you have been called." The empresario turned soldier got to work.

continued on page 12 ▶

▶ continued from page 11

of health, affecting his physical competency to discharge the duties of commander-in-chief of the army with that efficiency and promptness which were desirable, he was nevertheless convinced that the peculiar state of affair in camp left him without a choice as to what course he would pursue, feeling ready at all times to make any personal sacrifices when duty to the country required to be done; all of which considerations induced him to permit his name to be announced to the army as a candidate for commander-in-chief of the volunteer army of Texas. At the time indicated the army was paraded in good military order, and the election was conducted in an orderly but enthusiastic manner, and . . . Colonel Stephen F. Austin was elected without opposition.

OCTOBER 12

Accessibility became one of the hazards of being an elected commander-in-chief. Suddenly everybody had advice for Austin. Eli Mercer, an early settler from Georgia, had prospered in Texas, owning a 500-acre plantation on the Colorado River where he also operated a ferry. He was politically important in the state and felt obliged to give Austin military advice as well. The Army of the People should move on Béxar, Mercer wrote, and "if Coss and Ugartechea could be defeated and made prisoners, we would have time after that event to be in readiness for the next attack." Despite being warm for a fight in the streets of Texas' largest town, Mercer offered tactical advice that seemed at odds with house-to-house fighting. "Fight them from the Brush," he urged, "fight them from the Brush all the time; never take our Boys to an open fight our Situation will not admit of it. All must be deciplind before we can fight in the open field."

Mercer's good intentions and advice hinted at how the coming campaign must play out. Austin also received word of Captain Collingsworth's *coup de main* at Goliad. He urged the hotspur officer to bide his time before rushing against Béxar. "The fort of LaBahía must be retained," Austin insisted. "As at present advised it is considered that one hundred men will be amply sufficient, for that object." Everyone else should head to Gonzales or a future rally point and join the Army of the People. Austin would not have his various commands fling themselves piecemeal at the Centralists. The insurgents needed the strength that came from numbers.

Others arrived in camp. Ben Milam, fresh from La Bahía, brought in a prisoner, Captain Manuel Sabariego, a commander of the *rancheros* around Goliad. General Cos had placed Sabariego in charge of guarding the supplies at La Báhia until he could arrange to transport them to Béxar. Austin had no quarrel with the Tejano and freed him to return to his family in Goliad, but he ordered Milam to take him to San Felipe first to meet with Lorenzo de Zavala, who would brief the *ranchero* on the causes of the crisis. There was already a growing mistrust of the American colonists among the Tejanos, a belief that they were interested in seceding from Mexico rather than perfecting it as a Federalist republic. "The Cause we are defending," instructed Austin, "is the Constitution of 1824, and the Federal System." Sabariego believed otherwise. "He says that the General Opinion is that Texas has declared independence and that this opinion prevents the Mexicans from joining us." Perhaps De Zavala, among the highest-profile Federalists in Mexico, could give the cause some clarity.

With that chore handled, Austin wanted to make sure everyone in his command got the message but did not lose their military ardor. "You understand that the position taken by the people of Tejas is to support the Federal Constitution of 1824, and to oppose Centralism," he wrote Collingsworth at La Bahía. While an independent Texas might be an eventual outcome of the crisis, that cause would be too polarizing just yet, when Tejano support remained critical. That would have to evolve. One volunteer, 27-year-old Noah Smithwick, described the messaging problem that Austin faced. "Some were for independence; some for the constitution of 1824; and some for anything, just so it was a row," Smithwick wrote. "But we were all ready to fight. . . . we intended that it be quick, short, and decisive. Our plan was to rush on to San Antonio, [and] capture the garrison before it could get reinforcement."

With this matter addressed for the moment, Austin set his army into motion. After spending most of October 12 crossing the Guadalupe River from Gonzales, the army made camp on the right bank and settled in for the night. The Army of the People remained more of a mob than an army and reflected the society that had spawned it. "Buckskin breeches were the nearest approach to uniform," Smithwick observed, "and there was wide diversity even there, some being new and soft and yellow, while others, from long familiarity with rain and grease and dirt, had become hard and black and shiny. Some, from having passed through the process of wetting and drying on the wearer while he sat on the ground or a chunk before the campfire, with his knees elevated at an angle of eighty-five degrees, had assumed an advanced position at the knee, followed by a corresponding shortening of the lower front length, exposing shins as guiltless of socks as an Arkansas Senator's." Most of the volunteers wore moccasins or simple brogans. Boots were rare. Headgear varied widely as well. "Here a broad-brimmed sombrero overshadowed the military cap at its side; there a tall 'beegum' rode familiarly beside a coonskin cap, with the tail hanging down behind, as all regulated tails should do," Smithwick continued.[4] Gourd canteens swung at the hip of every would-be warrior. The animals with the army also reflected a cross section of Texas at the time. "Here a big American horse loomed up above a nimble Spanish pony ranged beside him; there a half-broke mustang pranced beside a sober, methodical mule." Overall, Smithwick observed, it was "a fantastic military array."

Centralist scouts galloped to Béxar to inform General Cos that the Army of the People, these self-styled Federalists, were on the move. He ordered his army to fortify the plazas as well as the Alamo, a half-ruined mission compound across the San Antonio River that was founded as a Franciscan mission in 1718 but turned over to civilian and military use in 1793. One of the two local companies of Mexican militia was currently housed in its buildings, and Lieutenant Francisco Castañeda, who commanded them at the standoff at Gonzales, owned two of the buildings along the west wall. Maverick, from his vantage point along the main thoroughfare through Béxar, noted the change in mood. "Great flurry and excitement by arrival of Mex. spies reporting that great crowds of Americans were on the road coming," he wrote in his diary on October 12. Mexican *soldados* came to the door and took away his housemate, the civil engineer John W. Smith, who would be forced to help construct breastworks, cannon emplacements, and trenches under military supervision. Fortifications started to rise on the streets of the town, while work details cleared fields of fire for the Mexican artillery and muskets. If the Army of the People wished to walk the streets of Béxar, they would pay for the privilege. Cos would welcome them with bullets, shot, and cannister.

3 THE ARMY OF THE PEOPLE ADVANCES

General Stephen F. Austin understood that his command needed to move with alacrity before the Centralists could dig in. He sent a report to the Committee of Safety at San Felipe emphasizing the importance of haste in sending forward reinforcements. On October 13, Austin got his army under way, but with only 300 volunteers, he knew his command had too few for the job ahead. If troops could come in from Goliad and join his column en route, it might help, but hundreds more were needed to have any hope of success. "I have therefore to request that you will use every exertion to press for Volunteers who may come up with us in time to give us important — perhaps indispensable aid, in the attack on S Antonio," he admonished the committee. "Fail not to use any possible exertion in this respect I beseech you. If there is any intelligence of troops coming on from Nacogdoches let an Express be dispatched to them immediately, urging them to hurry on by forced marches to join us and not to stay for the Tenoxtitlan Cannon or anything."[1]

The Army of the People needed more than volunteers to handle the muskets. It also needed powder and shot for its variety of muskets, shotguns, and fowling pieces as well as for its motley collection of artillery. Food, too, would soon run short. Austin urged his friends to send "provisions such as meat, beans, Sugar and Coffee and whatever else you may judge necessary for the troops." All he asked for himself were the necessary tools to run his makeshift headquarters: "I would have you send also 2 reams of paper — 2 bottles of Ink with a supply of quills, wavers and sealing wax."

Austin's instincts were correct, and the 700 Centralist troops transformed the once-sleepy streets of Béxar into an armed camp. General Cos declared martial law. In a circular to his troops, he made the stakes clear. "Soldiers: The veil which has long concealed the perfidious designs of the colonists is at length withdrawn," the document read. "These ungrateful men have revolted against our government, and assumed the right to live as they like, without any subjection to the laws of the republic. They are presumptuous enough to believe that the nation which has adopted them as her sons, has no sufficient power to subdue them and compel them to share that obedience to which they have sworn." He cast the men marching toward Béxar as arrogant liars and whiners who were ungrateful for the generous treatment they had received from Mexico. Now, under the guise of rebellion against tyranny, these American colonists revealed their motives to be "entirely contrary to the national interests." Cos believed his soldiers would easily dispel this rabble's enthusiasm for war. The army would not take the offensive until it was ready, but when it did, the matter would be settled quickly, he assured his readers.

But were his soldiers, and the civilians throughout Texas, loyal to the Centralist cause? Cos believed it was time for the Béxarenos and other Tejanos to show their allegiance to Mexico in what he cast as a general rebellion against their lawful rule. "Let us . . . rely on their exertions to support a cause which has become national," the circular continued, "and therefore common to all." Cos showed more faith in the reliability of his

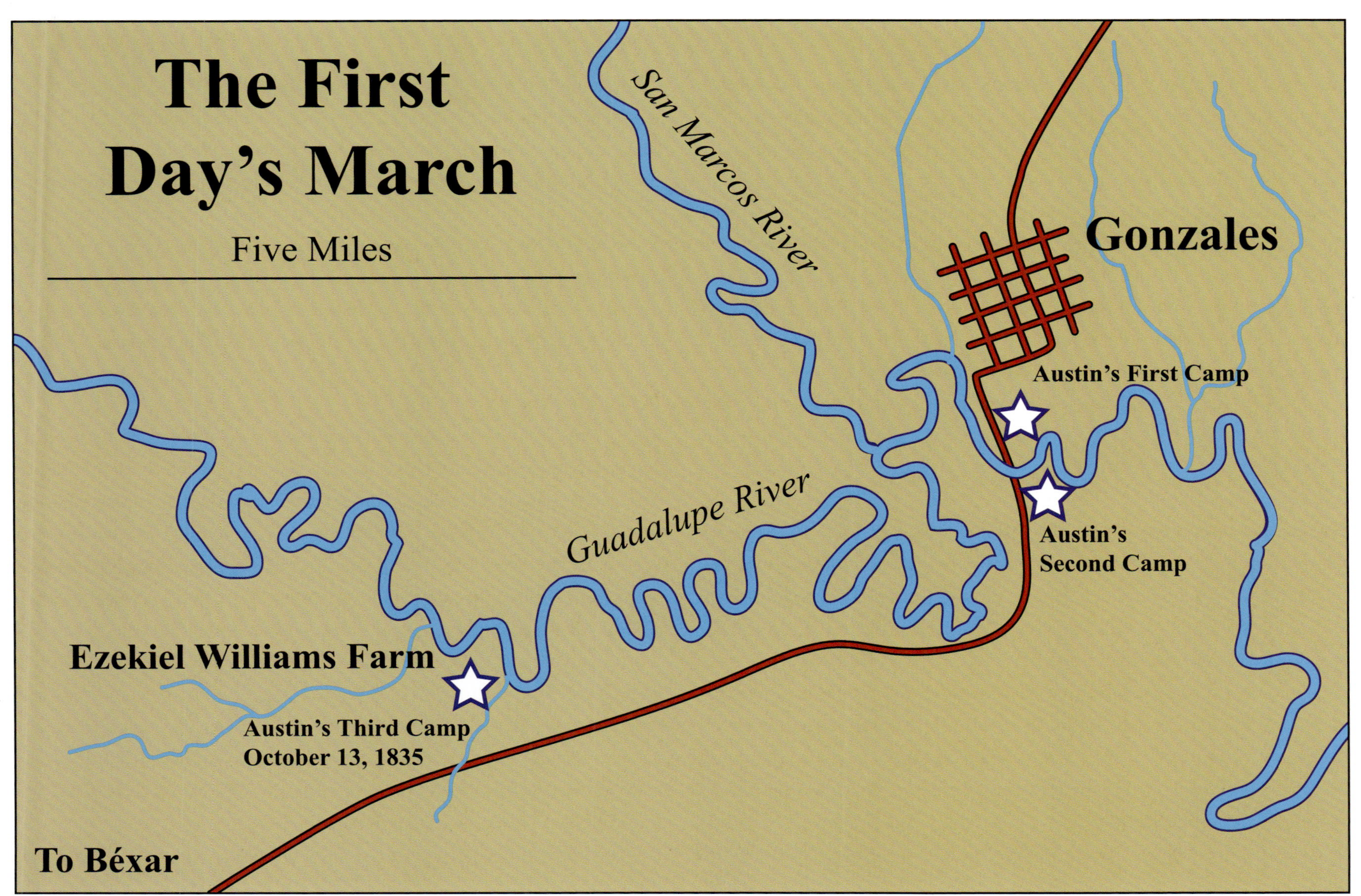

The First
Day's March
Five Miles
San Marcos River
Gonzales
Austin's First Camp
Guadalupe River
Austin's
Second Camp
Ezekiel Williams Farm
Austin's Third Camp
October 13, 1835
To Béxar

soldiers. "Comrades! I see with pleasure your enthusiasm. I view with satisfaction your high discipline, and with the other estimable qualities which distinguish you, I can easily foresee the result of a campaign, in which your valor will bring the rebels to repentance, who have thought the time had arrived to realize their plans as premature as they are injurious to the republic." He needed their hard labor now to fortify the main plazas of Béxar and bring the Alamo into repair so it could be used as quarters, a hospital, and an artillery position that would cover the northern approaches to town. "After fatigue comes repose," Cos promised. "We shall obtain it covered with glory; this will be the inevitable result of your valor."

In town, Sam Maverick noted the ax, pick and spade work under way on the streets of the once-quiet frontier town. "The military broke the figure of San Antonio," he recorded in his diary, presumably speaking of a statue of St. Anthony.

The Centralists troops fortifying Béxar would have plenty of time. By the evening of October 13, Austin's army has only made six miles' progress, pitching camp on the farm of Ezekiel Williams north of the Gonzales Road and along the Guadalupe River, the same location where the Gonzales standoff had occurred eleven days before.[2]

Austin's friends worried that his advance was premature, perhaps even rash. William H. Jack wrote from Goliad, congratulating his friend on his high command position but worried about his plans for marching on Béxar. "You will pardon me for expressing my views and opinions to you freely, fully and frankly," his compatriot wrote. In case Austin had missed this fact, Jack reminded him that he was heading toward a battle with fewer than 400 men — a fight in which the Texians would be badly outnumbered and poorly equipped. "I cannot conceive that it is seriously contemplated to attack Bexar with that number," he continued. "The fact

of Texas must not be risked upon one battle; unless the advantages are so decidedly in our favor, as to place the result beyond a Shadow of doubt." To Jack, the contest was not in question: the Mexicans would wipe out Austin and his army. "Though I have the utmost confidence in the firmness and bravery of our countrymen yet it is drawing too heavily on that confidence, to be willing to risk a general engagement, on which so much depends against such fearful odds," he lectured his friend. "They have a numerical strength. They have artillery, cavalry, muskets, bayonets, lances, against all these you present a band (brave perhaps to a fault) of untrained militia."

OCTOBER 14

The Army of the People spent the next day on the Williams farm reorganizing. Austin used the day to establish discipline in this ragtag group of volunteers. He outlined how his army would be managed going forward and posted general orders for his command. First, he directed, each man had to follow orders given by their superior officers. Next, all volunteers needed to keep their weapons clean and serviceable, their powder dry, and a good supply of bullets on hand. Sentries must stay awake and alert at their posts or face a court-martial. The troops were to keep good order in camp. "All riotous conduct and noisy clamorous talk is specially prohibited," he directed. Related to that rule, Austin reminded soldiers to not discharge their weapons in camp or along the march. To keep animals at hand and not wandering through camp, each horse was to be hobbled or tied when not in use.

Austin, who never served in any military capacity, nevertheless understood how difficult it would be to convert these hotspurs into soldiers. His army must be organized. Too many officers and not enough soldiers would cause even more chaos, and soldiers disgruntled with one officer might choose to slip over to a command led by men whom they considered more convivial. To clip this impulse, Austin directed that companies should have no fewer than thirty men, and all unattached volunteers needed to find a command and make themselves useful. Once organized, these companies would remain intact and maintain their position within the army for the duration of the campaign. Soldiers could, from this day forward, only leave their commands with their captain's permission. Those who refused to take Austin's orders seriously would suffer the consequences. "For every violation of duty or act of disobedience to orders — to which there is no fixed punishment in these articles," he promised, "the person offending shall be responsible to a court martial specially called to pass sentence upon and punish his offense."

This night, an omen appeared. Haley's Comet, which appears every seventy-five years, shone into view in the night sky. For those of a superstitious temperament from Mexico City to Washington D.C., the visitor seemed to mark 1835 as particularly auspicious.

OCTOBER 15

With the Army of the People taking on the form and function of an army, Austin put his command back on the road. The amateurs made good time, putting in fourteen miles before stopping for the day at the Sandies Creek crossing of the Gonzales Road, a mile beyond John Castleman's house. His was the last settler homestead before the long stretch toward Béxar. Austin took this moment to give directions on how the army should behave if it encountered the enemy. They would concentrate to avoid being broken up and defeated in detail, and the mounts would be secured. Centralist cavalrymen were patrolling in the neighborhood, and Austin didn't want any of his vanguard or rear guard getting cut off and destroyed. Knowing that a clash would come soon, he did what he could to make sure his men did not make poor decisions in the heat of the moment.

OCTOBER 16

Remarkably, the Army of the People leapt forward the next day. It reached Cibolo Creek, two dozen miles down the road, by nightfall. Austin ordered his command to pause at this strategic crossing, sending dispatches back the way he came. "I have dispatched this Express to inform the troops who are on the road," he wrote, "and to hurry them on by forced marches." Austin's scouts had pushed on toward Béxar, another two dozen miles down the road, and saw clear signs that Centralist cavalry were patrolling.[3]

OCTOBER 17

While he waited for more troops, Austin sent dispatches to Cos. One, with Austin speaking as the leader of the Army of the People (or, more formally, the Texas Division of the Federal Army), suggested a parley "to avoid the sad consequences of the Civil War which unfortunately threatens Texas" and to seek the "reestablishment of peace and confidence in Texas." He signed this note with the phrase "God, Federation, and Liberty." His second dispatch was more personal, an attempt at personal diplomacy with Cos. If the Centralist officer would agree to a meeting, "I can not doubt that thus will be opened the way for the satisfactory adjustment of all the affairs of Texas," Austin urged. "This is my desire, and I will contribute to the attainment of so important an object to the extent that my duty will permit."

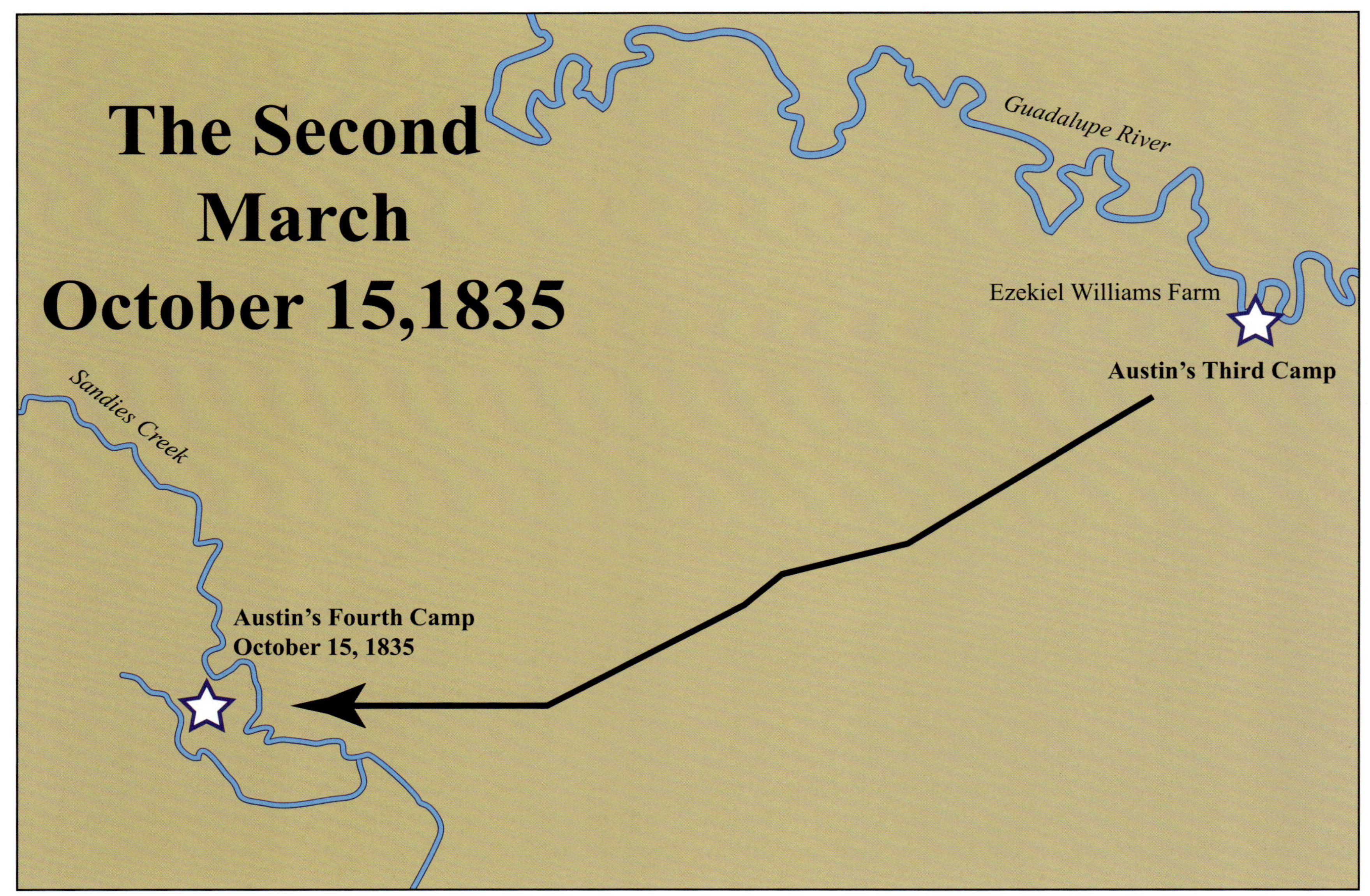

The Second March
October 15,1835
Guadalupe River
Ezekiel Williams Farm
Austin's Third Camp
Sandies Creek
Austin's Fourth Camp
October 15, 1835

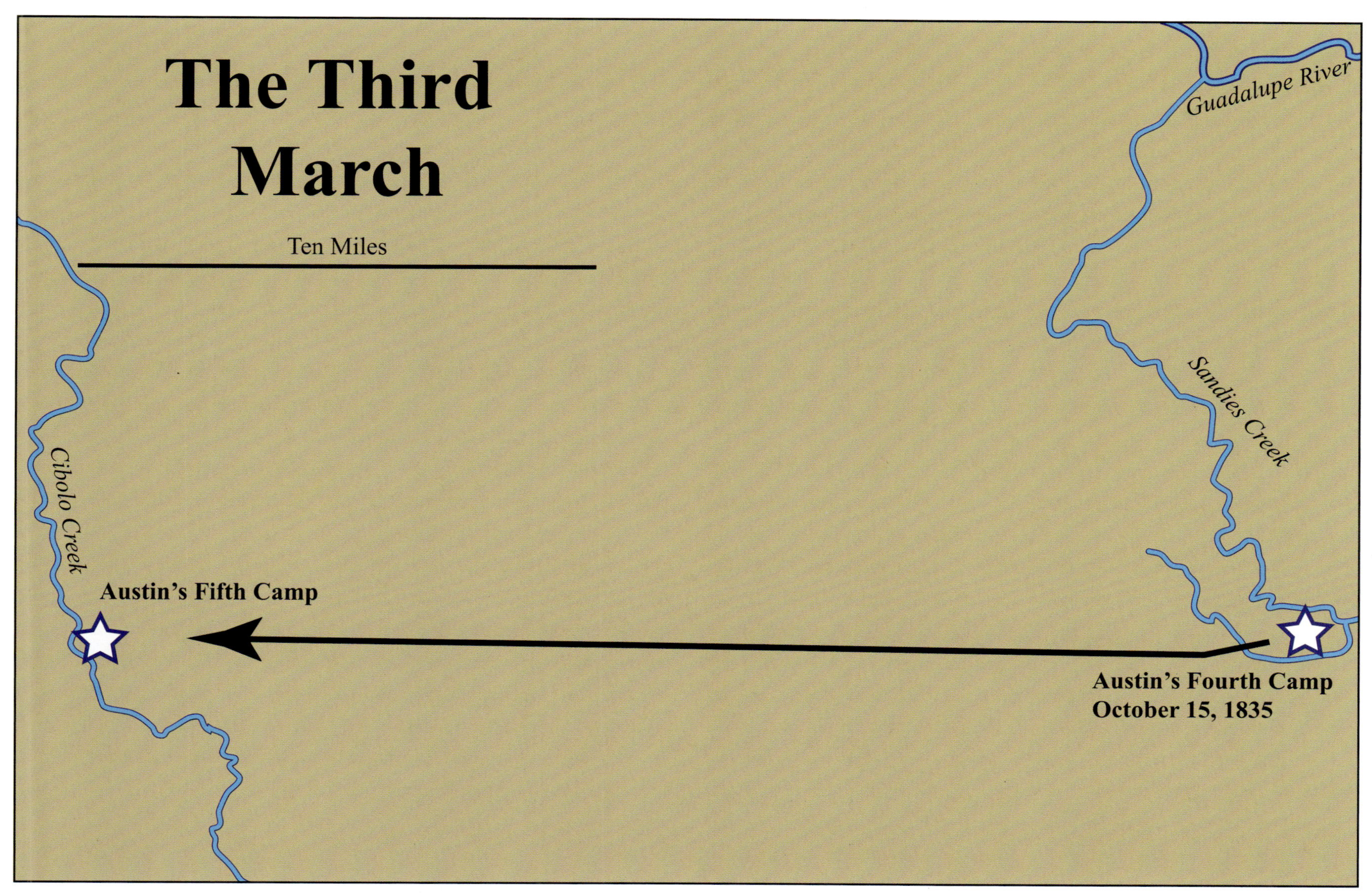

The Third
March
Ten Miles
Guadalupe River
Sandies Creek
Cibolo Creek
Austin's Fifth Camp
Austin's Fourth Camp
October 15, 1835

The next day, riders came into the camp on Cibolo Creek bearing a response to Austin's overture. Cos seemed dumbstruck that the usually reasonable and prudent Austin was leading the insurgent army. Even so, the time for a parley was over. Only when the Texians disbanded and returned to their homes would Cos have any authority to try to defuse the volatile situation in Texas. If the American settlers had grievances, they should appeal peacefully to their government for redress. "It is indispensable that you lay aside your hostile attitude, withdraw the people who accompany you, deliver up the Mexican soldiers that you have made prisoners, and place everything on the sole footing of petitions, and by no means resort to acts," Cos responded.

Austin and the Texians were paddling into deep waters, the Mexican general continued. He denied that there was a civil war in Mexico; on the contrary, Cos wrote, the defiance of the American settlers in Texas would unite the nation, and the rebellion would be crushed as a point of national pride. "I entertain the best disposition for arranging matters in such a way that the Colonists might not feel the effects of a disastrous War," he assured Austin, "but it is not my fault that they are presumptuous and are on the point of contending with the whole nation, whose pride is so great that she can never yield to the dictation of strangers and will finally chastise the guilty." The Texians had roused a dangerous enemy, Cos claimed. He acknowledged that some Tejanos would support the insurrection, but they did not represent the will of the people. "It is perhaps certain that some Mexicans, whether from private resentment or from private interest, or because no rule is without exception, will co-operate in the revolt of the Colonists," he wrote, "but the nation in general will oppose it with all her force."

Cos also questioned the very legitimacy of Austin's claim to be leading a part, the Texas Division, of a Federal Army of Mexico. "The term made use of by your official communication (to which I do not reply) of the 'Federal Army of Texas' is quite unknown," Cos wrote. There was only one Mexican army, he continued, "the one to which I belong." This same army, the general claimed, had never entangled itself with the various political uprisings of the nation and had never attacked the government of the Republic of Mexico. "It is desirous of peace, this army has sufficiently shown," Cos added, "but it does not decline to enter into War, inasmuch as that is its profession." If the shooting started, the cause and consequences would fall on Austin and his so-called army. "This shall be the last communication," Cos ended, "unless you should subsequently consent to my request of appearing in the character of a peaceable citizen, who ought certainly to be interested, in preventing the Mexicans from making of the Colonies a signal example."

Inside Béxar, Maverick watched as couriers rode back and forth on the road toward Gonzales. He also noted the preparations for war under way all over town. The day before, Mexican troops had mounted a cannon on a carriage, bringing their battery to four guns. San Fernando Church became the principal arsenal and magazine. The more than 600 troops were divided, with the infantry of the Morelos Battalion quartered in town on the Plaza de Armas or Zambrano Row, while the presidial and regular cavalry camped in the Alamo.

The following day, Maverick observed the arrival of a rider from the direction of the Texian camp with a message for Cos. The rider reported that Austin "had not come to treat but to fight; and if he (Cos) would not

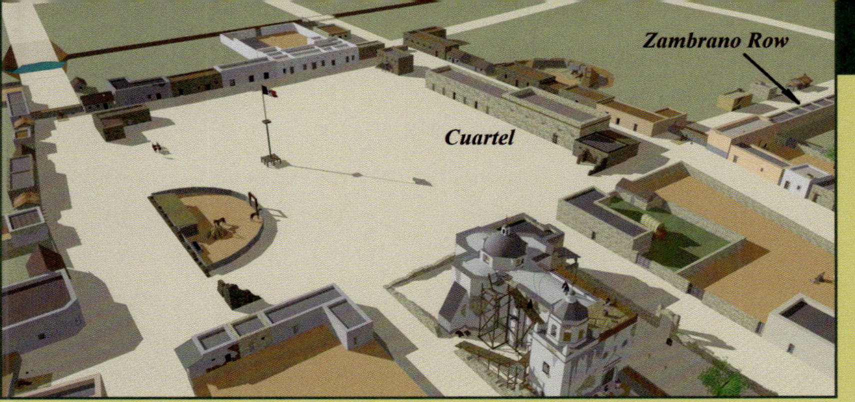

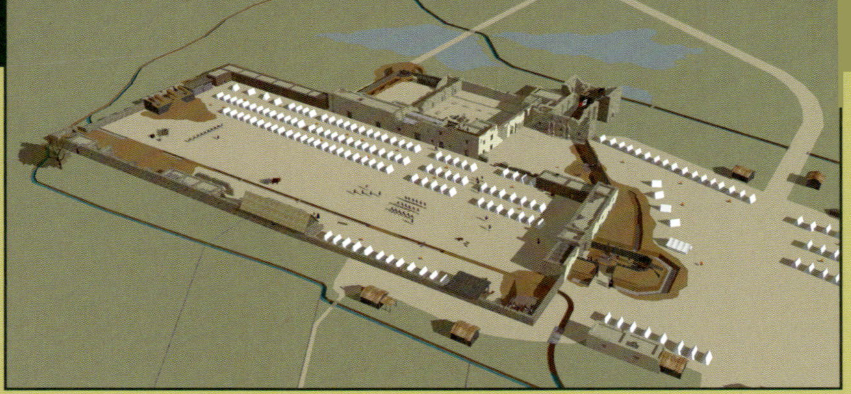

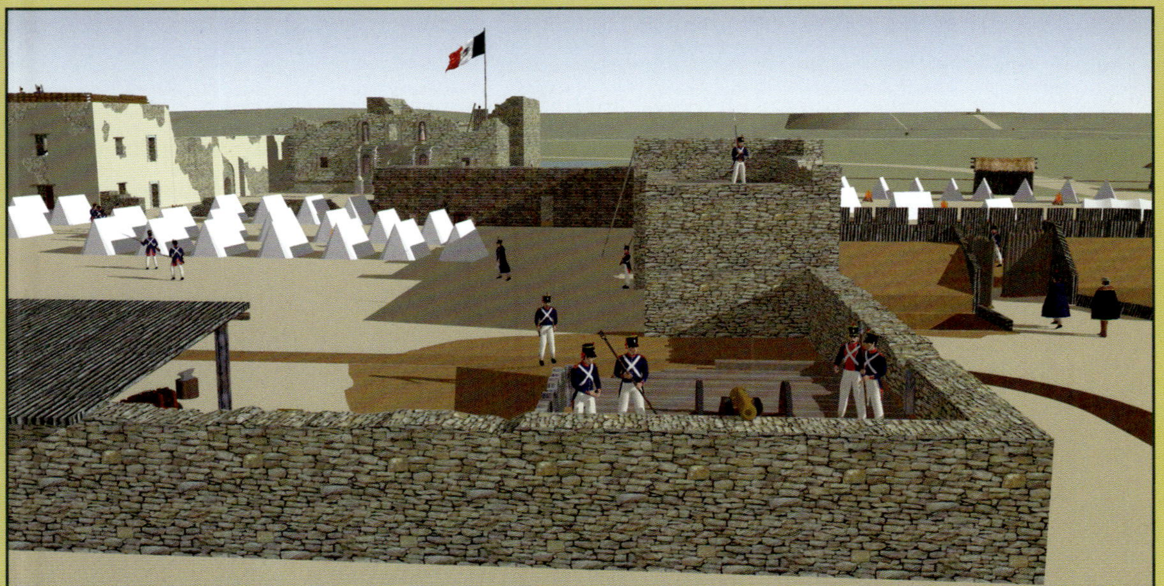

TOP LEFT: *Plaza de Armas. San Fernando Church (bottom) is now serving as the Centralists' powder magazine. The "cuartel of the infantry" of the Morelos Battalion in Maverick's diary refers to the long stone building labeled "Cuartel." Part of the Morelos infantry was also housed in Zambrano Row, along North Flores Street (upper right corner).*

TOP RIGHT: *The Alamo as fortified by Cos. Originally Mission San Antonio de Valero until 1793, it later became a military barracks and at this point is serving as a fort as well. Cos is keeping his cavalry here in addition to its resident presidiales.*

LEFT: *Cos' engineers have constructed ramps and platforms for cannon behind the old walls of the mission and raised the Mexican flag over the uncompleted and roofless Alamo church.*

meet him outside he would attack him inside of the town." The gauntlet thrown down, Cos responded in kind: "I want no more communications. Let the damn rascals come."

The exchange ignited something in Austin, who decided he could no longer wait on the Cibolo for the expected reinforcements from Nacogdoches and East Texas to arrive. He would move his command closer to Béxar — this time to Salado Creek, a mere five miles from the Mexican outposts — in a clear provocation. Austin believed the Béxarenos would rise in support of his army if they could see its campfires on the eastern horizon. "It is now well ascertained that the people of the town are well affected to our cause and will probably be ready, when occasion offers, to render us essential aid," he reported. Besides, his Army of the People was "in high spirits and eager to advance, but are at the same time not disposed to act precipitately or rashly." The faceoff with Cos and his Centralist troops, Austin believed, would end soon. "It is confidently expected that we shall be able to act conclusively within a very few days."

As the Texians broke camp and made their way closer to Béxar, a mounted party arrived from the direction of the town with news. Erastus Smith — a 48-year-old native of Washington, Duchess County, New York — had been living near Béxar since 1821. He had suffered hearing loss after a childhood illness, and most people referred to him as "Deaf" Smith as he settled into Béxar society. He had married a Tejana, Guadalupe Rúiz Duran, and raised four children. He had also earned a reputation as an excellent tracker and hunter and a frequent source of fresh game for the markets in town. His son-in-law Hendrick Arnold, a free man of color, had married Smith's stepdaughter Martina and was a frequent companion on these expeditions. They were returning from an extended buffalo hunt when they discovered Béxar fortified with guards at every street entrance. They were told that they needed to have permission from General Cos to be admitted and to "come back tomorrow." So they rode to the Texian camp to learn what they could.

Austin knew Smith's reputation and tried to enlist him as a scout. Smith refused. He and his Tejana wife would remain neutral. Smith and Arnold accompanied the Texians on their twenty-mile ride to the Salado and spent the night in camp. They would try once again to get home in the morning.

4 GATHERING AT SALADO CREEK

The next morning, Deaf Smith and Hendrick Arnold left Austin's camp on Salado Creek to attempt a return to Béxar — and to their homes and families. As they entered town, one of the guards grabbed Smith's reins and a squad of cavalry advanced toward them menacingly. Smith pulled away, spun his horse about, and sank his spurs into the animal's flanks as he and his son-in-law dodged bullets as they outran the pursuing cavalry. Their horses winded and lathered, the pair trotted into the Texian camp. Smith dismounted and stormed into Austin's tent. "General Austin, I told you yesterday that I would not take sides in this war but, Sir, I now tender you my services as the Mexicans acted rascally with me!" Smith sputtered. Austin, familiar with rude treatment by Mexican authorities, enlisted both Smith and Arnold as scouts.

Others arrived as well. Juan Nepomuceno Seguín, not yet 30 years old, rode into the Texian camp. He was no stranger to these men. His father, Erasmo, had been Austin's close friend since Austin arrived in Texas in June 1821. Erasmo and a group of Béxareños including the venerable Don Juan Martín de Veramendi had ridden to Nacogdoches to escort Austin over the arduous 306 miles back to Béxar in those promising early days of American immigration to Texas. In recent years, Juan had filled the positions of alderman, political chief, and *alcalde* of Béxar and was popular with the locals. The younger Seguín was a staunch Federalist like his father, and both were viewed suspiciously by the Centralists occupying their town. The Tejano hotspur offered his services to Austin's cause. "The military commander, Colonel Domingo de Ugartachea, considering me opposed to the existing government, ordered two officers to watch my movements in secret," Seguín explained, adding slyly that "this, however, did not prevent my working diligently to prepare for the intended campaign."

Austin was happy to have this charismatic leader, and son of a friend, join the cause. "The trusty patriot D. Juan Seguín is appointed captain in the federal army of Texas," Austin jotted as orders to his staff, "and as such is fully authorized to raise a company of patriots to operate against the centralists and military in defense of the constitution of 1824 and the federal system."

The newcomer brought other promising news. "Seguín also gave flattering accounts of the favorable disposition which prevailed among the citizens generally in San Antonio and its surrounding neighborhood," remembered William T. Austin, and "of their friendship to the cause in which we were engaged and their willingness to serve us." Seguín was as good as his word, and he lost no time in riding down the length of the the San Antonio River Valley, spreading the word of rebellion to the Tejano *ranchos* between Béxar and Goliad. He would return with thirty-seven mounted *vaqueros* to serve as the eyes and ears of Austin's army. Seguín also enlisted the aid of his family. His brother-in-law Salvador Flores arrived with forty more locals, many of whom had just defected from Béxar's presidial company and chosen to defend the Federal Constitution of 1824. The *alcalde* of Victoria, Plácido Benavides, arrived as well with twenty-six more Tejano Federalists. The reinforced Army of the People now had the backing of natives and newcomers alike.

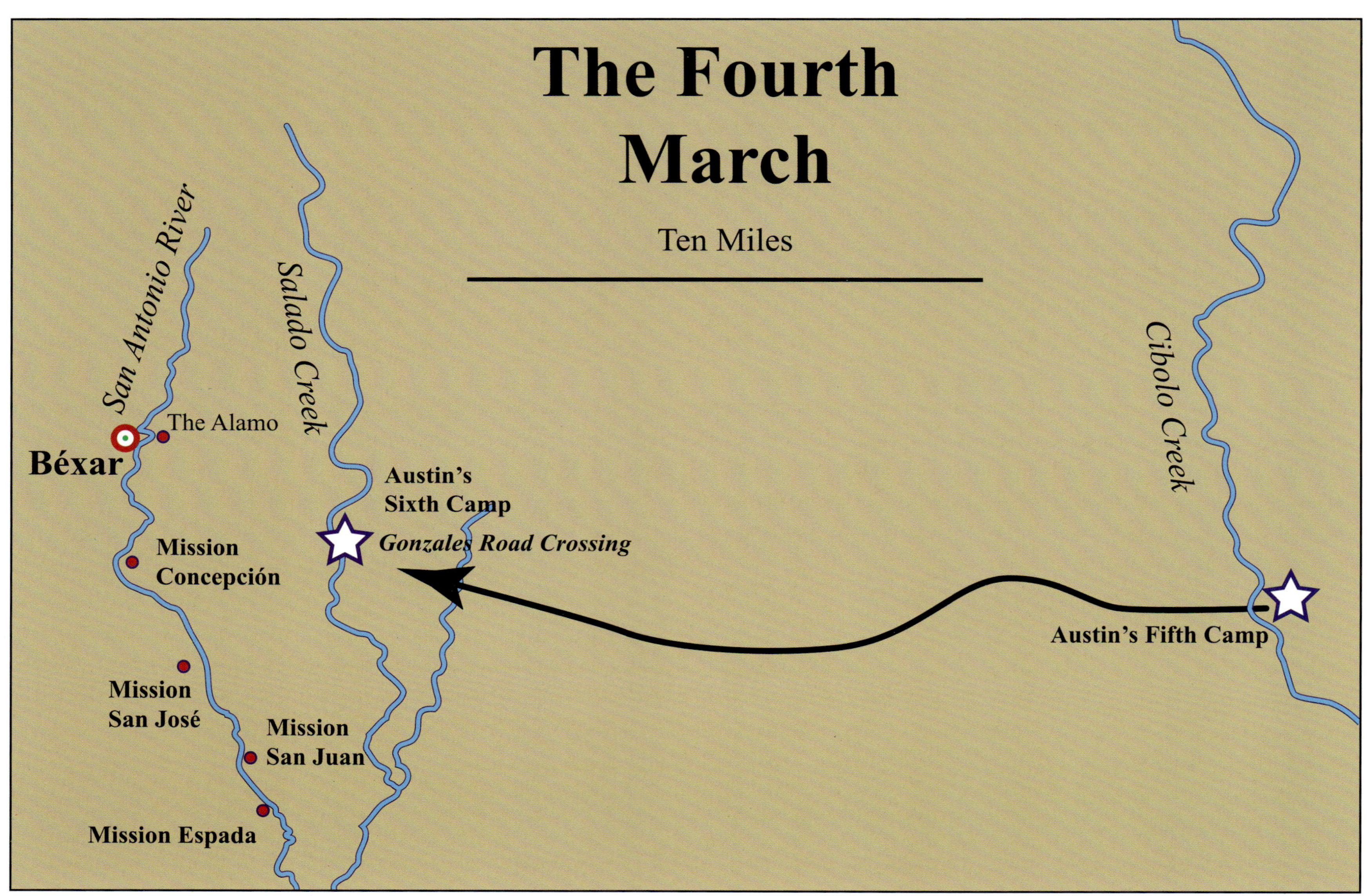

The Fourth March
Ten Miles
San Antonio River
Salado Creek
Cibolo Creek
Béxar
The Alamo
Mission Concepción
Mission San José
Mission San Juan
Mission Espada
Austin's Sixth Camp
Gonzales Road Crossing
Austin's Fifth Camp

Others arrived that day as well. James Bowie was another longtime resident of San Antonio who, like Deaf Smith, had married into the Béxareño community. In 1831, he had wed María Úrsula de Veramendi, daughter of Don Juan Martín de Veramendi (then vice governor of Coahuila-y-Tejas) and perhaps the most eligible woman in the region. Yet Bowie's joy — and his status as husband to the princess of Texas — was short-lived. In 1833, *Úrsula* and her parents died suddenly at their second home in Monclova, Coahuila, during a horrific cholera epidemic. Bowie grieved deeply, and drank heavily, for many months. But as he neared 40 years of age, he emerged from his melancholy to pursue the next phase of his life. He enlisted in the Army of the People. Austin, knowing Bowie's qualities as a fighting man and leader, searched for a way to utilize his unique talents to greatest advantage. Austin settled on appointing him colonel and aide-de-camp, keeping this man of action close to his headquarters against future needs.

William Barret Travis and his enslaved servant, Joe, also rode into camp. Travis, a brash 26-year-old lawyer and political gadfly, had praised and celebrated Austin when he returned from Mexico. He also had practically started the war single-handedly back in June. At the urging of local San Felipe malcontents, he had led twenty East Texas colonists in an attack on the Mexican customs house at Anáhuac on the coast and demanded the surrender of its forty-man garrison. Mexican Captain António Tenório, with the military and political situation in Mexico murky at best, asked for some time to consult with his officers. "Surrender immediately," insisted Travis, "or be put to the sword!" Tenório surrendered, and Travis crowed over his victory. Once he was back in San Felipe, however, conservative locals chastised Travis for having stirred the pot too soon. His prisoner, Tenório, proved charming and genuine, and many American settlers sympathized with his plight while Travis earned a reputation as a hothead. By October, Travis saw a chance at redemption with the latest crisis but missed the confrontation at Gonzales due to a bad case of the flu. Once he could ride, he reported to Austin's camp on the Salado. Everyone knew this firebrand was wanted by Centralist authorities. The Anáhuac affair had landed him on President Santa Anna's most-wanted list.

OCTOBER 21

In between greeting the various parties of reinforcements arriving on the Salado, Austin also pored over scouting reports and dispatches from other Texian commands. In Goliad, Captain Phillip Dimmitt, now in command of the Presidio La Bahía, had grown worried about the possibility of General Cos sallying out of Béxar to recapture his supply base and reopen communications with the coast. Word arrived that the Centralists, too, had received reinforcements — perhaps as many as 500 men via the overland route from the Rio Grande. "As soon as they should arrive," Dimmit reported, "he intended sending a strong force here, to retake this post. I enclose you intercepted letters on the same subject. They speak for themselves." In the same dispatch, Dimmit also reported what Austin must have surely already known. "All the squares of Bexar are fortified," the captain wrote, and "works are raised at every angle for the effective use of their artillery."

OCTOBER 22

Austin had a problem. He had focused almost entirely on planning the army's attack on San Antonio, but now there were larger strategic concerns to consider. To maintain communications between Dimmit's command at La Bahía and his force on the Salado, the Texians needed to control the San Antonio River Valley between those two points. Austin turned to Bowie. He ordered the veteran frontiersman to take several well-mounted companies to scout three of the four secularized Franciscan missions along the San Antonio River below Béxar, directing them to "proceed forth with to the Missions of San Juan, Espada and San Jose, for the purpose of gaining information in regard to the present condition of those places." Bowie's detachment would also scour these places for any food caches or horses and ascertain "the disposition of the inhabitants." If Bowie thought it prudent, he was to occupy one of these missions as a potential outpost link between La Bahía and the army outside Béxar. Captain James Walker Fannin, arguably the most knowledgeable military officer in Austin's command and a standout from the dustup at Gonzales, rode at the head of these mounted troops. At 31 years old, and with two years of training at West Point, this native Georgian and Texas plantation owner seemed the very image of maturity and experience among the amateur Army of the People.[1]

Austin sent a dispatch to La Bahía to calm Dimitt's jangled nerves, trusting the errand to Captain Seguín. Austin believed the presence of the Texas Division of the Federal Army on the Salado would keep Cos from making any risky advances against La Bahía. Dimmit needed to stand fast. In addition, Seguín would contract for pack mules to bring up salt and flour from the stocks at Goliad. "I have appointed Juan Seguín a Captain of the Federal Army," Austin explained to avoid any confusion, "and he will raise a Company of Mexicans. Inform your men, of this that he may be respected as such and as a devoted friend of the Constitution."

Meanwhile, Bowie's scouting expedition had yielded impressive results. Late in the afternoon, Fannin and his ninety troopers chased off four Centralist pickets and occupied Mission San Francisco de la Espada

(St. Francis of the Sword), the mission farthest downriver from Béxar. As the Texians settled in, Bowie spoke with the locals and then sent a galloper bearing dispatches back to Austin with details of all that he had learned. Refugees from Béxar were seeking shelter at the mission. The Centralists had pressed the locals into helping them build fortifications and their wives and daughters into making tortillas and preparing food for the soldiers. Those that could, fled, and were eager to tell Bowie about conditions in town. Cos had been caught off guard by the Texians' ride down the San Antonio Valley. "Great consternation was manifested there," Bowie reported, "when our approach to this point was made known."

Conditions in Béxar seemed to favor the insurgent cause. Dimmit's fears that Cos had received reinforcements appeared to be false, Bowie wrote. The Centralists had, however, stripped the region of horses, which they moved to Laredo while retaining a few hundred kept under close guard for the use of the cavalry. A Béxareño confirmed the number of troops in town at around 600. Cos and his command might soon run out of food, Bowie learned: "They have not got in corn or other provisions, and we find it all growing, or rather, yet in the fields." Apparently, the movement of his detachment had stampeded the Centralists. "When our approach was ascertained, the alarm was great, and 14 Beef Cattle was ordered to be penned up," he continued. "The men with whom we have conversed — are decidedly of the opinion, that in five days, they can be starved out."

Not all of the news out of Béxar was as encouraging. The Centralists had fortified both town squares, built parapets of freshly made adobe bricks on the roofs of houses covering the approaches to the streets, and mounted eight 4-pounder cannon to cover the approaches into town. A larger gun, too, would soon be emplaced. San Fernando Church had become a citadel. The Centralists "have removed all their ammunition to it," Bowie continued, "and enclosed it by a wall, made of wood, six feet apart and six feet high, filled in with dirt, extending from the corners to the ditch, say sixty yards in length."

There was other news. Austin's friend Erasmo Seguín remained in Béxar. "General Cos has threatened to make Seguín and others of the most respectable citizens to sweep the public square," Bowie reported, "and in case he whipped us, to make their Ladies, grind tortillas for his soldiers."

Bowie also forwarded other troubling reports. Food was going to be scarce for the Texian Federalists, too. One of his local guides had been to the two other missions upstream and found nothing useful. San José had a garrison of five men; San Juan had none. Both were barren of groceries. "We learn that no public stores are collected at either place," Bowie reported. "The Bean crops are entirely destroyed." The fields bordering the San Antonio River, though, abounded with unharvested corn. Bowie was reluctant to seize it without paying for it. "The principal owners are in Town, and Couriers will be dispatched early for them, to make contracts with [them] for the army," he wrote. "There is corn here, but owned by men who rent the land, and will sell for cash only, and only in small quantities."

Bowie would continue his scout upriver, using Mission Espada as his base and a communications link between Dimmitt's command at Goliad and Austin's outside Béxar. The frontiersman did have a suggestion for his commander: move the army over to the San Antonio River above Béxar, while he operated on the river below. "This will alarm and intimidate the enemy and inspire our friends with renewed confidence," he suggested. "Should you concur with us, and determine to occupy the position above, inform us of it, that we may co-operate with you, and wind up the job speedily." Meanwhile, should more men arrive, Bowie wanted another fifty sent his way. "We will then be entirely able to take and hold any position you may please to designate," he boasted.

OCTOBER 23

The next day, Bowie found conditions at Mission San Juan and Mission San José just as he had been told. "At the Mission of St Juan, they only planted three pecks of corn, and it is yet in the field, and very fine," he wrote. Several families lived there, and the walls were in good shape and could offer a good defense. "The Citizens are well disposed, and now look to us for protection," Bowie continued, "and should the enemy attempt to withdraw their corn, information will be forthwith received from them." There was no corn at Mission San José, but there were patches of unripe peas. Only one family took shelter within its crumbling walls. Bowie thought the large mission compound might be perfect for housing his men but changed his mind. Drinking water from the river was too far away and could be cut off by a Centralist advance. As he turned back toward Mission Espada, the Texians heard a smattering of gunfire coming from Béxar — shots fired between Texian scouts and an enemy patrol that broke and ran for safety. Sometime during the day, Bowie added, Centralist Captain Marcos Barragán and thirty troopers had arrived to strengthen the garrison, no doubt bringing news from beyond the Rio Grande as well.

Unknown to the Texians, Centralist cavalrymen under Colonel Ugartechea were following Bowie back to Mission Espada.

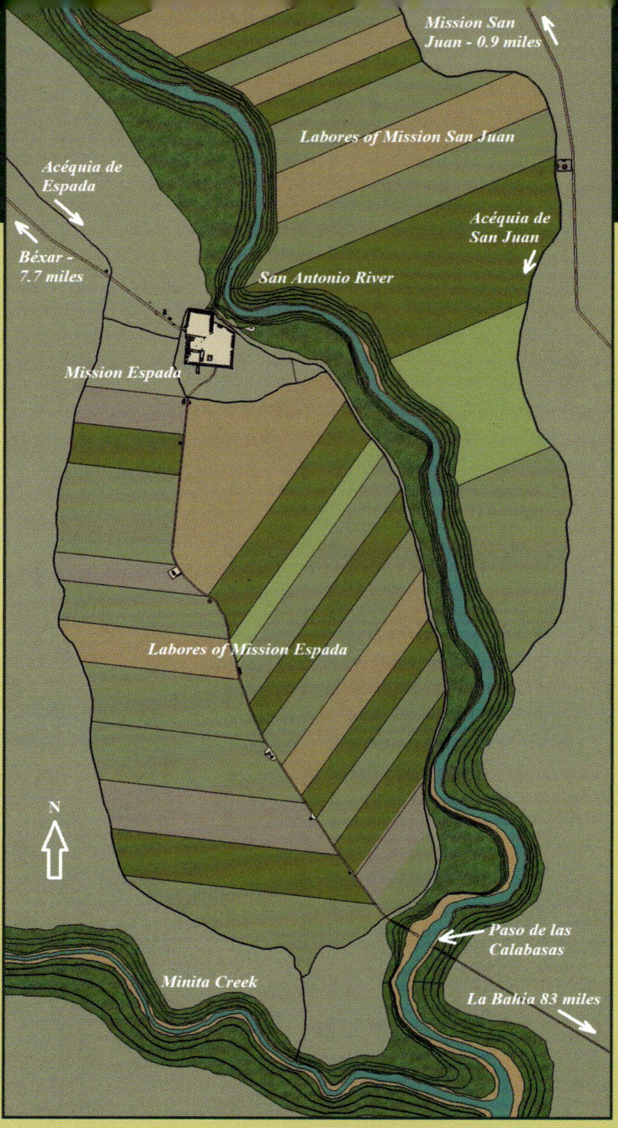

TOP: *Mission San Francisco de la Espada (Mission Espada) looking south over the San Antonio River and the irrigated labores (mission farms) beyond. Originally owned by mission Indian converts, now in 1835 most of these fields are owned by Béxareños since the mission was secularized in 1824.*

RIGHT: *Map of Mission Espada and its labores on the west side of the San Antonio River. Across the river to the east are the labores of Mission San Juan de Capistrano located a mile north of Espada. The four missions were deliberately built on alternating sides of the river to provide more space for each mission's farms. The fields in this map are still in operation today.*

ABOVE: *Looking east over Mission Espada's partially ruined convento. The back of the past church of this secularized mission is on the left.*

The past church of Espada with the remains of the convento connecting it to the plastered and whitewashed building at the left. This building was originally the mission cosina and anticosina (kitchen and anteroom) probably owned in 1835 by Rafael Casillas. He was granted legal title to it in 1824 and has occupied it as a resident of the mission since 1799.

Looking northwest over Mission Espada with Bowie's camp of ninety-two men within the compound.

OCTOBER 24

Around sunrise, the Mexicans advanced on Mission Espada. In the early morning light, Texian riflemen reported seeing' about fifty Mexican troopers moving close enough to exchange shots, but dust in the distance indicated several hundred more in the vicinity. Clearly, the Centralists were determined to learn what they could about the Texian Federalists' strength, and to pen their enemy in his defenses. Bowie unconcerned over the incident, reported "the place is in a good condition, or can be made so in an hour, for defense, and until we know, of the advance of some aid, or what was intended by this feint, we will continue to occupy this station," he wrote, "where we have provisions enough for the army provided means are supplied to purchase." Ugartechea would keep the nosy Texians away from Béxar and shut up within the walls of the Espada compound.

Clearly tensions were growing. Bowie remained hobbled at Espada. He had planned on renewing his scout toward Béxar — perhaps to within a mile of the enemy defenses — but now hesitated until he knew what Austin's plans might be. Together, the two Texian forces might throw a strangling loop around Béxar. "Permit us to again suggest — nay urge, the propriety — the necessity of some movement, which will bring us nearer together, and shut in the enemy, and either starve them out, whip them out, or dishearten and beat them in small parties," Bowie wrote. He had once advocated holding positions above and below Béxar with the Centralists squeezed between. Now he argued for the two to draw closer together for mutual defense. General Austin was inclined to agree. Centralist probes of his pickets had become a daily affair, and blood had been drawn. In the skirmish this morning — a few hours after Bowie was facing off with Ugartechea's cavalry — Texian rifles along Salado Creek felled nearly a dozen Centralists *soldados*. How long would it be before the Mexican forces made a serious attempt against either, or both, of the Texian positions?

The enemy was learning the strength of the so-called Federalist Army of Texas with the lives of its soldiers. There would be a reckoning. Inside Béxar, Centralist casualties dribbled in from the gun battles south and northeast of town. "Infantry come in with one man wounded (shot through the head)," observed Sam Maverick. "We heard at least 100 reports." Another rumor he noted claimed soldiers had also been wounded in the fighting around Mission Espada. The Centralists surely had learned much from the encounters.

Austin felt the burden of command. Not only was the enemy coming to life, but his own army would soon be hungry. He first turned to men with means among his command to make a loan to the army. He then made plans to secure funding from prosperous farmers and planters back east, or even from investors in New Orleans. Short of cash and with little to be had from passing the hat among his troops, he knew he needed credit. He turned to Captain Seguín to find provisions from the *ranchos* along the San Antonio River toward Goliad and to convince the owners to sell based on faith in the cause. He believed the army needed nearly 300 bushels of corn for men and beasts, and at least ten of beans or peas. "Contract with the inhabitants or owners of ranches," he instructed

Seguín, "at the current price, delivered in the encampment of the army, with the understanding- that payment will be made in money, or that bills of exchange on [New] Orleans will be given, and that in addition to the public faith of the people of the departments of Brazos and Nacogdoches the principal capitalists of Texas, who are now in this army, are pledged for the faithful and due payment of the value of the corn and of all else that is bought from the inhabitants."

At this critical point in the spontaneous and reactionary uprising, Austin fretted over the meaning of it all. How could he keep hungry men, eager for action, at the tedious task of besieging a superior force without defining the cause for which they were suffering? They had been the Army of the People, then the Texas Division of the Federal Army. Lately, he had taken to calling it the Federal Army in Texas. The men would need clarity. So would he. He hoped the convening of a governing body calling itself both the "General Council" and the "Consultation" would deliver some precision on the matter. William T. Austin, a Connecticut native, merchant, and fellow agitator along with William Travis, reported the confusion in camp. "The country also being without a head and in a state of chaos and confusion," he wrote, the general "deemed it important . . . that a declaration should be made by that party to the world, setting forth the principles which the army was defending and the cause in which it was engaged."

While Austin fretted, another newcomer arrived on the Salado: Sam Houston. "He rode into our camp alone, mounted on a little yellow Spanish stallion so diminutive that old Sam's long legs, incased in the conventional buckskin, almost touched the ground," remembered Noah Smithwick. Austin assembled the army. The former governor of Tennessee and member of the Consultation from the settlements around San Augustine passionately addressed the volunteers. He urged caution in the coming days. "He did not favor active operations but advised delay for drill and preparation said that our troops were hastily assembled, composed of citizens, untrained, that the Mexicans were regular soldiers and in a fortified town, and that we were not prepared for an active campaign and the reduction of San Antonio," wrote William Austin. Houston also advised retreat "to the east side of the Guadalupe until the army was reinforced, trained, and provided with artillery."

General Austin, mounted but still clearly weak from his long illness, spoke next. "He delivered a very feeling and patriotic address, in which he clearly represented the true position of the army and the cause in which it was engaged," William Austin wrote. "He alluded to the disorganized state of the country and the necessity of organization instantly; he recommended that the delegates then in the army should proceed to San Felipe and unite with members there and go into session at the earliest possible moment."

The general's nephew Moses Austin Bryan admired his uncle's grit. "In his short speech he told them that he would remain as long as 10 men would stick to him, because the salvation of Texas depends on the army being sustained and at the same time the meeting of the Convention." There were nearly thirty elected members of the Consultation in the ranks. These soldiers debated the merits of getting on with the business of governance or deferring until Béxar had fallen. "A large majority were in favor of the members returning with the exception of those who belonged to the staff, and those who might volunteer to remain," Bryan remembered. "When the thing was first talked of, I thought it would be the means of disbanding the army as I heard most everyone say that he would return [home] if the members of the Convention left." One member of the Consultation set the example, stood by General Austin, and helped quiet the debate. William Barrett Travis volunteered to remain with the army.

General Austin sent a letter with those returning to form the Consultation outlining his views. The men forming this makeshift government should act prudently, he urged, and be clear that they were acting on behalf of Mexican Federalism. The men under his command were loyal Mexicans, he argued, but faithful to a vision they had been promised under the Constitution of 1824. Simply stated, they were opposing the Centralist dictatorship of President Antonio López de Santa Anna. The details of Texas' future within the restored Republic of Mexico could be discussed later.

There were practical matters to address. His army needed money. Indians needed to be kept happy and peaceful so they would not enter the conflict. There needed to be a system of dispatch riders so messages could pass swiftly between the troops in the field and their government. Most importantly, though, Austin needed troops and Texas needed an army.

The army — of the people or of the Federalists, it was hard to say — emerged divided. Many volunteers resented the departure of the Consultation delegates, while others clearly resented what they saw as a veiled attempt by Houston to disband their army. Austin's patient wisdom won the day. The men remaining continued in the field, bidding farewell to their friends and comrades who were members of the Consultation as they headed back east, Houston among them.

With the matter settled, Austin decided to move his army. Reports from Bowie were encouraging. The four missions along the meandering San Antonio River south of town provided the perfect steppingstones for the army's approach, each one serving as a secure base as the campaign developed. Most were ruins but still populated by Tejanos who were, for the most part, friendly and willing to keep Austin's army supplied. When, and if, reinforcements from Nacogdoches and other East Texas towns arrived over the next few days, Austin would surely have enough men to worry General Cos and ultimately to take the town. Gallopers rode away from Austin's headquarters with the necessary instructions for the army. A detachment would mark a route from the crossing of Cibolo Creek to Mission Espada. Austin also directed Colonel John A. Moore to form a useful mounted command armed with pistols and shotguns. Austin could count only 400 men and believed he faced twice that number in the growing defenses of Béxar.

In town, Maverick watched from his house as the Centralists' positions grew stronger. He counted five cannon covering the fortified squares and another posted to defend what had become the town citadel, San Fernando Church. The Alamo, too, bristled with guns. *Soldados* emplaced seven there," he wrote, "of which one, the 18-pounder, is on the top of the old church."[2]

Austin faced other concerns. He was fading. "My health is very bad," he admitted in dispatches back to San Felipe. The disease he contracted in Mexico continued its deadly work. His nephew was more optimistic. "Uncle is better this morning than he has been for several days," he wrote, "although slightly salivated."[3]

5

CONCEPCIÓN

In the gray light of dawn, Austin's little army moved the six miles from their camp at Salado Creek to Mission Espada. By midday, the Federalist Army of Texas reunited with the detachment under Bowie and Fannin, and Austin settled in and continued shaping his army to face the tasks ahead.[1] He found a use for Captain William Barret Travis: he would lead a cavalry company. The mounted troops would provide cover to the army as it advanced, concealing its strengths — and intentions — from the Centralists. With this in place, Austin directed Bowie and Fannin to push upstream to find the army's next position. "Select the best and most secure position that can be had on the river," Austin instructed, "as near Bejar as practicable to encamp the army tonight, keeping in view in the selection of this position pasturage and the security of the horses, and the army from night attacks of the enemy." Once Bowie had chosen his ground, Austin wanted him to scout the edges of the Mexican positions in town. "You will also reconnoiter, so far as time and circumstances will permit, the situation of the outskirts of the town, and the approaches to it, whether the houses have been destroyed on the outside, so as to leave every approach exposed to the raking of cannon," Austin continued. Fannin and Bowie led four companies under captains Andrew Briscoe, Robert Coleman, Michael Goheen, and Valentine Bennett upstream.

The column of mounted Texians moved up the San Antonio River. Dr. Joseph E. Field traveling with the group, describing them as "a detachment of ninety men, many of whom were boys from fourteen to twenty years of age." The column passed Mission San Juan with only a short stay and then continued north. Juan Seguín and his company of Tejano horsemen joined the youngsters; together the men reached Mission San José and considered its advantages but continued upriver to Mission Concepción. Mexican pickets spotted the Texians and then disappeared. "The only opposition we encountered was from a party of Mexican soldiers who came up and fired on us at long range," remembered Noah Smithwick, a friend of Bowie's and along for the adventure. "We returned the compliment and they retired, leaving the road clear."

When the Centralist pickets rattled into town and delivered their report, General Cos emerged from his headquarters. "He went out in person with a small number of infantry and two hundred thirty horses

Looking south-southwest over Austin's camp at Mission Espada, October 27, 1835.

Mission Concepción.

in search of them," remembered staff officer General Vicente Filisola Somehow the opposing columns missed each other along the banks of the San Antonio River. "At La Misión de San José he learned from two men that the enemy had gone along there about three o'clock in the afternoon with some one hundred men," Filisola reported, "and that they had crossed the river near Concepción, the mission nearest to Béxar." Clearly the Texians were looking for a way into Béxar, but the day closed with no action. Cos turned his command around and headed back. Tomorrow he would find and drive away the pesky Texians.

Bowie, Fannin, and Seguín settled on Concepción and, instead of returning to Mission Espada to lead the whole army forward, bedded their command down for the night. The officers opted against taking a position within the mission compound itself and instead chose ground in a bend of the San Antonio River just a few hundred yards upstream on the east bank. The location had many advantages. Water would be secure, and the army would be out of sight as it camped in the river bottom. Creed Taylor described it as "a low ground or bottom with high banks skirted with timber in front and the river in our rear." Any attempts to approach the

Looking over the ruins of the walls of Mission Concepción toward the river bend lined with trees 500 yards to the north-northwest.

Texian camp would face other challenges. "On the other side of the field was a morass," observed Field, "making the entire opposite boundary, except a narrow opening along the river." The Texians were now just two miles from the Centralist positions in Béxar.

Bowie sent a rider back to Mission Espada explaining his thinking. "We . . . selected our ground in a bend of the river San Antonio, within about five hundred yards of the old Mission Conception," he wrote Austin. "The face of the plain in our front was nearly level, and the timbered land adjoining it formed two sides of a triangle, both of which were as nearly equal as possible; and, with the exception of two places, a considerable bluff of from six to ten feet sudden fall in our rear, and a bottom of fifty to one hundred yards to the river." Bowie's command occupied ground that served as a natural breastwork that would funnel attackers into a crossfire of Texian rifles. He described it as an open triangle. Fannin and his men would cover the right, or southern leg, while Captains Coleman, Goheen, and Bennet and their forty men would cover the left.

All the Texians knew the Centralists would come, and they remained edgy. Seguín prepared his men for what must surely come. "Passed the

Since the eighteenth-century century outer walls and their stone and adobe houses are in ruins, local Tejanos at Concepción now live in quickly built jacales (cedar post shacks roofed with river grass) built inside and outside the compound.

night in making preparations to resist an attack which we considered eminent," he wrote. "We were not deceived." A priest from the mission arrived at the Texian camp with warm greetings. Creed Taylor did not trust him. "It was suggested that he was a spy and should be detained," the Texian wrote, "but Jim Bowie coming up recognized the priest as an old friend and assured the boys that the padre was a trustworthy man, and so he was allowed to go unmolested." The people living at Concepción were clearly agitated. "This gave us reason to believe that a runner had been sent to warn General Cos of our presence," Taylor concluded. "Thus, forewarned, we used the utmost caution for the night." The Texians picketed their horses in the river bottom, posted pickets, and Lieutenant Robert James Calder took a half dozen men and posted as lookouts in the tower of the Mission Church.[2]

When one of Bowie's officers arrived at Mission Espada with news that the scouting detachment would not be returning that night, Austin grew anxious. He believed Bowie had blundered and had acted counter to

Mission Concepción from the river bend where Bowie's men will camp for the night, the bank just beyond the trees serving as a parapet if they are attacked.

his intentions. "This disobedience of orders gave the commander-in-chief great discomfort," noted William Austin. "The party being weak, he well knew the enemy would regard it as a good opportunity to attack it." Bowie, by putting himself in a position to be cut off and destroyed, had upended Austin's plans. If the Mexicans took advantage of this opportunity, which surely they must, General Austin would have to march the army to Bowie's rescue. He would face a strong enemy in the open. "This consideration induced him to abandon the thought of making any further preliminary preparations to laying the siege," the Texian soldier noted, "and to march the army with all possible haste to the new position."

OCTOBER 28

At first light, General Austin, still fuming, ordered his 300 men north to save Bowie from his own recklessness. It would prove to be a long six miles. A deserter from the Texian ranks caused a stir, and the tumult surrounding his discovery and recapture delayed the departure. With the sun climbing

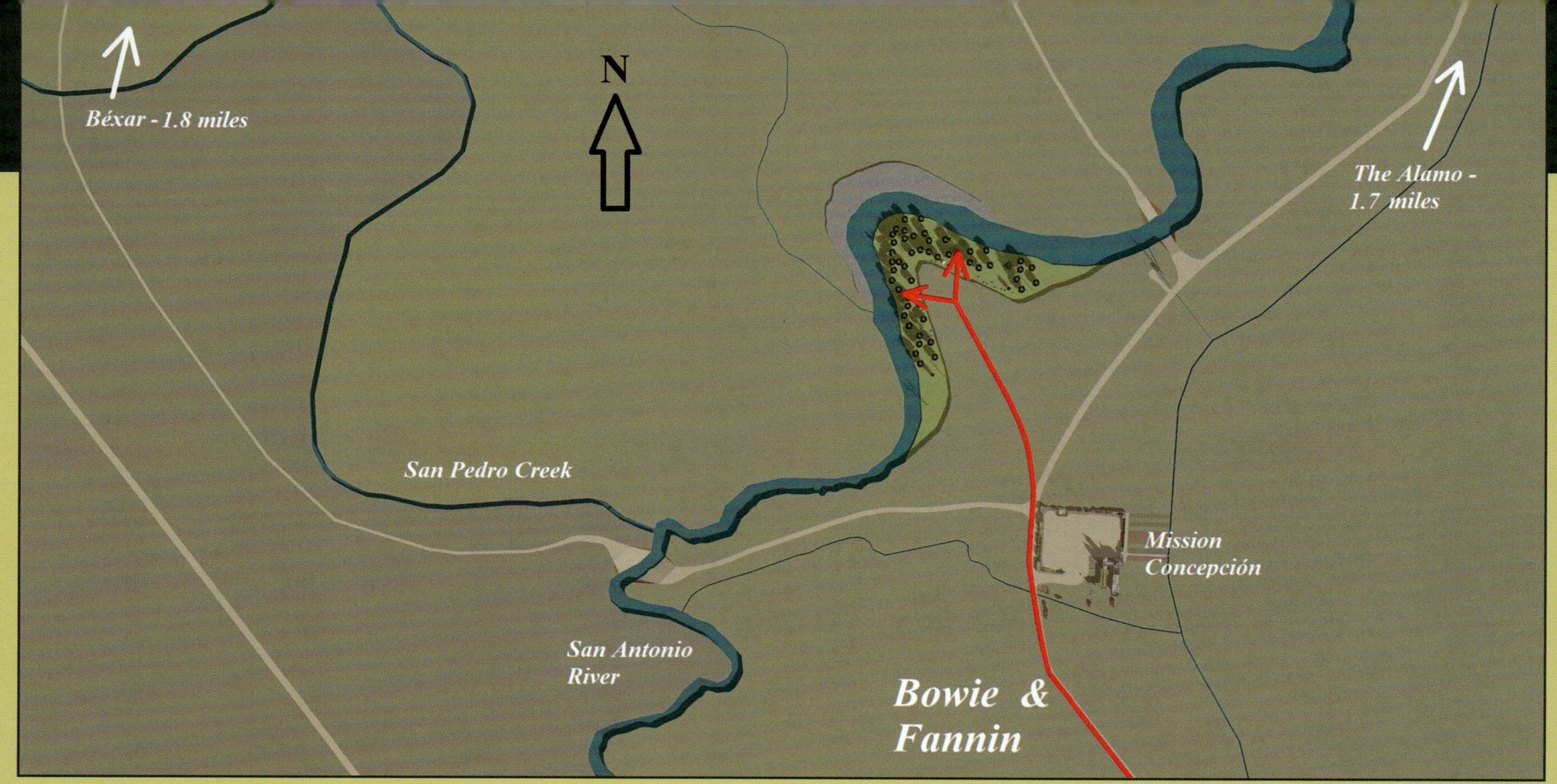

Mission Concepción and environs. Bowie and Fannin continue "above" the mission and camp in the 70-degree angle of the river, Fannin to the left and Bowie to the right. (River bends drawn from the 1903 USGS topographical map, before being straightened in the twentieth century.)

in the sky, and sure that his plan would now be obvious to the enemy, Austin ordered his command to be ready for action. "Expecting to meet the enemy on this march, the commander-in-chief took the precaution to have the army formed in proper order to meet any emergency," remembered William T. Austin. "It was formed with the picket-guard in advance and guards upon the right and left flanks, the camp-guard in the rear, and the mounted company under Lieutenant Travis in the extreme advance. In this order the army moved on without the slightest alarm and began to stir after a quiet night. There was a new danger, though. "At dawn of day, every object was obscured by a heavy, dense fog, which entirely prevented our guard, or look-out from the Mission, seeing the approach of the enemy," Bowie reported.

The Centralists were certainly on their way, even the Texians could not see them coming. Under the command of Captain Rafael de Ugartechea, 209 cavalry rode down the mission road along the east bank of the San Antonio, through the gloom, toward Mission Concepción. To isolate the battlefield, the captain detached a mounted company from the Presidio del Rio Grande and sent it downstream to see if Texian reinforcements might be coming from Mission Espada—and to raise the alarm if they did. Meanwhile, his main force scattered a mounted Texian patrol, forcing them to flee to the safety of the mission bell tower where they abandoned their mounts and clambered to safety. The successful Centralists rounded up the enemy horses and then prepared to move against Bowie's camp.

Ugartechea's men controlled all the roads leading to Concepción, and his command had approached with little commotion. With luck, the Centralists would annihilate Bowie and Federalists detachment. The insurgents had chosen a position with the San Antonio River to their rear and no way to retreat. The Mexican captain could not believe his luck, and he sent a hasty note to Cos in Béxar. "I sent the message that the enemy were hemmed in," he reported, "occupying the woods and the Mission." Close behind, Lieutenant Colonel Don José María Mendoza and around seventy foot soldiers of the Morelos Battalion arrived with a light field piece to add their muscle to the upcoming brawl. They pressed ahead of the cavalry and formed a skirmish line to probe the fog for the enemy line while pushing their cannon into a position on the left of the line to shell the Texian positions down the length of the high bank.[3]

The sun was up, but the river valley remained murky. The Texians at Bowie's camps remained unaware of the enemy presence. By 7 a.m., the men started to cook breakfast. "I and brother Josiah had saddled our horses and breakfasted when two or three of our comrades came along and asked us to go with them to the picket line to relieve the guards for their breakfast," remembered Creed Taylor. "Josiah declined the invitation, but leaving my horse in his care, I took my gun and went along."

When the Texians reached the picket post, a rise of ground on the road heading toward the mission, they spied the silhouette of their comrade Henry Karnes through the fog.[4] The soldier was stooping and peering through the gloom as if trying to locate some object. "In a low tone he told us to listen, that he believed he heard the sound of hoofs," Taylor continued "A few moments later we were fired upon by a large body of Mexican infantry which had silently approached under cover of the fog, and the continued blaze of their guns made a lurid scene." Shocked by the flash of gunfire and the whizz of bullets, the young Texians fired blindly at their attackers and stumbled back toward the river. "Just before we scampered down the high bank, and while yet exposed to the enemy's fire," Taylor wrote, "Karnes exclaimed 'Boys, the scoundrels have shot off my powder horn.'" Mexican bullets cut down a Texian. "We thought he was killed," observed Noah Smithwick, "but, on examination, found that his only injury consisted in a sick stomach caused by a bullet striking and breaking a large Bowie knife which, he carried stuck under the waistband of his pantaloons directly in front. The knife saved his life."

Recovering from the surprise, Bowie went to work as bullets continued to zip and whizz overhead. "The men were called to arms; but were for some time unable to discover their foes, who had entirely surrounded the position," Bowie wrote, "and kept up a constant firing, at a distance, with no other effect than a waste of ammunition on their part." Officers ordered their men to the crest of the high bank where they were to cut

Mission Concepción from Bowie and Fannin's camp in the trees of the river bend. The "Road of the Missions" crosses left to right and directly in front of the mission walls. Captain Ugartechea's skirmish with the Federal outposts was near the grist mill at the left edge of the picture, between the road and the river.

away all brush and improve their fields of fire. If the Mexicans wanted them, they would have to root them out of this strong position. Bare hands and hunting knives tore and hacked away at the underbrush as young men, full of adrenaline and fear, prepared for battle. Others gathered the horses and pulled them close under the cover of the high bank.

Through the mists, Bowie and his men could barely make out the Centralist troops coming into position. "The work was not completed to our wish, before the infantry were seen to advance, with arms trailed, to the right," Bowie reported, "and form a line of battle at about two hundred yards distance from the right flank. Five companies of their

BATTLEGROUND BÉXAR

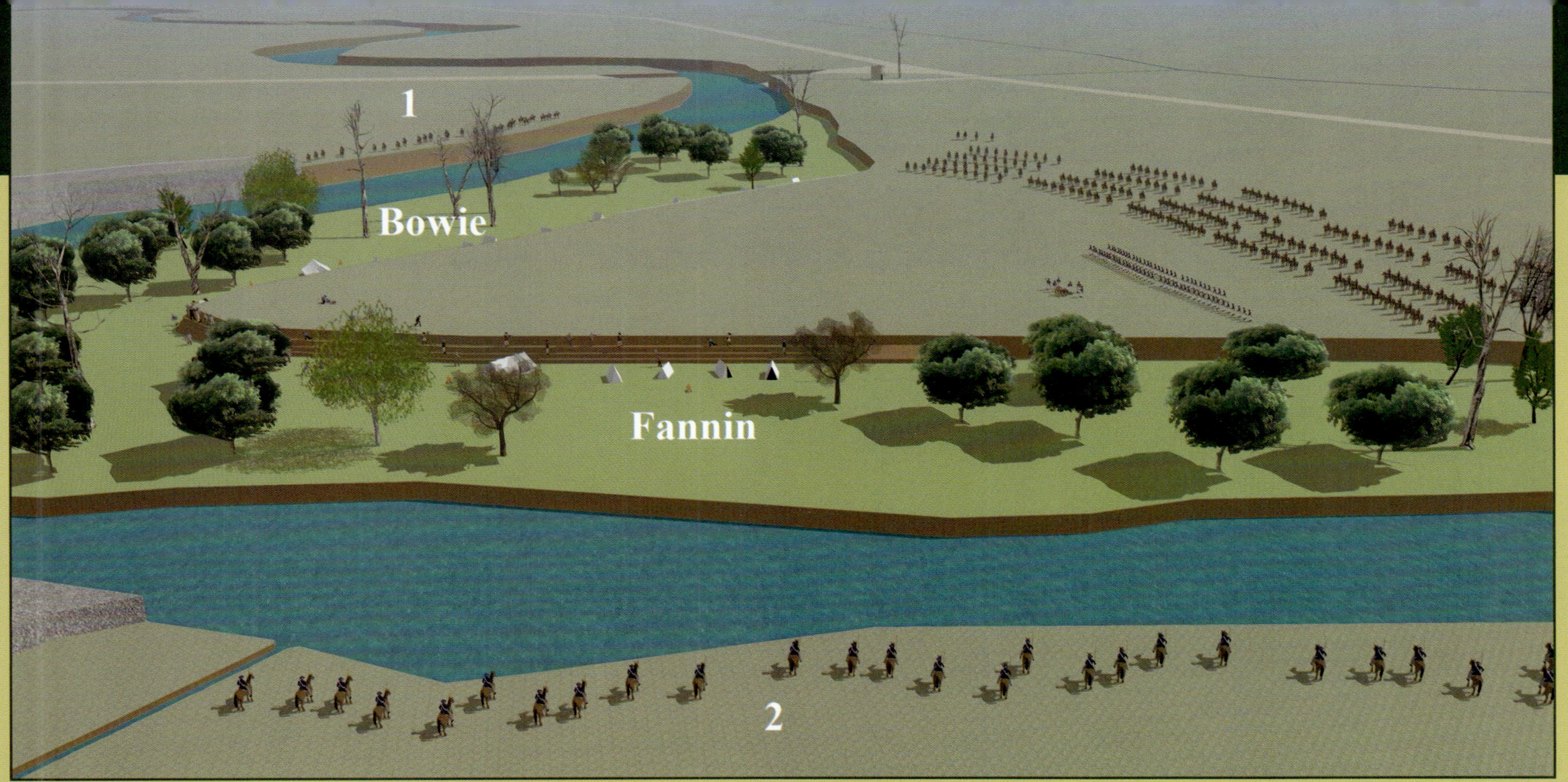

Looking east-northeast over Captain Fannin's camp with the attack about to begin on the plain. Two companies of Béxar presidial cavalry (numbers 1 and 2) of thirty men each are stationed across the river to block possible escape routes.

cavalry supported them, covering our whole front and flanks. Their infantry was also supported by a large force of cavalry." Bowie and his command faced annihilation, and as the morning sun burned away the vapors, the plight of the Texian force became clear. "When the fog rose, it was apparent to all that we were surrounded, and a desperate fight was inevitable," Bowie wrote, "all communications with the main army being cut off."

There was cause for hope. The Centralists would have to cross an expanse of open ground to close with the Texian Federalists. Bowie's men had timber for cover, and the shelter of a steep riverbank where they could reload. Across on the west side of the river, heavy timber and a steep bank protected them from gunfire or, worse, artillery. Presidial troops commanded by Lieutenant Francisco de Castañeda were posted to seal the trap. "Across the river, to cut off retreat, were two companies of cavalry," remembered Smithwick, "but retreat formed no part of our programme."

The Centralists' plan of attack was simple. They would pin each of the Texian flanks, with cavalry threatening the enemy left and the artillery raking the enemy right. The Morelos Battalion would advance in skirmish order on the Texian center. Around 8 a.m., the Mexican soldados advanced.

A rifle shot on the extreme right of the Texian line rang out. The rest of Bowie's men then rose from behind cover and "gave them a volley that broke their line and threw them into disorder," remembered Dr. Field. The misty battlefield erupted in thunder and smoke, flash and flame. "The discharge from the enemy was one continued blaze of fire, wilst that from our lines was more slowly delivered, but with good aim and deadly effect, each man retiring under cover of the hill and timber to give place to others, wilst he re-loaded," observed Bowie.

The rattle of war rolled up the San Antonio River Valley and washed over Béxar. From the house in town where he was being held prisoner, Sam Maverick had no trouble hearing the battle. "At 7 1/2 o'clock," he noted in his diary, "firing commenced, which continued nearly 2 hours."

The amateur soldiers on the Texian firing line found the violence astounding. "It was my first taste of real war and it was a nerve-trying experience," remembered Creed Taylor. "Captain Bowie urged the boys to be cool and deliberate and to waste no powder and balls, but to shoot to hit." Noah Smithwick noted: "Bowie was a born leader; never needlessly spending a bullet or imperiling a life. He repeatedly admonished us, 'Keep under cover, boys, and reserve your fire; we haven't a man to spare.' "

The Mexicans advanced toward the Texian right and prepared to rush the position. Bowie adjusted his lines in response to the unfolding battle, extending his right (or southern) wing by drawing troops from his left (or north) "so that they might be enabled to rake the enemy's, should they charge into the angle, and prevent the effects of a cross-fire of our own men," he explained. "Bowie ordered Coleman to the support of Fannin, and, in executing the movement, the foolhardiness of some of our men caused the only casualty of the engagement," remembered Smithwick. "We scarcely waited, really, for orders, but broke for Fannin's position. Excited and eager to get a shot, some of the boys mounted the bank and cut across, exposed to the fire of the whole Mexican army. They got there before we did, who went around."

The Texians suffered their first casualty. A Mexican bullet cut down one of the more eager of Colemen's men. "The first man I saw as I came around was Dick Andrews, lying as he had fallen, great drops of sweat already gathering on his white, drawn face, and the life blood gushing from a hole in the left side, just below the ribs," Smithwick continued. "I ran to him and attempted to raise him. 'Dick,' I cried, 'are you hurt? 'Yes, Smith,' he replied, 'I'm killed; lay me down.' " Smithwick laid the stricken man down and made him comfortable by elevating his head. "It was the last time I saw him alive," Smithwick remembered. "There was no time for sentiment. There was the enemy, outnumbering us four to one, charging our position, so I picked up my gun and joined my comrades."

The Federalists faced a new danger. The Centralist cannon on their right flank came to life and threated to rake their line. "The battle had not lasted more than ten minutes, before a brass double fortified four-pounder

RIGHT: *The arrival routes of the Centralist forces on the morning of October 28, 1835.*

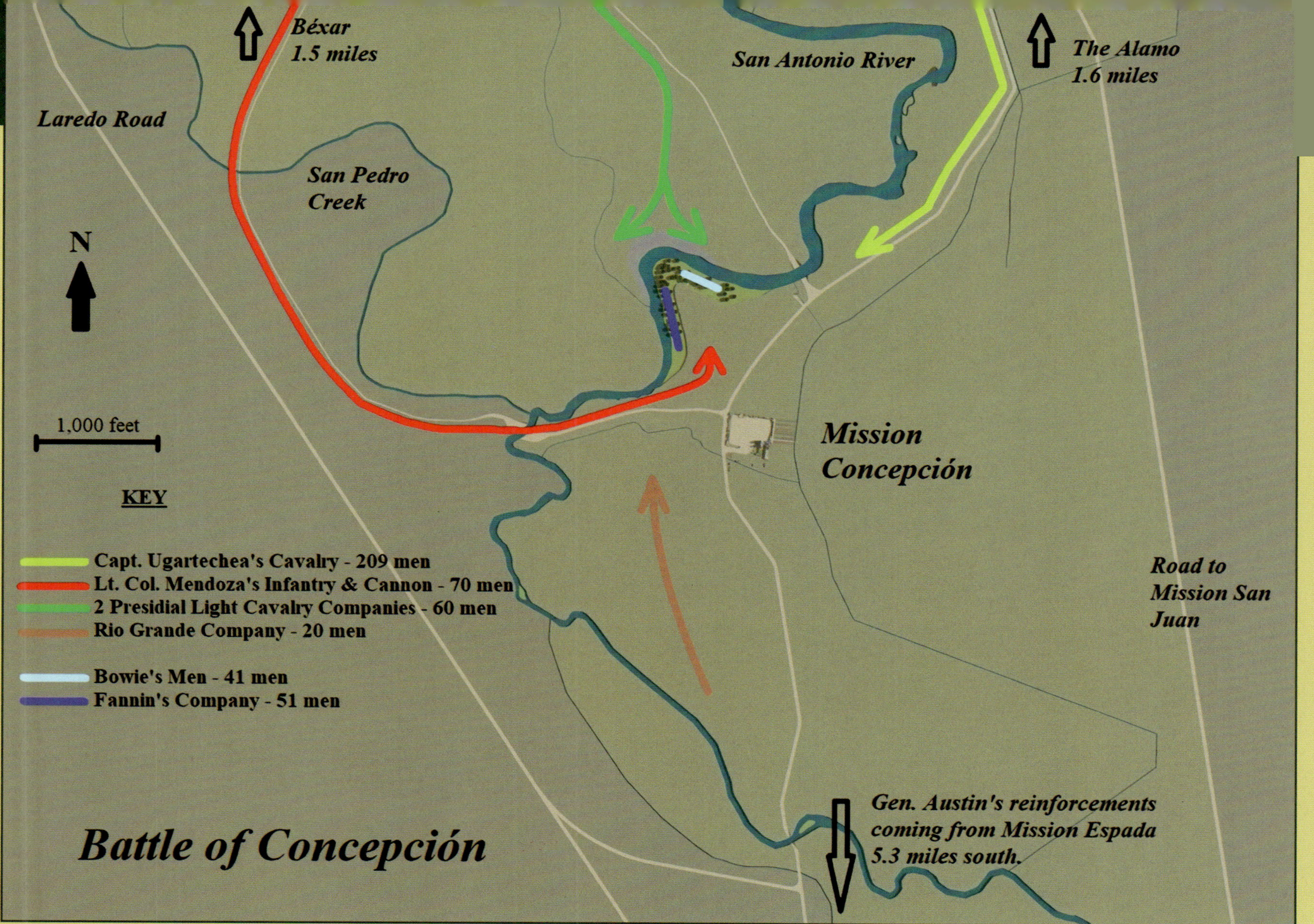

Béxar
1.5 miles
Laredo Road
San Antonio River
The Alamo
1.6 miles
San Pedro
Creek
N
1,000 feet
KEY
Capt. Ugartechea's Cavalry - 209 men
Lt. Col. Mendoza's Infantry & Cannon - 70 men
2 Presidial Light Cavalry Companies - 60 men
Rio Grande Company - 20 men
Bowie's Men - 41 men
Fannin's Company - 51 men
Mission
Concepción
Road to
Mission San
Juan
Gen. Austin's reinforcements
coming from Mission Espada
5.3 miles south.
Battle of Concepción

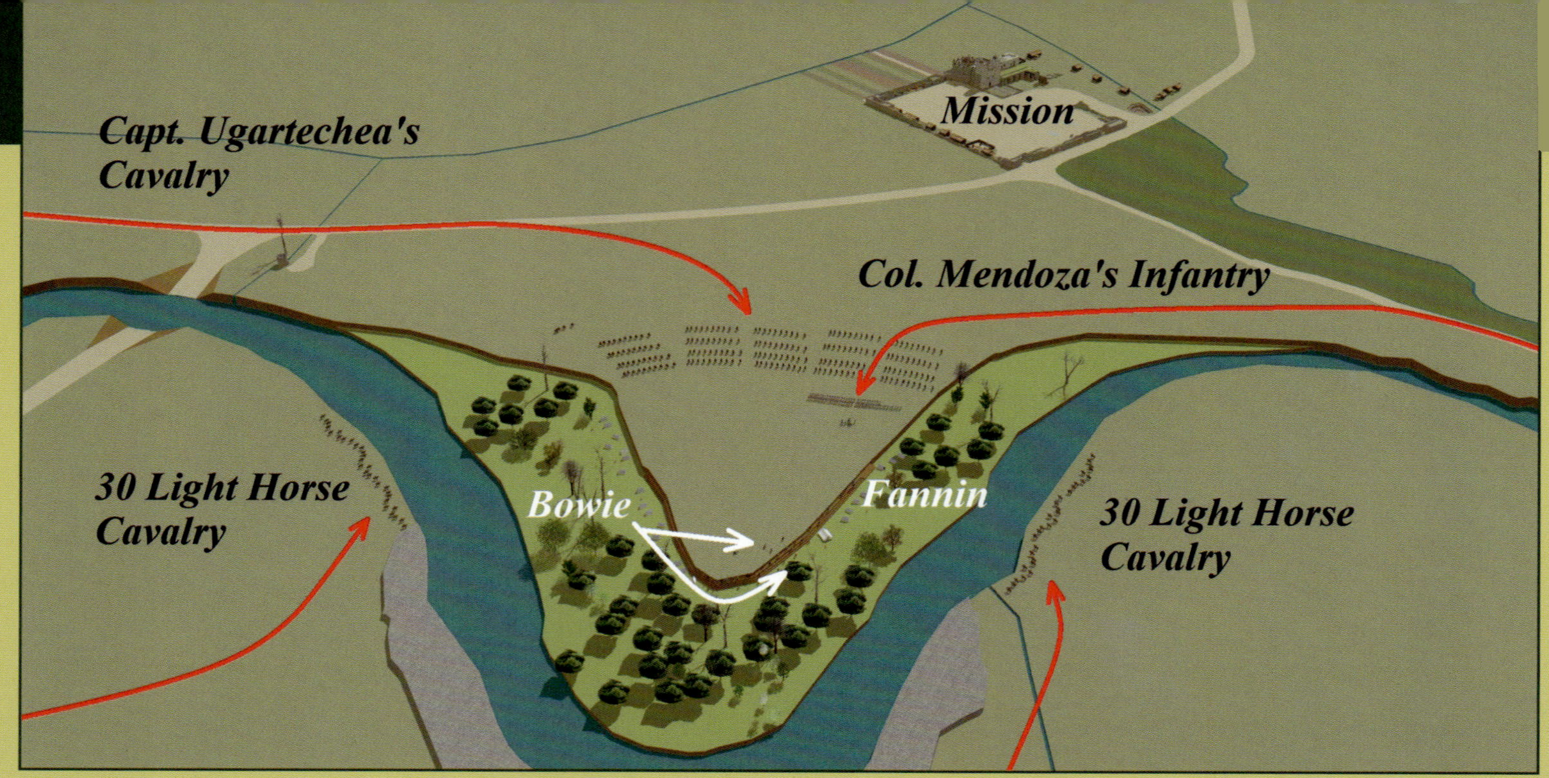

Bowie leads a move (lower white arrow) around to Captain Fannin's side of the river bend with some of his men taking a shortcut (upper white arrow) across the exposed field, or "crossing the angle," as Bowie said.

was opened on our line with a heavy discharge of grape and canister, at a distance of about eighty yards from the right flank," Bowie reported. Bugle calls among the Mexican Centralists announced that bayonets, lance tips, and sabers were made ready to end this fight. The Texians' time had come.

Bowie's men, though, responded confidently. The crew of the enemy cannon, for all its noise, were handling it poorly. Most of its cannister flew over the Federalists' heads, rattling among the branches of the timber and cutting down leaves but doing no harm among the sheltered men. Emboldened, Texian riflemen began cutting down the Centralist gunners. "The gunners became targets for the crack riflemen along that part of the line nearest the cannon," observed Creed Taylor. "It seemed that at one volley every artilleryman hit the dust, and those who took their places

Mission Concepción with the battlefield beyond.

shared a like fate." Bowie was pleased. "The cannon was cleared, as if by magic," he noted, "and a check put to the charge."

Two miles away, the echoes of the battle continued to roll through the streets of Béxar. Sam Maverick noted "9 rounds of artillery are heard, and brisk firing for 20 or 30 minutes."[5] He also watched as brightly uniformed Mexican couriers galloped in with news and led two mules loaded with ammunition toward the fight. Another cavalry company rode out of town, escorting a heavy cannon. The Centralists might, with this additional piece, create a crossfire on the Texian position and dislodge them from their cover. Then the cavalry could do their deadly work with sword and lance.

Would these reinforcements arrive in time? On the banks of the San Antonio, Bowie's Texian Federalists swept the field with their rifles. The

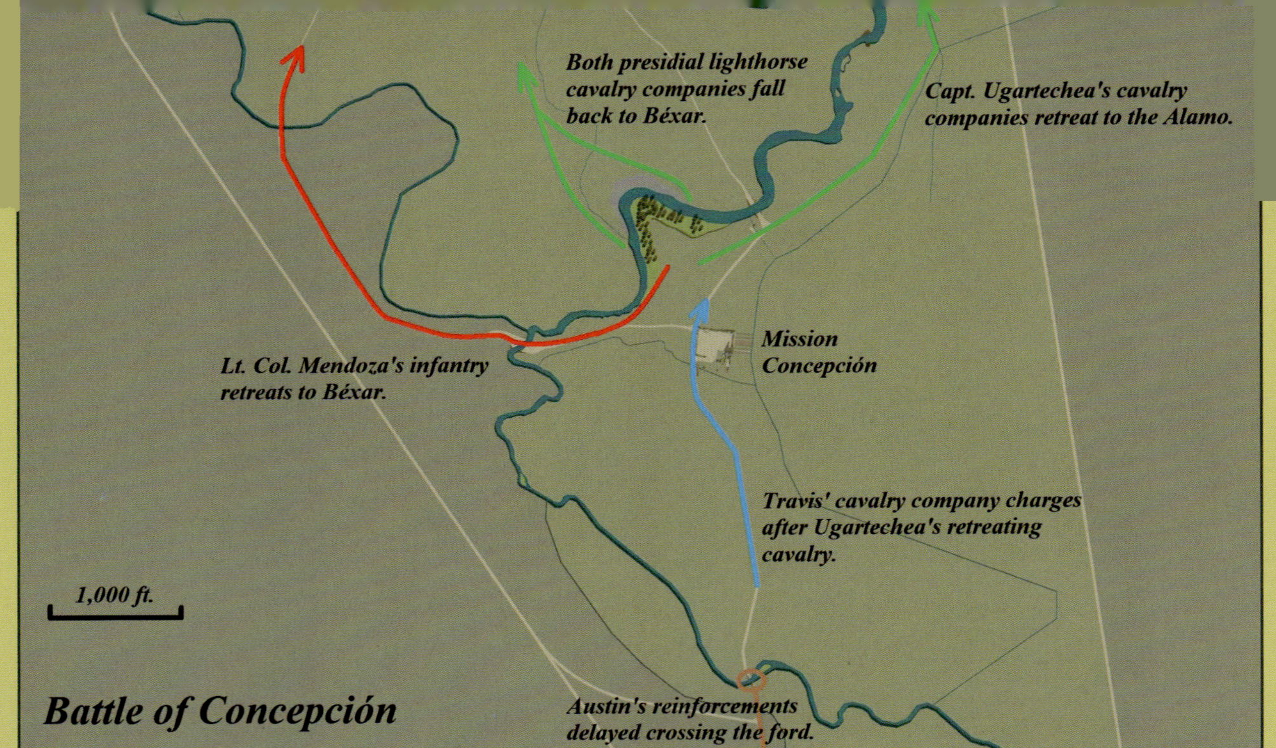

Austin's reinforcements have been delayed crossing the river ford a mile south of the battlefield, and Lieutenant Travis violates orders by leading a cavalry charge pursuing Captain Ugartechea's cavalry.

fog had lifted, and now the clumps of blue uniforms more than a hundred yards away proved easy targets. The Centralists, outgunned, had to close the deadly distance toward Bowie's command to come into range for their smoothbores and pistols, or work up the nerve to dash in and among the insurgents and pit bayonets against tomahawks and hunting knives — a challenge even for veteran and motivated troops. The men of the Morelos Battalion lost their nerve. The Texians, although trapped, proved vicious, and three different advances by the Centralist infantry fell apart under the constant and accurate fire coming from the high bank of the river. The Mexican officers planted the colors of the battalion on the cannon and urged the men to rally there for one more attempt to throw the rebels out of their hole.

Bowie recognized that the moment of decision had arrived. Creed Taylor recalled "While their officers were vainly trying to rally them on their colors, which had been placed on the cannon, Jim Bowie shouted, 'The cannon, boys! Come on and let's take the cannon' and with a wild cheer the men rushed forward." The Centralists fled, their flag fluttering to the ground, as a bugler blew signals after the fact and officers streamed after their men. "'The cannon and victory' was truly the war-cry," crowed Bowie. The insurgents wheeled the loaded gun around and fired a parting shot at the Mexican soldados. "They retreated in great confusion, leaving ten of their dead on the field and several wounded," noted Dr. Field, "and also their cannon for those who know better how to use it." As the Mexicans rode past Mission Concepción, the Texians posted there (or who had taken cover there) fired at them, adding to the Centralist humiliation.

The arrival of the Centralists reinforcements — the cavalry company and second field piece — halted the rout. The Mexican troops rested and reorganized while Captain Ugartechea sent a dispatch to Béxar asking for instructions while also noting the arrival of Texian reinforcements. The answer returned with the hour: fall back into town.

General Austin had arrived with the rest of the Federalist Army of Texas, 300 men, at the crossing of the San Antonio River a little less than a mile south of Mission Concepción. Travis and his mounted commanded splashed across, but the bulk of the troops halted on the opposite bank while crews crossed over the baggage wagons and artillery train. Travis received orders to cover this movement, and from his advanced position he kept a wary eye on the Mexican troops. When the enemy began to disappear toward Béxar, the young lawyer turned warrior led his three dozen riders in pursuit, leaving Austin and his command uncovered amid a river crossing. "Lieutenant Travis, observing the enemy about taking flight as he arrived in sight of the position at Concepcion, instead of giving notice to the army, as would have been proper, pressed rapidly on with his company in pursuit of the panic-stricken, retreating Mexicans," noted William T. Austin. He was too late. As the pennants of the lancers dipped over the horizon, Travis wheeled his command around and returned to the army.

When the Centralists dragged into Béxar, their officers could not believe the disaster that had occurred at Concepción. General Vicente Filisola put his spin on the news, describing the fights as an ambush by more than 200 Texians, who were "able to fire point blank and with great accuracy. Thus, in less than ten minutes almost all fifty brave men of the Morelos group were lying on the ground either dead or wounded, and their artillery piece was in the hands of those traitors." The Mexican cavalry had suffered less. "The loss that I had for my part consists of one corporal and two wounded lancers, two dragoons from Aguaverde and one of Activos wounded, four dead horses and eight wounded," reported Captain Ugartechea.

The Texians claimed their victory. "Thus a small detachment of ninety-two men gained a most decisive victory over the main army of the central government, being at least four to one, with only the loss of one brave soldier (Richard Andrews), and none wounded," Bowie boasted. "The enemy suffered in killed and wounded near one hundred, from the best information we can obtain, which is entitled to credit; say sixty-seven killed, among them many promising officers. Not one man of the artillery company escaped unhurt." The frontier adventurer was proud of his troops. "Every man was a soldier, and did his duty, agreeably to the situation and circumstances under which he was placed."

Austin believed the fight was far from over. "Immediately on arriving on the field upon which this battle was fought, the commander-in-chief believed it to be an auspicious opportunity to put an end to the campaign by following up the victory instantly," reported William T. Austin. "I was riding by the side of the general and heard him say, 'The army must follow them right into town!" remembered Moses Austin Bryan. The general, still mounted and with a sense of urgency, urged his troops to pursue the enemy "and attack him during his excitement and panic."

The men who had just delivered the victory objected. "Colonel James Bowie, supported by Fannin, upon hearing the determination of General Austin, went to him in person and implored him to abandon the project," William T. Austin recalled. The general called his troops to a half, and the officers of his army gathered to discuss the next move. "The views of the general were given that now, then, was the time to capture Bexar, as there would be confusion and consternation," Bryan wrote, "but the

Austin's encampment at Concepción.

**Head Quarters, Mission of Conception
1-1/2 Miles From Bejar, October 28, 1835.**

To the President of the Convention of Texas

Sir — I have the honor to inform you that the enemy, to the number of about three hundred cavalry and one hundred infantry, as nearly as can be ascertained, with two pieces of cannon, at sunrise this morning, attacked a detachment from the army, consisting of ninety men, under the command of colonel Bowie and captain Fannin, who were posted at this place; and after a warm engagement of three hours, were repulsed with the loss of one piece of cannon, (a six-pounder) and about thirty muskets, sixteen men left dead on the field, and, from the best accounts, nearly as many more were carried off. The number of wounded we can only conjecture, with the exception of two that remained on the field. It is with great regret I have to say, that on our side we had one man, Richard Andrews, of Mina, dangerously wounded — I fear mortally. But we have sustained no other loss, except a few horses.

The main body of the army came up, in about thirty minutes after the enemy had retired. A more circumstantial account of this action, which has resulted so gloriously to the federal army, and more particularly to the individuals immediately engaged, will be given as soon as it can be made out.

The overwhelming superiority of force, and the brilliancy of the victory gained over them, speak for themselves in terms too expressive to require from me any further eulogy.

I have just learned that the cavalry of the enemy was commanded by Ugartechea, and the infantry by Colonel Mariano Cos, brother of the general, Martin Perfecto.[7]

S. F. Austin

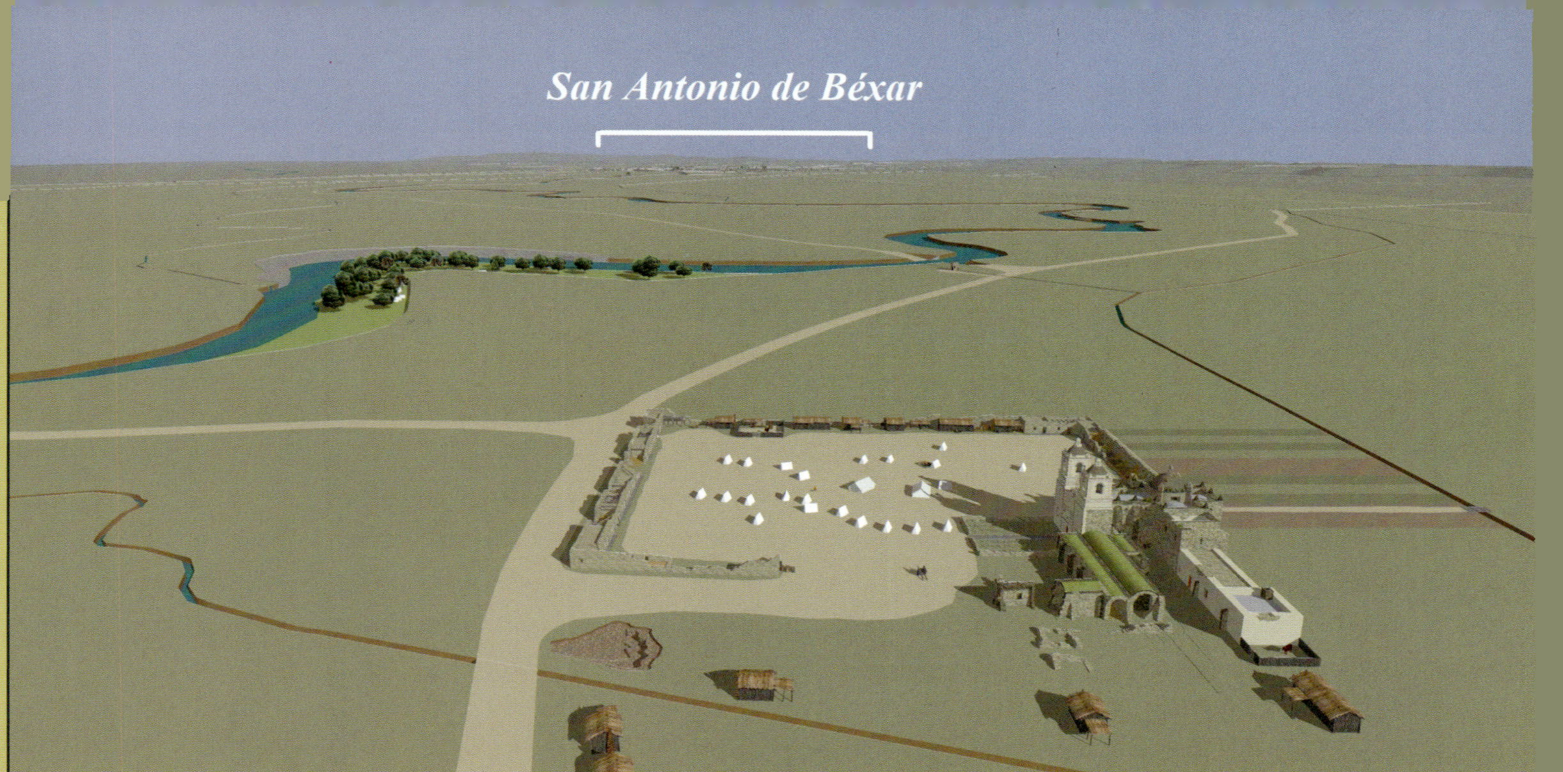

The goal, San António de Béxar, is 2.3 miles due north of Mission Concepción.

council decided against the measure." The Texian Federalists settled for the victory at hand instead of pressing their advantage. Bowie blamed this missed opportunity on Austin's late arrival. "Had it been possible to communicate with you, and brought you up earlier," Bowie declared, "the victory would have been decisive, and Béjar ours before twelve o'clock."[6]

The Texian newcomers gawked at the battlefield they inherited. "We arrived here about the middle of the day," remembered Bryan. "16 Mexicans were left dead on the ground and several wounded and dead were taken off by the cavalry. Capt. Richard Andrews from the Colorado was shot in the stomach. It is supposed he will die." Filing into the compound of Mission Concepción, the Army of the People set up their encampment to await the next move. To the men in the Texian command, Bowie and Fannin emerged as heroes. Austin, his headquarters in place, penned his account of the battle.

To all present, the Battle at Concepción looked very much like war. The grand adventure for which many had turned out had taken a serious turn. General Austin believed reinforcements from Nacogdoches and East Texas were only a day or so away. He believed he had been denied the chance to finish driving the Centralists from Texas, so now he would have to bide his time until a sizable, and proper, army could form. He issued orders to his command. "The Army is now in presence of the enemy — prompt Obedience to Orders and strict discipline will soon effect the great objects of the Campaign, but without them nothing but disgrace and ruin will be the result," he lectured. "It is therefore expressly ordered that any Officer who disobeys orders, shall be immediately arrested and suspended from his Command, until a Court Martial decides his case." The Federal Army of Texas might have won its first battle, but the next step — a giant one — remained. Béxar must fall.

Meanwhile, Sam Houston continued to bet against Austin's success. Houston arrived in Gonzales on the way back east from his unsuccessful attempt to scuttle Austin's plans, and continued to do all he could to abort the Béxar venture. George Huff and Spencer Jack, both Austin supporters, wrote to the Council in San Felipe to provide a report on Houston's additional attempts at sabotage. "Today Sam Houston of Nacogdoches arrived in this place on his return to the consultation of all Texas," they tattled. "His conduct here has evidenced the most discontented & envious of spirits mixed with the most unmeasured vanity." Houston ordered artillery headed for Austin's army to turn around. "He has endeavored to discourage our men by ridiculing the siege and alleging the impracticability of taking Bexar," Huff and Jack continued. "He has tried to induce our men to return by declaring we ought not to march against San Antonio — he has even attempted to persuade one of our waggoners, to refuse to proceed farther — but to leave the cannon and return, he had the impudence to order the blacksmiths who were at work on the cannon to stop — in fact he has in the course of two or three hours stay in this Town done more to convince every reflective mind, that he is a vain, ambitious, envious, disappointed, discontented man, who desires the defeat of our army — that he may be appointed to the command of the next."

In Béxar, Austin ignored Houston's machinations and moved his army to Mission Concepción[8] until the arrival of reinforcements. As they set up camp, a report arrived that troops from East Texas were only one day out. Encouraged, Austin sent a courier and guides addressed to the "Commandant of the Nacogdoches Volunteers" to welcome them into the army and put them immediately to use. "You can safely march in sight of Bejar without going much out of your way — This will have a good effect, in discouraging the troops of the enemy, giving them an idea that we are rapidly reinforcing," Austin wrote. "It will be well . . . . to march in such order as to make the great display possible."

6 ON TO BÉXAR!

More good news arrived at Austin's headquarters. The two battering cannon deemed necessary for breaching the Béxar fortifications were on the road from the coast. The chairman of the Permanent Council at San Felipe, R. R. Royall, conveyed the news in a letter to Austin with a promising addition. "We are happy in announcing to you the arrival among us of 60 or 70 fine young men from New Orleans well equipped and in complete uniform, and who are already on their March from Brazoria to Goliad," he wrote. "Another vessel containing many more is hourly expected. Seventy-five men have gone up Red River also from New Orleans, intending to come by land from Nachitoches, where no doubt they will receive such accessions as to augment the number to 300 men." A 12-pounder gunade was indeed on the way, but a large (and heavy) 18-pounder tube unfortunately had been delayed on the coast since it was too heavy to transport without large wheels.[1]

OCTOBER 30

Finally, the 200-man reinforcement led by red-haired, 31-year-old Captain Thomas Jefferson Rusk arrived. Austin sent orders on where these men should report, and the troops' deliberate approach to Béxar was observed by Sam Maverick from the Nixon house: "In the afternoon a large reinforcement; 2 or 3 hundred, coming to the American army came almost into the town (supposed by mistake) and then turned off." Since Rusk's force arrived from the east, they approached the town on the Gonzales Road over Powder House Hill just a few hundred years south of the old Watch Tower and Powder House known collectively as "La Garita." These reinforcement for the Federalist Army included some veterans, some of whom fought in an 1832 skirmish at Nacogdoches. The skirmish at Gonzales had drawn them, and scores of enthusiastic newcomers to Texas, toward the front.

OCTOBER 31

The arrival of these 200 men from East Texas raised Austin's army to around 600, making it nearly equal in number to the Centralist forces. Thus strengthened, Austin decided it was time to put the vise grips on General Cos. Following Bowie's earlier suggestion, Austin marched most of the army around to the north side of Béxar, leaving Bowie and Fannin with four companies at Concepción. While on the move, Austin's scouts brought promising news. "I have certain information that all the surplus horses except about 250 or 200, were started to Laredo last night," Austin wrote to Bowie. "The number that left is reported at 900 — The escort does not exceed twenty or thirty men." Austin turned to his cavalry commander, Captain Travis, to pick off this Centralist detachment. "He has good guides," Austin assured the officers at Concepción, "and I have no doubt will succeed." Austin had another task for Bowie and Fannin. "I wish you to send to Seguíns Ranch for some rockets that are there — 2 or 3 dozen," he explained. "In Spanish they are called quetes pronounced

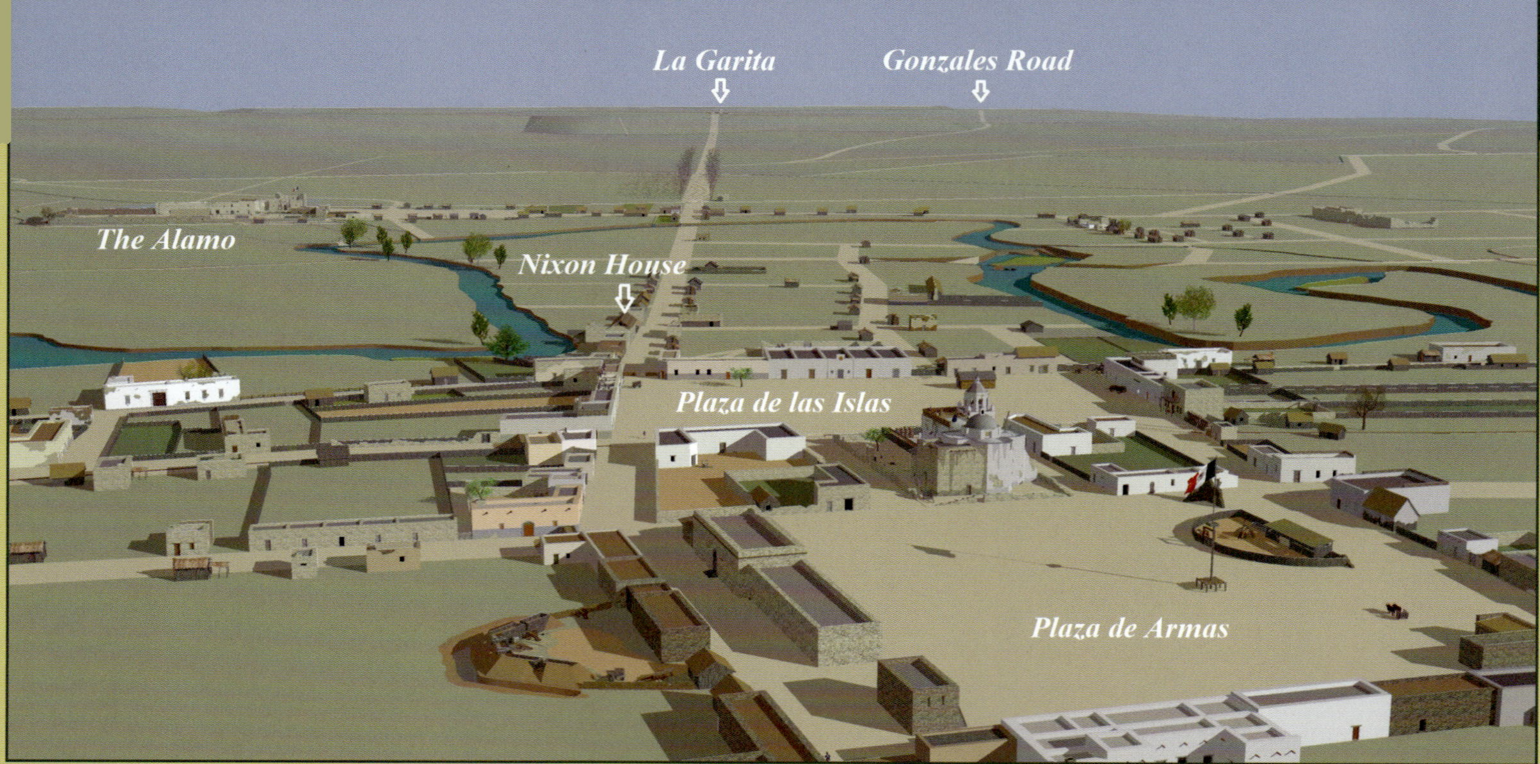

Looking east over the Béxar central plazas toward Powder House Hill. The Nixon house on Calle del Potrero is where Sam Maverick is being held captive by General Cos. Captain Rusk's reinforcements most likely approached Béxar, as per Austin's orders, down the Gonzales Road.

quates — we may want them." These small pyrotechnics might come in handy for signals and momentarily lighting a large area at night. Austin hoped his men could bring them in before Cos caught wind of them.

While Austin maneuvered, Bowie played a different gambit. He sent a dispatch into Béxar providing Cos with a way of diffusing the situation. "You are aware of the position of the forces under my command below Bexar, as well as that of Gen. Austin above town," Bowie wrote. "The two bodies are now prepared to act in concert with each other." Bowie explained that no one needed to die.

There was another way. "I am induced by the most friendly and humane considerations for my Mexican fellow-citizens to open a communication with you in order to close the war & avoid unnecessary effusion of

BATTLEGROUND BÉXAR

blood," Bowie pleaded. He explained that, although he had repulsed the Centralist forces at Concepción, he pledged to respect a flag of truce to discuss an acceptable settlement. "In this event the war may be speedily and honorably closed & the rights of all secured." Bowie explained to Cos that his troops were not bloodthirsty mercenaries but instead were men of principle "just from their homes, accustomed to agricultural pursuits [and] only fought you like soldiers and men resolved to live free or die. They have sworn to support & maintain the Federal Constitution of 1824; and they hold to that as their sheet anchor and will sooner part with life, than abandon it without further effort." Bowie claimed that these men, now roused, would see the job through. "It is with much difficulty these brave men can be now restrained, having been reinforced by a large number of their countrymen and recently flushed with victory purchased with no loss on their part." Cos apparently did not respond.

A negotiated settlement would have to come quickly or the Texian Federalists would bring even more weapons to bear on Cos and his command. Back in San Felipe, R. R. Royall assured Austin that the long-awaited cannon would soon arrive. "If they afford no other advantage you can plant them where they will knock a few of their Houses about their ears," Royall crowed. He was overly optimistic: while the 12-pounder was indeed on the way, the still-unmounted 18-pounder sat useless on the beach at Dimmit's Landing. There simply weren't wheels and carriage large enough to bring the heavy gun forward.[2]

Other promising news arrived at Austin's camp north of town. A local Béxareño reported that two Mexican companies wished to defect. Hopeful, Austin forwarded the news to Bowie and Fannin. "I have to inform you that a servant of Antonio de la Garza came into camp today bringing a proposition from the greater Part of the S. Fernando Company of Cavalry,

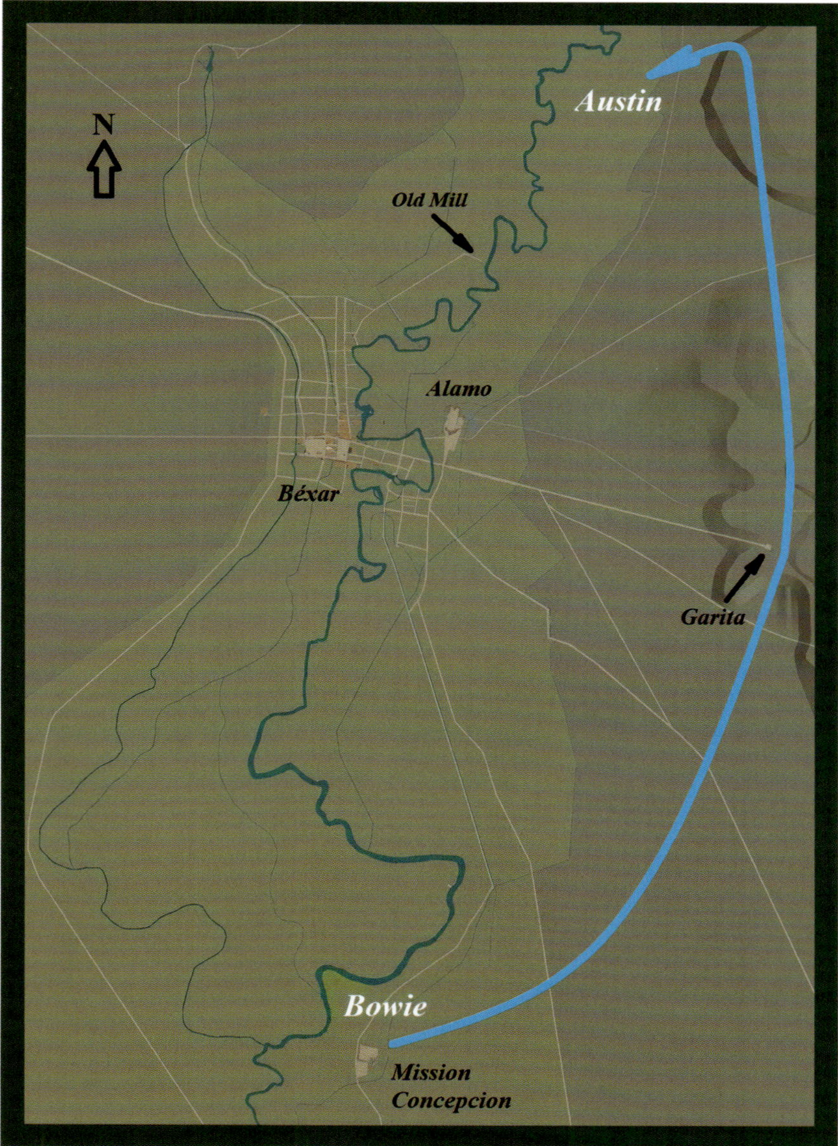

The probable route of General Austin's division as it moves from Mission Concepción to the north side of Béxar. Riding along the top of Powder House Hill gives them an excellent vantage point from which to see the enemy in town and at the Alamo — and to be seen by them, as with Rusk's reinforcements. Bowie's division remains at Concepción.

and the one of Rio Grande — to desert," Austin wrote. "This man was sent to procure a guarantee for them when they come out. I have given the guarantee and have now to communicate, to you, the mode in which they will come out to us." Austin wrote that Bowie and Fannin should create some distraction the next afternoon that would raise the alarm in Béxar. These two companies would sally out to meet the challenge and then simply keep riding away from Béxar and out of this strange siege. "These troops are stationed in the house of Padilla in one of the lower labors," Austin wrote, knowing that Bowie would know the exact spot. "Give these men the chance to come out," Austin urged, "and then escape."

NOVEMBER 1

Bowie and Fannin obliged General Austin and moved their men up to a point along the San Antonio River within a few hundred yards of the edge of town, but by late afternoon nothing Austin had predicted had happened. "We have made all the display possible," Fannin and Bowie reported. When no reaction came from the Centralist garrison, Bowie and Fannin decided to hold their new ground. "We determined to occupy it, and have in consequence brought up the Baggage . . . from Concepcion, and have thrown a rough bridge across the River, and thus occupy both banks. We are resolved to hold it as long as our numbers can justify it, and it meets your approbation." The two companies of deserting Mexicans never appeared. However, Bowie and Fannin believed Cos would answer the challenge soon enough. "We are exposed, and they must certain know our force, and may in all probability attempt to dislodge us," they reported. "As we are here in a very exposed situation much more than you are we earnestly request that you immediately send us a reinforcement the troops will not be satisfied without it."

In town, the Centralists apparently believed Bowie's call for a surrender, followed by his advance up the San Antonio River, might be a buildup to a Federalist assault.. They exaggerated the threat. "A party of 3 or 4 hundred, with Bowie, came up on this side of the river near to town," Sam Maverick wrote in his diary. "The banter not being accepted, after staying till evening, they went down again."

There were other distractions in Béxar that day. Austin sent in his own messenger asking Cos to surrender. "A foreigner with a white flag brought me an officer of Señor Austin," Cos recounted. "I ordered him to turn around and go back, and I told him that we would not receive any flag of truce while the colonists met us with weapons in hand." Austin's plan had failed, and the enemy commander remained resolute. "Gen. Cos stated that his duty would not permit him to receive any official communication

Looking north toward Béxar. Bowie, Fannin, and their men move up to a position (circled in red) on both sides of the San Antonio River "about 800 yards below town." The "house of Padilla" (José António Padilla) is circled in white at the southern edge of town.

and of course it was returned, unopened," Austin wrote. "He in a short time after sent out Padre Garza with a flag [of truce] to say to me, verbally that he had absolute orders from his Government to fortify Bexar and hold it at all hazard — that as a military man His honor and duty required obedience to these orders, that he would defend the place until he died, if he had only ten men left with him." Austin, rebuffed, moved up a piece of artillery supported by a few riflemen and cavalry. The Federalists, in position, opened fire but drew a quick response from the Centralists' 12-pounder. "One shot (Ball) passed over our heads and one of grape fell in the lines but fortunately injured no one," Austin told Bowie and Fannin. In town, the Centralists felt good about the day's event. "From the cannonade they received," Cos smugly reported, "they were obliged to promptly withdraw."

After such a lackluster showing, and with Cos committed to a fight, Austin finally acknowledged that this siege would be drawn out. He broke the news to Fannin and Bowie. "From every information the fortifications are much stronger than has been supposed and the difficulty of storming of course much greater," Austin wrote. "The system of alarms will be kept up as much as possible night and day, and the place invested as closely as practicable." Austin moved part of his army across the San Antonio River to the Zambrano sugar mill — called by locals the "Old Mill" — to put forces on three sides of Béxar.

Austin had to reevaluate his plan. Bowie and Fannin had moved precariously close to Béxar and had asked for reinforcements to hold their ground. Austin had none to give. "The forces are not so unequally divided as appears at first view," the general explained. Travis and his horsemen were never in camp, as they had to handle a host of chores requiring speed and endurance. Whether escorting the long-awaited cannon or chasing

Mexican horse herds, Travis and his troops were constantly on the move. Austin had also divided his command and placed forces on both sides of the San Antonio River, which also left him short-handed. There was another drag on his army's strength. "Our prisoners are daily increasing," Austin explained, "and require a strong guard." Austin also reported quite a few sick in his camps.

He wanted Bowie to know that his excuses were not unfounded. "Everything shall be done on my part possible for the service and to keep up harmony," Austin continued. The ground he occupied, though, also brought challenges. "Our position here is far from being a strong one — we have no bank for defense — a good position cannot be found without going too far off," he concluded. "I submit these matters to your calm

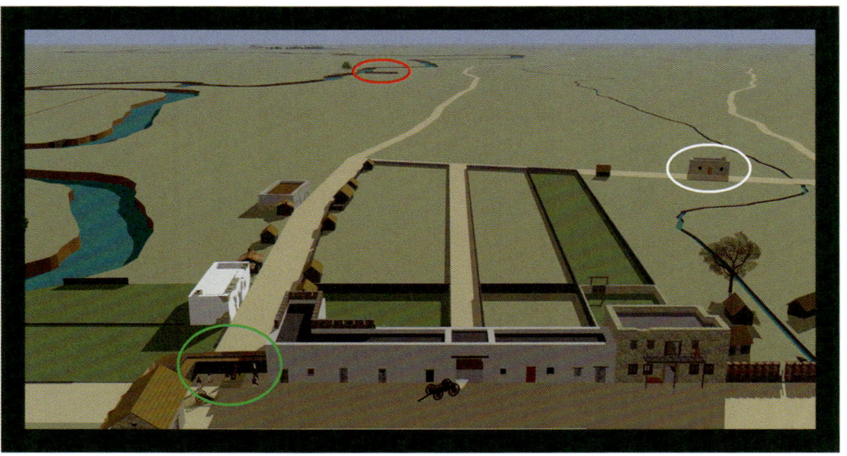

Looking south from Plaza de las Islas toward Bowie and Fannin's position (circled in red), we see how direct a cannon shot at their position would be if fired from the Mexican battery at Quinta Street (circled in green), if they had been ordered to fire. For some reason, however, this order was never given. José António Padilla's house on Nueva Street is circled in white.

Austin places his adjutant general and most of the northern division in the area on the west side of the river just above the Zambrano sugar mill (commonly called the "Old Mill") while he, his immediate staff, and (no doubt) a small company of men continue to camp across the river near the Alamo acéquia.

judgement — It is known that headquarters are here, and the main attack will be here if any is made." The initiative, and momentum, gained by Bowie's battle at Concepción had been frittered away.

Cos was more prudent after that fight. He now understood how deadly these insurgents could be in a fight out in the open. His Centralists had fortified the town and the Alamo well and now chose to stay behind their walls to await developments. Sam Maverick watched it all from within Cos' fortifications. "Cannons now mounted," he recorded. "The place could much easier have been taken with 200 men after the affair of Gonzales than it can now with 1500 men." The American reported the Alamo as "very strongly fortified" and "the streets to the plaza here well-guarded." The Centralists had also cleared fields of fire. "All trees, grass, fences and other lurking places and barricades removed and being removed," he scribbled in his journal, "in order to see the Americans when they come up."

Clearly, San António de Béxar has been turned into a fortress. Events would now make it into a battleground.

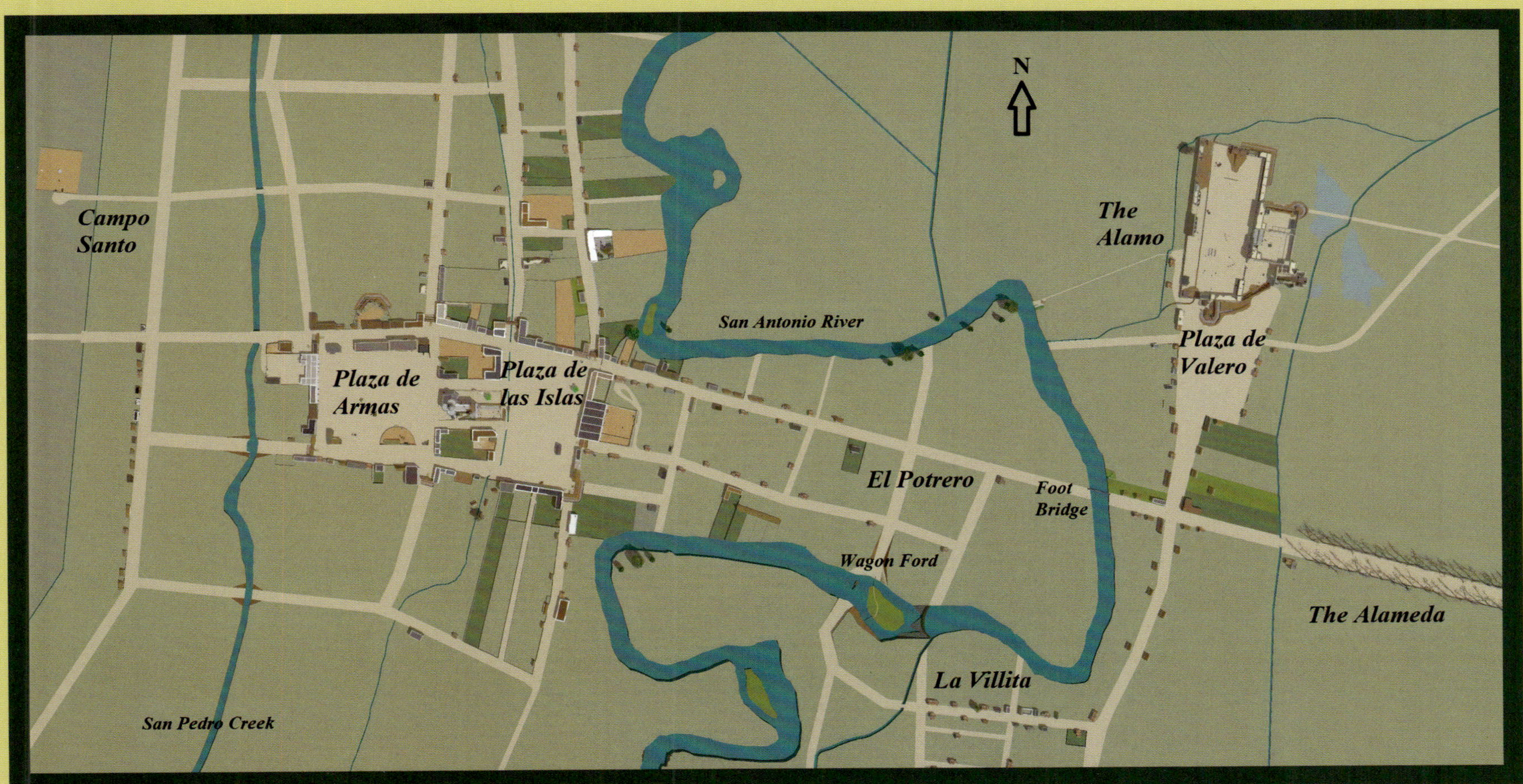

Map of San Antonio de Béxar labeling principal features. The area within the large horseshoe bend of the river was known as El Potrero (the horse pasture). In 1835-36, Béxar and the Alamo were connected only by the wagon ford to La Villita and a footbridge from Potrero Street to the Alameda (grove of cottonwood trees lining the road). There was no wagon bridge.[1]

Béxar looking east-northeast. The back of San Fernando Church is seen beyond the Mexican flag on Plaza de Armas. The Alamo and the Alameda can be seen in the distance at the top of the picture beyond the horseshoe bend of the San Antonio River.

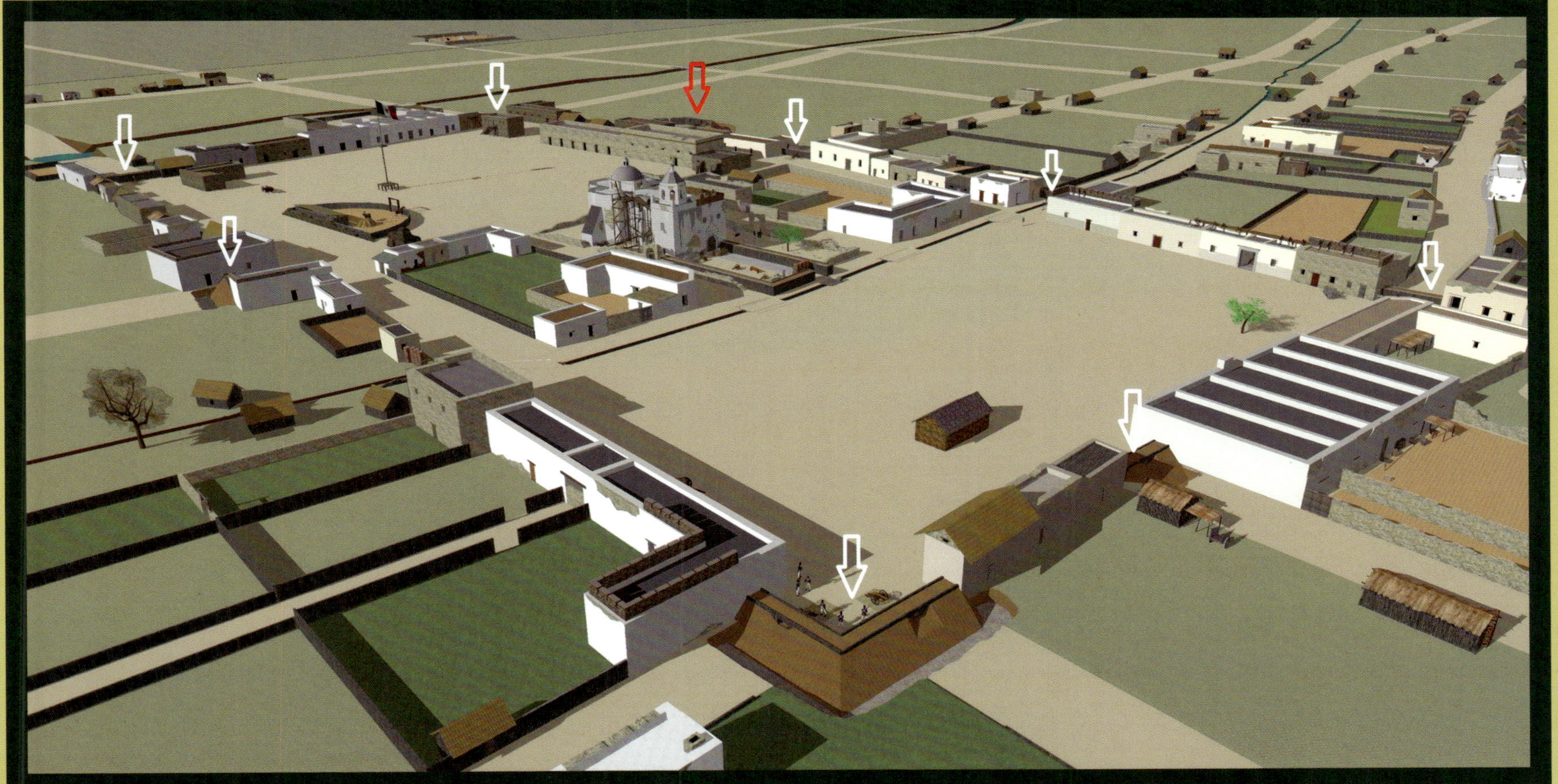

The Béxar Plazas looking northwest. Every street entrance except one is blocked by a palisade breastwork (indicated by white arrows). Each has a cannon port in the middle as well as loopholes for small arms. A three-cannon redoubt (red arrow) outside the north side of Plaza de Armas covers the northern part of the town.

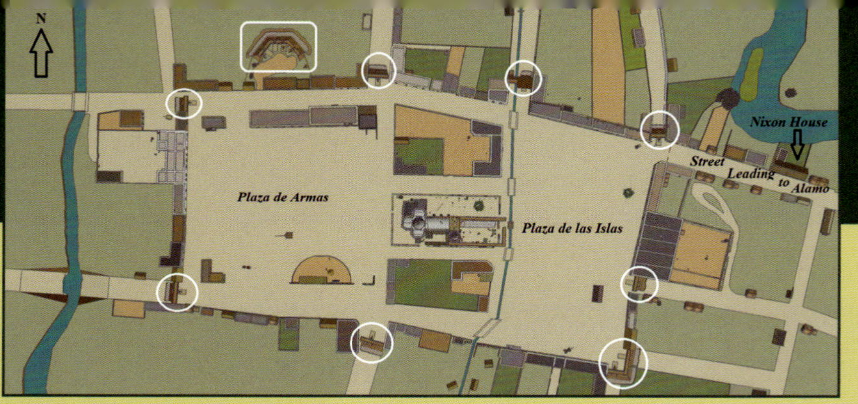

ABOVE: *Fortress Béxar. In this map view, the breastworks are circled, and the northern three-cannon redoubt is indicated by a rectangle. The only street not blocked is the "street leading to the Alamo," the Calle del Potrero (now renamed East Commerce, at the right edge of illustration) since it was considered to be within Cos' fortifications, which included the Alamo and access to it. San Fernando Church with its cruciform footprint separates the plazas and faces east. The Nixon house, where Sam Maverick, John W. Smith, and A. H. Holmes are being held under house arrest, is identified right under the elbow of the river (upper right).*

TOP RIGHT: *Looking west into Plaza de las Islas from the breastwork on Calle del Calabosa (now Market Street). The rear of the town jail (calabosa) is seen right of center, and the Casas Reales (town government buildings) are to the right of the jail.*

MIDDLE: *San Fernando Church has been commandeered by Cos and is being used as a magazine for storing gunpowder. Regarding cannon emplacements, Bowie's report to Austin from Espada said: "They have none on the church — but have removed all their ammunition to it, and enclosed it by a wall, made of wood, six feet apart and six feet high, filled in with dirt, extending from the corners [of the church building] to the ditch . . ." The ditch referred to is the San Pedro acéquia (irrigation and drinking water canal, lower right), which originates 1.54 miles north-northwest of the plaza above a diversion dam on San Pedro Creek just south of its headsprings. It runs down part of Acéquia Street and through the plaza directly in front of the churchyard and continues south, watering the Labores de Abajo (Lower Farms). It then empties into the San Antonio River across from the Concepción battlefield. These hand-dug acéquias are the life of San António de Béxar and environs.*

BOTTOM: *A ramp for easy access to the roof of San Fernando Church has been constructed by Cos' men and is topped by a crane capable of lifting cannon barrels to the roof.*

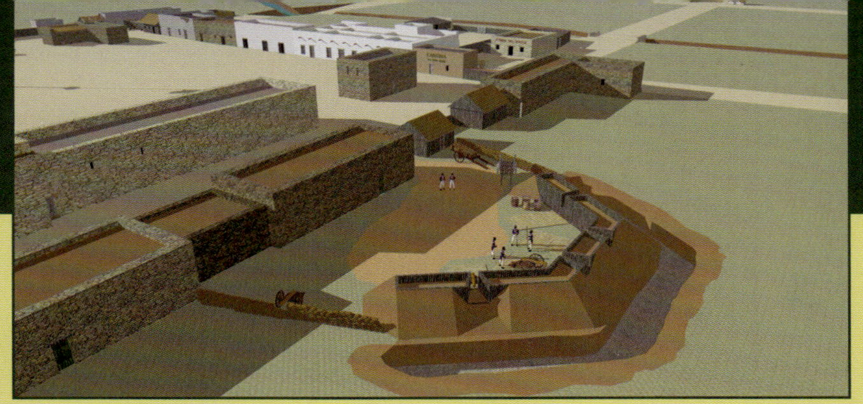

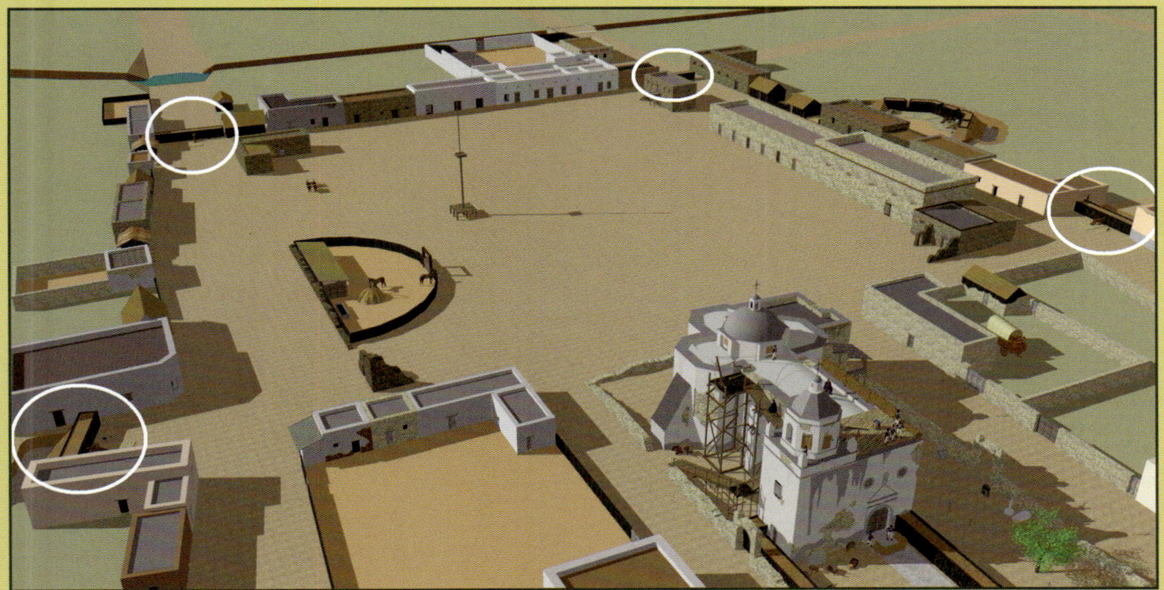

TOP LEFT: *San Fernando's roof and bell tower offer an excellent view of Béxar as well as a good location for artillery, fusiliers, and riflemen. Its use as a powder magazine makes it a prime target for the Federal forces under Austin.*[2]

TOP RIGHT: *The redoubt built beyond the north side of the Plaza de Armas provides a position for several cannon. Their field of fire can thus cover a 180-degree arc, the whole northern part of the town. This is most likely the redoubt that Cos' Mexican soldiers dubbed Fortín de Santa Anna (Small Fort of Santa Anna) in honor of their Centralist president.*

LEFT: *Plaza de Armas, behind the church, also has four street entrances barricaded with palisade breastworks (circled). The houses on this plaza had built up around the remains of the Presídio de Béxar, the never completed eighteenth-century Spanish fort. The ruins of the presidio's corner buildings can be seen within the square. The old cuartel (the long stone barrack building to the right of center) is the only part of the original presidio still intact in 1835. It is now occupied by part of the Morelos Infantry Battalion and will remain standing into the late 1800s.*

The street "leading to the Alamo" starts at the northeast corner of Plaza de las Islas and was named Calle del Potrero (modern-day East Commerce Street). Laid out by the military decades before, it is perhaps the only straight street in town and shoots east across a large area called El Potrero (the Pasture), due to the early Spanish custom of grazing horses there. The potrero is surrounded on three sides by the horseshoe bend of the San Antonio River. Potrero Street is lined part of its length by houses of stone or adobe and others of jacal construction (vertical posts chinked with mud and roofed with a river grass called tule). The stone house with the gable roof on the left side of the street 200 feet from the plaza is the Nixon house, where Sam Maverick is being held. This street leads to a small footbridge crossing the river to Plaza de Valero (a barrio of more jacales) and the Alamo compound (previously the Franciscan Mission San António de Valero until its secularization in 1793). A ford in the river on the south side of the loop (see illustration below) enables wagons to cross to a barrio called La Villita and then continue around the bend to the Alamo.

The wagon ford crosses the low water just below Concepción Dam that feeds the Pajalache, another hand-dug acéquia leading to Mission Concepción 2.3 miles south. The road leads through La Villita (on the right) to Camino de las Misiones (Road of the Missions) which connects the Alamo to the other four missions along the river below town.

The Alamo and Plaza de Valero lie to the left of the road, which leads from the footbridge to the Alameda, the double row of planted cottonwood trees flanking the road. As the eastern extension of Potrero Street, this road is commonly called the Road to the Powder House, because it was laid out by the Spanish military in the first decade of the nineteenth century when they built the Powder House and Watch Tower 1.37 miles east of the footbridge.

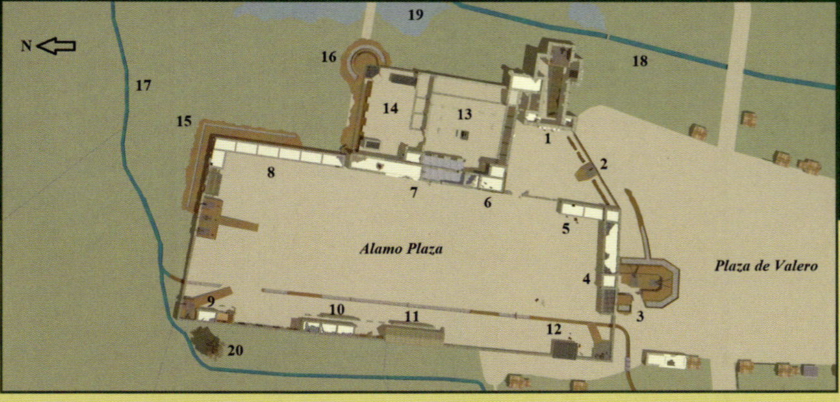

Fortifying the Alamo

TOP: *Plat of the Alamo as occupied and fortified by the Centralist forces under Cos: (1) Roofless Church. (2) Palisade breastwork. (3) Entrance to the tambour protecting the main gate. (4) Main gate through the Low Barrack. (5) Kitchen. (6) Hospital upstairs and storeroom downstairs. (7) Long Barrack (old convento). (8) Adobe houses. (9) North Castañeda house. (10) South Castañeda house. (11) Treviño house, probably used as Cos' quarters during the December Battle of Béxar. (12) Artillery work shed. (13) Convento courtyard used as a horse corral. (14) Cattle pen with latrines (next to east wall). (15) Log and earth revetment (unfinished) reinforcing the outer walls of the adobe houses. (16) Circular palisade and ditch protecting a cannon in the northeast corner of the cattle pen. (17) Acéquia del Alamo, with a branch going through the plaza and now blocked off. (18) Acéquia running to La Villita. (19) Flooding from acéquia due to poor construction and heavy rainfall. (20) Pecan tree.*

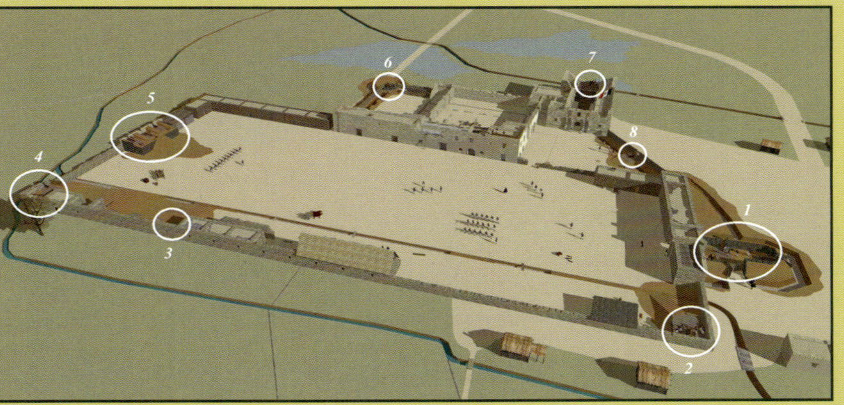

MIDDLE: *Artillery emplacements. Cos' cavalry and the two resident presidial companies, roughly 400 men, occupy the Alamo. His engineers and sappers have built a tambour (No. 1), a semicircular barricade built to protect the main gate. Additionally, cannon platforms have been built to allow artillery to fire over or through the outer walls (Nos. 2-8).*

BOTTOM: *The Centralist soldiers also have built a 114-foot palisade fence to block the gap between the Low Barrack on the right and the southwest corner of the unfinished church of the Mission San Antonio de Valero. They emplaced a cannon (No. 8 in Figure 87) in the middle and a firing step for fusiliers along the whole length of the stockade.*

TOP: *In the rear of the unfinished church, they have built a cannon platform (No. 7 in Fig. 87) supported by stone from the fallen arches that had been built to support the roof that was never added. A wooden ramp has been constructed reaching from the front entrance to the twelve-foot-high firing platform. This eastern (rear) wall was apparently deliberately knocked down to a height of fifteen feet by the Centralists to enable the artillery to fire over it and fit a ramp (still maintaining its regulation 6-to-1 grade) within the building.*

BOTTOM: *There is room on the platform for three cannon facing east toward Powder House Hill. It is probable that Cos has placed the 9-inch pedrero here, the largest cannon he has. The centralists have named the battery Fortín de Cos in honor of their general.*

BATTLEGROUND BÉXAR

The Alamo and the town plazas 800 yards away have been transformed by the Centralists into two distinct fortresses that the Federal army of General Austin will have to breach and capture in order to win this war. Unfortunately, to accomplish this, Austin needs a battering cannon — the wayward 18-pounder.

8 LAYING SIEGE

General Austin was floundering in the face of the Centralists' defenses. He held a council of war with the officers of the northern division, twenty-six men total. The goal in this democratic army, according to Austin, was "to have the opinion and determination of the officers in regard to the best measures of immediate operation on the enemy, whether by closer investment simply or by storm." Would he command a siege or spectacle? Only Major Benjamin Smith voted for an immediate assault; the other two dozen-plus had no stomach for such a bold move. Austin took the side of prudence and ordered his men to move into positions "as would best secure it from the Cannon shot of the enemy and enable it at the same time to carry on offensive operations." Meanwhile, he would wait for his heavier artillery, wherever it might be and whenever it might show up.

Austin sent word to the lower division of the army at Concepción to get their opinion from his officer there. Since he had decided that a siege was the way forward, he asked his subordinates downstream if "the whole force ought to be united above town where corn is plenty and harass the enemy by keeping out beeves by means of detachments and wait until the battering cannon and reinforcements arrive." Or should the Federalist Army of Texas remain posted as it was, above and below Béxar? With his strategy coming into focus, the general began to be bothered by new worries. Compared to Cos's troops, Austin's army remained light on artillery. He had only the gun brought from Gonzales and the cannon captured at Concepción, but others were coming: another 6-pounder and a pair of 4-pounders. None of these guns had the reach needed to face

off with the heavy ordinance in Béxar. The Centralists counted sixteen cannon in their defenses.

Austin's army moved into their new homes. Colonel Edward Burleson took his 200 men to the Zambrano sugar mill and positioned his camps behind the stone aqueduct of the millrace — a seven-foot-tall natural breastwork that ran from the northwest down toward the river. This arrangement kept his position safe from the cannon batteries on the

Béxar looking north over Plaza de Armas and Plaza de las Islas. The Old Mill camp upriver is circled in red.

Looking south over the Old Mill and Federalist camp (bottom) toward the Alamo and Béxar. The mill is on the town side of the river. The Alamo is across the river and 1,000 yards south of the mill.

Alamo's north wall, 1,000 yards to the south. Burleson and his men, thus emplaced, would be within a mile of the Béxar plazas as well as on the same side of the river. Austin maintained his position on the upper Alamo acequia on the east side of the San Antonio River. His avenue of approach, when the day of battle came, would be dead ahead toward the Alamo.

While Austin settled in, his forces at Concepción were unraveling. The officers there had held a council of war and had concurred that a siege would be more prudent. They had also agreed that the safe course of action would be to reunite the army north of Béxar to avoid any chance of being defeated in detail. But something else was brewing. Bowie resigned his position within the army. "I deem it of the utmost importance for you to effect a union of the two divisions of the army as soon as practicable," he wrote to Austin. "Great dissatisfaction now exists in the division and unless counteracted by the measure suggested I seriously apprehend a dissolution of it. The causes which have produced this state of things will be explained when I see you, when I will also explain my motives for taking the step, I have taken in reference to myself." With the prospects of action receding, the troops had turned to bickering. One faction favored Sam Houston's campaign strategy. These men plotted to abandon Béxar and General Austin, join Houston, and assemble a new command somewhere east of the Guadalupe River.

NOVEMBER 3

With the army on the defensive and fissures growing among the various volunteers, Austin knew time was precious. The general obsessed about his hoped-for "battering cannon." Without it, his siege would be pointless, and clearly his officers did not have the nerve to assault the Centralist fortifications. His army would fall apart, and with it, he feared, the cause of Texas. He penned a letter to the president of the Consultation, which was finally in process at San Felipe de Austin, with clear if sardonic instructions. "I have dispatched this express to urge on with all possible dispatch the battering cannon and round shot — I must again repeat that it is useless to send Cannon without round shot as well as grape or musket balls," he wrote. His big gun — and his biggest hope — remained without wheels a long way from Béxar. It also had no ammunition. Austin thought he knew where there might be some. "There is considerable round shot at Anahuac and some at Harrisburgh," he urged. Beyond the need for something to fire at the enemy, and something to shoot it with, his impatient army was facing a winter encampment. "The army will need Blankets, Shoes, Course cloth, for pantaloons and Jackets, Socks," Austin continued. "I am ready to mortgage all my estate to raise funds." Whiskey, though, was already too common in camp, and he urged that no more be sent.

Clearly this campaign was personal, and Austin was prepared to lose everything in his estate to see it victorious. The volunteer Army of the People, expecting as they were that the war would be over in a week, had left home in early October without winter clothing or even, in many cases, without tents. Now November promised to bring sudden Texas northers that could plunge temperatures with little notice.

NOVEMBER 4

News of the squabbling in the Texian Federalist camps drifted into Béxar. "A report is abroad among the citizens that the Americans are quarreling, and particularly Austin and Bowie," noted Maverick. There were other rumors spinning around as well. The Consultation — the leaders of Texas — believed Austin had everything he needed for victory. No more troops need go to Béxar. "On this subject I have to assure you I am decidedly of the opinion that without very strong reinforcements Bexar cannot be taken," Austin responded, "nor with them without battering cannon and from one to two hundred shots for battering down walls."[1]

Austin started to lose heart. The hard math of war worked against him, as did the nature of a democratic army. "In the last few days more than 150 men have left this camp to return home for winter clothing and other purposes, so that the effective force is only about 450 men after deducting the sick," he wrote to San Felipe. "This force, it is known to all, is but undisciplined militia and in some respect of very discordant materials." These men, including himself, were amateurs, Austin continued. "With such a force, Bexar cannot be effectually invested — All that can be, has been done." Cos still had between 600 and 700 men at his command.

What had been accomplished in the last few weeks had been impressive, and Austin believed the support of the men assembled at San

Felipe were crucial to victory. "The enemy have been beaten and driven within their walls, with loss in every instance where they have made sorties," Austin wrote. "At Concepcion they were defeated . . . with the loss of 1 Cannon and 70 men killed wounded and missing." There was much to celebrate. "Our army has so far done wonders," Austin pointed out. "It has confined a superior force within strongly fortified walls. It has struggled against all manner of privations and sufferings, against want of discipline, desertion, dissention." Austin, peeved by the foot-dragging going on in San Felipe, blamed much of the low morale emerging in his command on the "coldness and tardiness in sending out reinforcements." The general could feel the burden of his command. "I repeat, Bexar cannot be taken without 1,000 men at the very least and the battering cannon of which I have spoken," he repeated. He could keep his army intact if he could tell them, honestly, that reinforcements were on the way. "Those who have left have all promised to return," he concluded. "It is to be hoped they will have sufficient patriotism to do so."

Even if the American colonists and their Tejano neighbors were cooling off about the insurrection they had started a month before, Americans from east of the Sabine would stoke the fire. "I last night received dispatches informing me of the gallant Army of patriots who have volunteered and are volunteering from Orleans," the general continued. "This news is cheering and has [raised the spirits] of the army very much."

Austin did not trust the Consultation to support him. Hedging his bets, he ordered his adjutant general Warren D. C. Hall and his aide-de-camp Colonel Peter Grayson to go east personally after supplies, men, and cannon. Perhaps they could also stir the Consultation into supporting the army. "You are to proceed forthwith to the Colonies, for the purpose of bringing on with all possible dispatch, reinforcements for the Army of men, clothing, tents, and all other necessaries — as well also of hurrying on the large Cannon with the proper munitions of ball powder Cartridges," Austin ordered, "all which are indispensably necessary to the Success of the Present Campaign."

While Austin struggled to keep his army together, the Consultation wrestled with defining the cause — the purpose — of this war. D. C. Barrett, a delegate from Mina (later renamed Bastrop), prepared a first draft of a statement of causes for the revolution and a declaration in support of the Federal Mexican Constitution of 1824 that Santa Anna had abolished. "We fight to preserve our rights (thus invaded) under the constitution & laws and to put down the usurped power which has trampled them under foot and restore the full operation of their provisions & the establishment of our rights," his document read. "We fight to establish unchangeably our fidelity to the constitution and laws which we have sworn to support and unite with the friends of Liberty among Mexican fellow citizens in the same glorious object." Barrett and his compatriots hoped to cast their military action as but a part of a much larger Federalist rebellion against Centralist control.

This was not a war of their choosing, these settlers claimed. "We are not the aggressors," the colonists declared, "and that it is our duty to defend our unalienable rights against all who attempt to subvert our liberties, although citizens of the same country." The document repeatedly swore allegiance to the Constitution of 1824 and declared that this was not a war against the Mexican people. The enemy, the document claimed, was Santa Anna. "We are at war and fight against the usurper, Santa Anna, and all who unite and confederate with, aid, support and advise, or council with him in his unjust and tyrannical measures for destroying the established government and all rights guaranteed to the citizens or colonists."

Not every volunteer was so principled. In Gonzales, colonist Launcelot Smither, suffering from a beating he had just received, sent General Austin a disturbing dispatch. A group of volunteers who had passed through town on their way to reinforce Austin's army at Béxar had ransacked the place. Since most of men from that town were with the army, these newcomers helped themselves to personal property in the largely empty town. They also harassed the unprotected women. "The men," sputtered Smither, "broke open all most Every house in town and Robed all that they could Lay ther hands on and such Insults wire never offered to American women before. Thire is no tribe of savages or Mexicans that would be guilty of such conduct." When news of this sacking of Gonzales by supposedly friendly volunteers reached Béxar, it would accelerate the collapse of the army's morale. "If the authority of this army dos not take some steps to stop such conduct," Smither wrote, "the wild savages would be preferable to the Insults of such Canebols."

For the troops in both armies, a siege meant tedium punctuated with daily harassment. Austin's cavalry companies prowled the edges of town, taking the occasional shot at the Centralist pickets, especially near the town cemetery, the *campo santo*. "This evening at 7 o'clock," Maverick reported, "the Mexican Guards, whilst passing in the vicinity of the grave yard, received a couple of shots and came in." There was another reason for the patrol to hotfoot it back into town: a Texas norther blew in a chilly wind, dropping the temperature twenty degrees from a mild day into a blustery night and chilly morning.

While Austin's army flailed away to no avail and other Texians plundered Gonzales, insurgents elsewhere attacked Centralist garrisons still lingering in Texas. Captain Ira Westover and thirty men left Goliad to attack the Mexican Fort Lipantitlán on the Nueces River across the stream from the settlement of San Patricio. Most of the Centralist garrison had left the post to patrol for Texians operating in the area. Knowing that only a few of the fort's garrison were still there, Westover's troops proceeded by forced march and entered the vicinity of the fort about thirty minutes after sundown on November 3. After placing guards at the two nearby fords of the Nueces, they moved up to within seventy or eighty yards of the fort under cover of some *jacales*. Earlier, they had captured an Irishman named James O'Riley who had been aiding the enemy; he offered to go into the fort and try to induce the remaining garrison to surrender. "The fort surrendered at 11 O clock [p.m. on November 3] on conditions of being set at liberty on parole and not to take up arms against us during the war," Westover reported. The Texians disarmed and released more than twenty Centralist soldiers and gathered in more weapons and supplied as well as two small cannons.

Lipantitlán, however, was a poor excuse for a fort. John J. Linn, who was with Westover's force, later remembered it as "a simple embankment of earth, lined within by fence-rails to hold the dirt in place, and would have answered tolerably well, perhaps, for a second-rate hog pen."

However, it had been garrisoned by Mexican soldiers repeatedly since it was established in 1825. Cos, on his way to Béxar in October, had placed ninety men there under the command of Captain Nicolás Rodriguez. Most of this force was somewhere on the main road between Lipantitlán and La Bahía, searching for Westover's force that had travelled from La Bahía to Lipantitlán over a different road.

In the afternoon of November 4, Westover started his men back across the Nueces at the De Leon Crossing, a few hundred yards east of the fort,

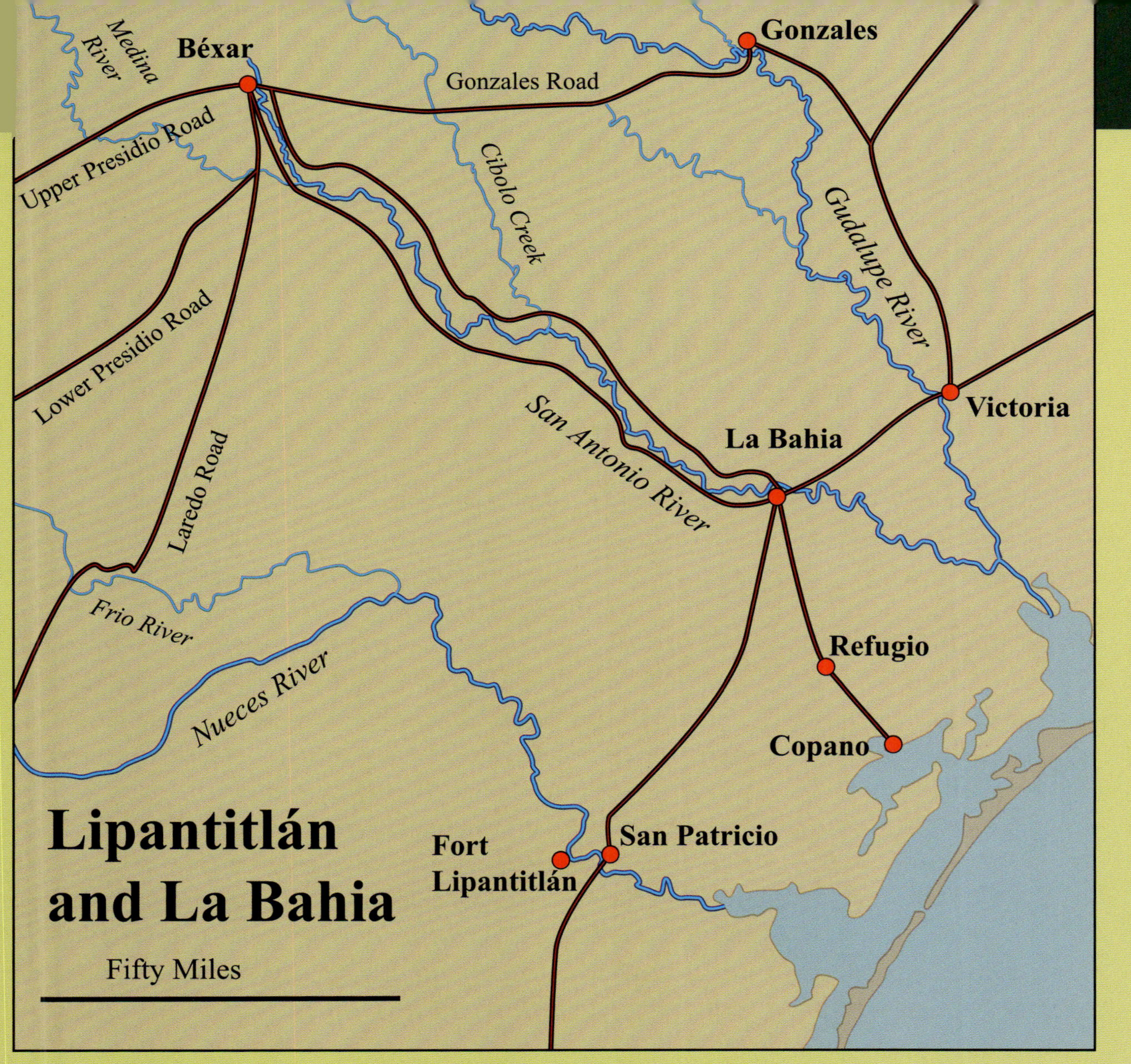

Medina River
Béxar
Gonzales
Gonzales Road
Upper Presidio Road
Cibolo Creek
Guadalupe River
Lower Presidio Road
San Antonio River
La Bahia
Victoria
Laredo Road
Refugio
Frio River
Copano
Nueces River
Lipantitlán
and La Bahia
Fort
Lipantitlán
San Patricio
Fifty Miles

but they were caught midstream. "As soon as the troops were put in motion seven or eight of the enemy appeared in view watching our movements," he wrote. "We proceeded immediately to cross the river leaving six men on the high ground to watch the enemy and after passing about half of our men over the river in a Canoe . . . word was sent down the river that the enemy was coming down with all their force to attack us seventy-three in number." Out of time to consolidate his command, Westover determined to make a stand. The Texians took cover in the timber lining the river, while the Mexican dragoons advanced to dislodge them, aided by Irish militia from San Patricio. The Texian rifles on both sides of the Nueces cut down the Centralists as they advanced, dropping more than two dozen *soldados* as well as three Irishmen. "Lieutenant Marcellino García was mortally wounded and died the 2d day after the action," Westover continued. "We had but one man injured, Sergeant Bracken, who had three fingers shot off from his right hand and the other fractured with the same ball."

After the battle, Westover's company finished crossing the Nueces. Shortly after dark, a cold, wet norther blew in. This made it virtually impossible for them to drag the two cannons captured from the fort back to La Bahía due to the soaked condition of the prairie, and the Texians dumped them in the river. Capturing Fort Lipantitlán had eliminated, at least temporarily, Cos' only line of communication between Béxar and Matamoros, his source for supplies.

NOVEMBER 5

The change in weather accompanied a change in circumstances for Austin's army. The three light pieces of artillery arrived, as did 180 men from East Texas — perhaps including the disreputable "cannibals" who had ransacked Gonzales. Discipline, already brittle in the army, might erode further. Austin, forewarned of the newcomers' rowdy nature, pleaded with the Consultation to withhold the fuel of such miscreants. "In the name of Almighty God," he wrote, "send no more ardent spirits to this camp — if any is on the road turn it back, or have the head [of the cask] knocked out [and the contents dumped]."

Austin refused to get his hopes up even while grateful for the reinforcements. "I must however say that the taking of Bexar is very difficult," he reminded the Consultation. "We have in every instance driven the enemy within his fortifications which are very strong." Austin assured these leaders that he would press the campaign with vigor, but "the convention however must not be surprised should Bexar hold out for a long time." His conditional language telegraphed his own doubts.

One of the thorniest issues was how to starve out the Centralist garrison. The local *granjeros* and *rancheros* continued tending their crops and herds, which put plenty of provisions within easy reach of Cos and his troops. "The corn and country around Bexar might be laid waste," Austin explained, "but this will ruin the inhabitants who are our friends." His army could make it tough on the garrison to feed its horses and miles. "The grass will all be burnt from Rio Grande to Bexar — I shall send parties for this purpose but the other measures of laying waste to the country around Bexar, I think too hard on the inhabitants."

Comforting news arrived from home. Austin's friend Gail Borden (the future inventor of condensed milk), his brother Tom Borden, and Joseph Baker had recently established the first significant newspaper in Texas, *The Telegraph and Texas Register*. His friend reported the Convention's warm support for the Constitution of 1824. But Borden also worried about

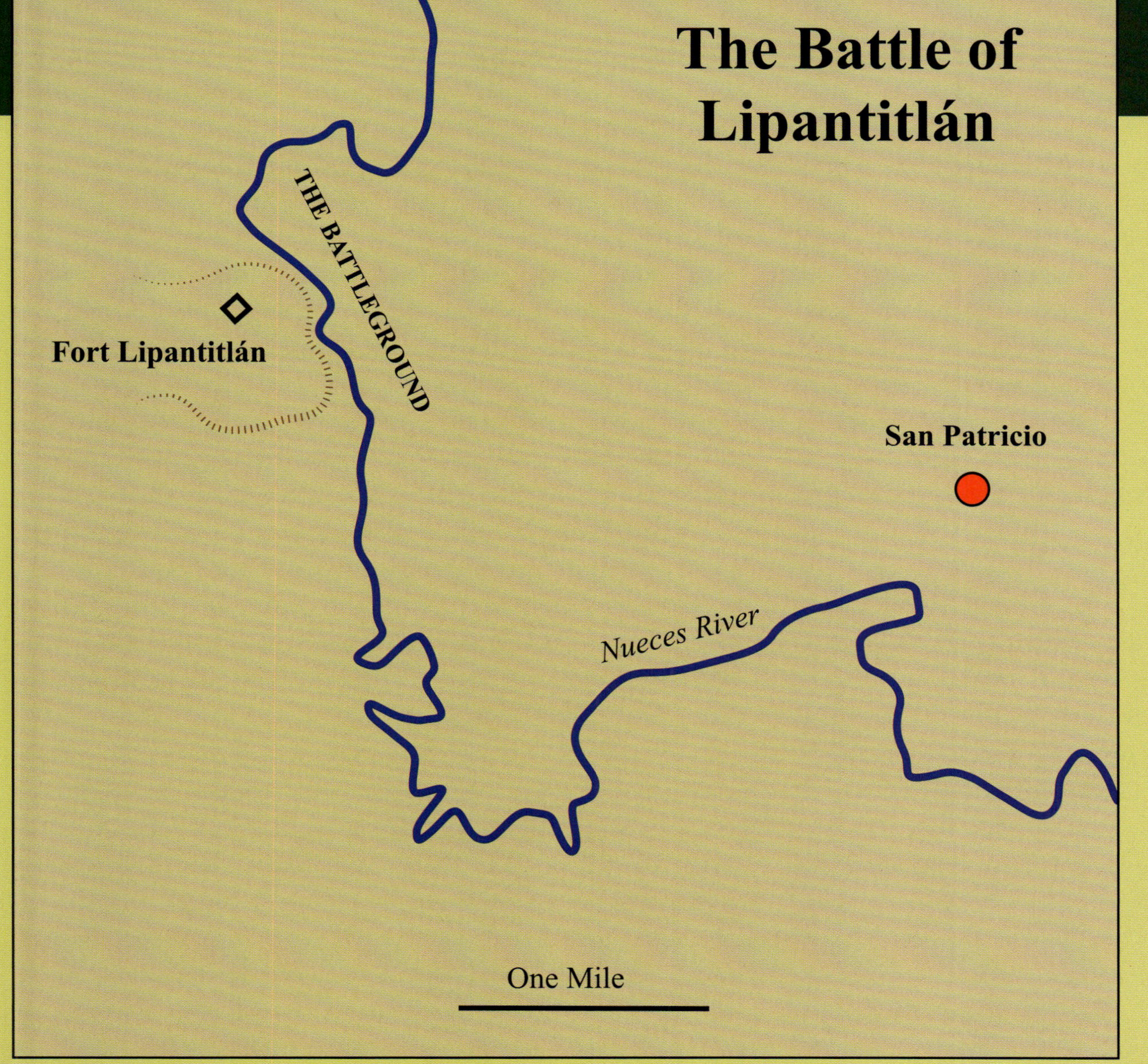

The Battle of
Lipantitlán
THE BATTLEGROUND
Fort Lipantitlán
San Patricio
Nueces River
One Mile

Austin's health. "Last night was a cold and stormy night, and I thought of you and the army — that perhaps you were in the broad prairy without cover and perhaps destitute of wood," he wrote. "I regret to hear your health is not good and fear, the hardships of the Camp and what is worse, the labor of the mind will endanger your health."

Warmed by these sentiments, and by the arrival of the field pieces and hundreds of reinforcements, Austin decided to reorganize the army in hopes of instilling some esprit de corps. First, he needed to replace the officers he had sent east. Bowie, who had tried to resign, instead decided to stay on as the new adjutant general. Austin named Thomas Rusk as his aide-de-camp. The changes would begin by assembling the army. "A General Review and Inspection of the Army now at Head Quarters above San Antonio," Austin's orders read, "take place tomorrow morning at Sunrise."

NOVEMBER 6

Not everyone liked the changes. After the review, the camps came alive with grumbling and second-guessing. Austin's trusted cavalryman, William Barret Travis, quit the army. "Sir — Believing that I cannot be longer useful to the army without complaints being made," he declared, "I herewith tender to your Excellency my resignation as Capt. Of Cavalry." The young officer had come up short when sent to capture the Centralists' horse herd the week before. There were certainly rivals in the army who rejoiced at Travis' embarrassment. Austin refused to accept his resignation and instead ordered him back out, this time after another, much larger herd of horses being driven south. Captain Fannin wrote to the leaders at San Felipe with his concerns over the state of the army. No matter the number of rifles in camp, they needed heavier artillery. "With two 12s or 18s battering pieces, Bexar would have been ours on the sixth hour after setting down before it," he complained. "We have about 600 men in Camp — but whether all will remain, until they [the cannon] do arrive, I am unable to say — but I fear." If the Centralists remained pinned down and if no one came to save them, the Federalists might still prevail, but not without the right cannon.

Travis' bruised ego and Fannin's pessimism were part of a chorus of grumbling. Captain F. W. Johnson and other officers believed Austin was too soft on the locals. If the Federalists were going to starve out Cos, the local Tejanos needed to be controlled. None of the locals should be allowed to gather their own crops. Fourteen men signed a statement to this effect, including Austin's own aide, Rusk. Two men declared themselves opposed to locals being allowed in camp under any circumstances, and another wanted to make sure that Tejano volunteers must stay with the army; the practice of letting them return to their ranches and homes needed to end. The American volunteers were starting to view every Tejano — perhaps even trusted men like Juan Seguín, Salvador Flores, and Plácido Benavides — as potential turncoats. Béxareños who had been frequent visitors to the camp seemed especially suspicious.

As if the rumblings among Austin's own army were not enough, the Centralists seemed to be springing to life as well. Reports arrived that Centralist reinforcements might be on their way. Since Travis had resigned, Austin turned to Captain Andrew Briscoe and his mounted company to scout the roads leading toward the Rio Grande. While Briscoe was prowling west of Béxar, he should also capture or destroy any food or fodder that the garrison might be bringing into their lines. Austin also ordered the captain to look out for two key developments: couriers carrying mail and a payroll caravan. Either one might answer niggling questions about Cos, his army, and his intentions. Beyond that, Austin explained, Briscoe should spend his time "harrassing the enimy in evry in any way possible."

NOVEMBER 7

Other developments buoyed Austin's hopes. If Béxar continued to resist, perhaps pressure from another quarter might influence events in Texas. He sent a dispatch to the Consultation relating a promising rumor. General José Antonio Mexía, a Mexican Federalist in exile, was forming an army in New Orleans to invade his home country and fight Santa Anna. "I know of no movement that would serve Texas so efficiently as an expedition against Matemoras or Tampico," Austin gushed. Mexía, a veteran officer who was fluent in English and intimately familiar with Texas, had been a senator, but when Santa Anna suspended the Mexican legislature, the soldier-politician rebelled. His campaign lasted just two months before Centralist forces ran him to ground in Jalisco. Santa Anna, instead of having him shot, ordered this influential figure into exile. Like many Mexican revolutionaries before him, Mexía wound up in New Orleans. There, eager young adventurers met with him to discuss a scheme to recover his fortunes by capturing Tampico. Austin caught wind of this plan and sincerely hoped that, if true, Mexía's expedition would further erode the Centralists' grip on the country. The general of the Federalist Army of Texas had no way of knowing, but the day before, November 6, Mexía and a band of three dozen American adventurers had set sail in the schooner *Mary Jane,* bound for the coast of Mexico.

At the Texian camps, morale plummeted. One of the volunteers, R. B. Irvine, reported camp rumors to Sam Houston that the army at Béxar was falling apart. "Gen Austin has resigned his command and will retire,

CAPT. JOHNSON AND OFFICERS TO AUSTIN: We the undersigned — assembled at this place with the hope of compelling Gen. Coss to surrender — and expecting to accomplish that result by starving him out — must Solemnly Protest against any Mexican under any pretence save those belonging to our army being permitted to gather corn-Beef or any provisions of any Sort —

San Antonio November 6th 1835

F. W. Johnson Capt	J. H. Money
J. Eberly	Albert Martin
A. Somervell Majr.	P. D. Mesesser
John M Bradley Capt.	George English Capt.
Geo. M. Poe Capt Artillery	R. B. Irvine
Parrott	W. H. Wharton
Ben R Milam	J. W. Fannin Jr.

I am opposed to Mexicans entering the Camp at all

P. B. Irvine   T J Rusk

In addition I am opposed to permission being given to them to return when once entering the army

Wm Scott.

tomorrow, with the disaffected portion of the army to San Felipe," he said. "Col. Bowie will remain at the head of such as are actuated under a sperit of patriotism, for the purpose of driving off cattle, halling off all the corn, and burning the grass, in the vicinity of the town when they will also be compelled to retire, unless reinforced." Yet Austin had not resigned, and the army was not breaking up. Austin's nephew Moses Austin Bryan wrote to his friend James F. Perry that "Uncle has had a trying time of it on account of dissatisfaction, disorganization [and] aspiring men to deal with. But thank God that has nearly all passed and things are going on straight."

NOVEMBER 8

Despite the aggravations, Austin sent word to the Consultation that he was staying with his troops at Béxar. "The determination of the army as expressed today is to remain here at all hazards," he wrote. "I shall remain with them." He told the leaders of the insurrection that he would maintain the siege, but "all now depends on the speedy arrival of strong reinforcements."

Other Texians, though, had lost faith in the cause. William H. Wharton, a Houston man and vocal member of what became known as "The War Party," advocated for aggressive action and had always disliked Austin for his patience with Mexico and now had little faith in the army. Frustrated, he resigned. "Sir, I take this opportunity of tendering to you my resignation of the office of Judge Advocate," he wrote. "It is useless and unusual to give reasons for so doing. I will however say that from a failure to enforce general orders and from an entire disregard of the grave decisions of councils of war I am compelled to believe that no good will be achieved by this army except by the merest accident under heaven."

News from the field did little to increase confidence. In Béxar, Maverick heard news of a dustup west of town. "A spying party of Americans said to be seen west of town a mile out," he recorded in his diary. A squadron of Centralist cavalry sallied out and chased the intruders. The Texians took cover in a gully but abandoned some of their mounts in their flight. Fearing the Texian rifles, the cavalry fell back with their plunder. "They took 6 horses, two frock coats and two hats," Maverick remembered, "on which account the church bell was rung in joy." Later that evening, jumpy Mexican troops believed the Texians had returned; signal rockets raced skywards from the Centralist fortifications, "which threw things into a little helter skelter," Maverick wrote, "and turned out a false alarm."

AUSTIN'S CAVALRY

NOVEMBER 9, 1835

Since Bowie, Fannin, and the other officers in the southern division chose to move their companies north on November 2 and join the main branch of the army at the Old Mill, General Austin had now moved his headquarters back to Mission Concepción to keep a presence below town as well as above. This would hopefully amplify General Cos' feeling of being surrounded.

It was also a better location from which to send cavalry companies on patrols to the south and west of Béxar and cut the city off from supplies and reinforcements coming from Mexico. Austin had been sending cavalry south regularly, and Juan Seguín and his company of Tejanos had even seized a letter meant for Cos explaining that some Centralist troops destined for Béxar had instead been diverted south to fight against Colonel José António Mexia and his attempt to capture Matamoros or Tampico.

For Austin, covering the area to the south and west of Béxar had now become doubly important because word had reached headquarters that other Centralist reinforcements were indeed headed to San Antonio from Laredo. Sam Maverick, still under house arrest in Béxar, recorded the rumors he was hearing. "[It is] reported that 4 or 5 hundred soldiers are coming on to Cos from Laredo (having some reluctant Mexicans as prisoners). The Americans are keeping a good lookout for this reinforcement." The question remained as to which road the reinforcements would use. (See map below.) While the Laredo Road was more direct, the Centralists, trying to slip by Federalist forces searching for them, also could cross northwest from the Laredo Road to the roads coming from Presídio del Rio Grande near present-day Eagle Pass. As a result, the troops coming to support Cos might be approaching Béxar from the southwest rather than from the south.

Austin needed to know. He issued orders for Fannin, explaining that he would be outnumbered nearly two to one but that he would find William Travis and his command prowling around that area. They would be welcome additions to the expedition.

NOVEMBER 10

Other irritations abounded. Many area Tejanos continued to run in beeves and flour to Cos' troops. "We warn all the inhabitants," Austin proclaimed

Mission Concepción church and convento.

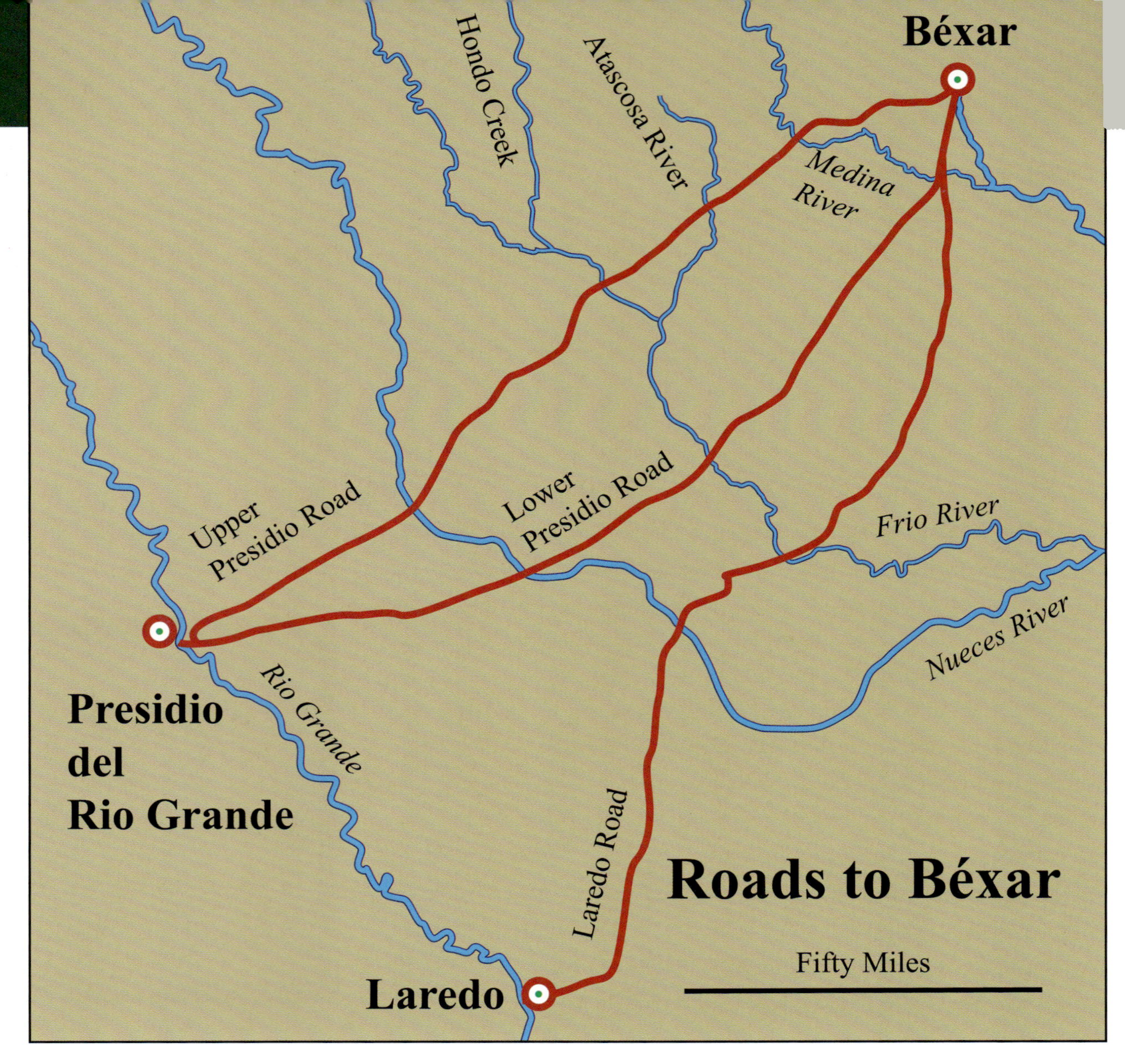

Béxar
Hondo Creek
Atascosa River
Medina River
Upper Presidio Road
Lower Presidio Road
Frio River
Nueces River
Rio Grande
Presidio del Rio Grande
Laredo Road
Roads to Béxar
Laredo
Fifty Miles

in a circular, "not to take beeves or other resources to the enemy centralists and military in Bexar." The general also bared his fangs. "There will be necessary punishment to all those who violate this measure as enemies of the cause of the Constitution and Freedom. Likewise, all communication of any nature with the Bexar plaza must stop."

In Béxar, though, rumors continued to circulate reporting the growth of the Texian army. Maverick reported the arrival of artillery in Austin's camp. "The Federal Army (of Austin & Co.) have from time to time been receiving cannon," Maverick jotted in his notebook. "Just heard they received yesterday one requiring six yoke (of oxen) to haul. Suppose an 18 pounder." This must have been an exaggeration of the arrival of the 6-pounder and two 4-pounders on November 5.

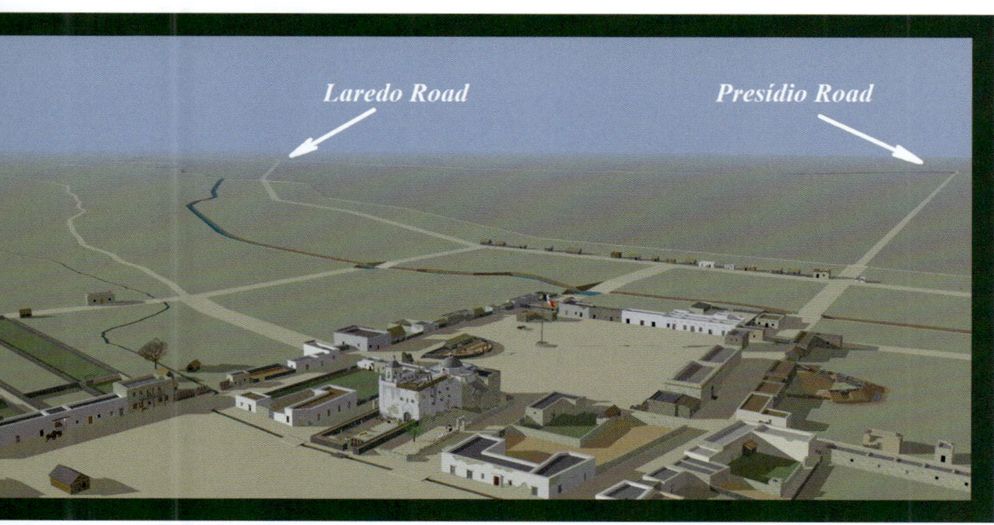

Looking southwest from Béxar at the Laredo Road and the Upper Presidio Road as they disappear into the fog. The Lower Presidio Road branches off the Laredo Road twenty-two miles south of town.

Head Quarters Concepción November 9th 1835

To Cap. J W. Fannin,

Information has been received from various channels — that a large number of packs with supplies of flour and other articles for the enemy in Bexar, escorted by fifty or sixty men who are also bringing on seventy or eighty convicts as recruits for the besieged, are on the road from Laredo. It is of the greatest importance to the service that these supplies should be taken and the party destroyed or dispersed who are bringing them on, so as to prevent their reaching the enemy. You will therefore proceed as speedily as possible with not less than one hundred nor more than 150 men with the best guides you can procure, in the two encampments, in the direction of the Laredo road to intersept the said convoy.

Your detachment will be composed of as many men of your own company as have horses able to perform the trip; of Volunteers from the Nacogdoches battallion and by a detail from Col. Burlison's command above town.

In the discharge of this duty much must be left to your own discretion. According to the information the convoy ought to reach the Atascosa, distant about thirty miles from here, to night, at or before reaching said creek it will leave the road probably on the north side and travel principally in the night through the woods and bye paths. This will render it indispensably necessary for you to keep out spies in every direction so as to find the trail and examine every road and bye way for which purpose it will be important to establish a stationed camp at some concealed place on the Atascosa so that your spies may know where to find you. This however you will regulate according to your own judgment and circumstances.

The greatest dispatch and rapidity of movement is necessary to succeed in this matter. You will therefore loose no time.

continued on page 76 ▶

▶ continued from page 75

You will have the enclosed directions delivered to the inhabitants on the Medina and Atascosa prohibiting them from taking any beeves or any other supplies to Bexar or having any communication with that place.

Travis was to have stayed at Salinas rancho on Atascosa last night. You will inquire for him and incorporate his party with yours. Since writing the above I have additional information that the guard of the Convoy is 200, and the Convicts, 300, your force will therefore consist of 150 men.

S. F. Austin

NOVEMBER 11

If these rumors troubled General Cos, he did not show it. The commander of the Centralist garrison reported to José María Tornel, minister of war and marine, that "nothing remarkable has happened of which to inform you because the rebels remained encamped in the vicinity of this city without having the daring to attack." Neither would he make the first move, he added; instead, he had "limited my operations to annoying the enemy as much as possible."

That same day, Austin sent gallopers out to find Travis and ordered him to support Fannin's attempt to intercept the reported Centralist reinforcements. "Every point must be watched," Austin urged. "This reinforcement must be cut off." The Texian force would number nearly 200 men, but Austin grew convinced that the Centralists were coming toward Béxar. A regular foraging detachment left Béxar on the Presidio Road to cut grass for the garrison's animals, seeming to confirm that this would be the preferred rout for the enemy reinforcements. "But," Austin hedged, "[they] still may come in below."

After dark, gunfire in Béxar disturbed an otherwise peaceful night for Maverick. "Two hours after dark an alarm, and in about twenty minutes four or five hundred muskets discharged and three cannon," he wrote. Two of the muskets went off near his quarters, so he shifted about to see if he could stay out of danger. Before he could, a Centralist officer and a squad of *soldados* burst through his door, with the commander of the band claiming someone had shot at him, as he had heard the bullet pass overhead. "In his lingo he demanded who shot off the guns and why, and in a very menacing, hurried manner ordered his men, who at the word formed in a good position, cocking their muskets, and held them at a present (with bayonets)." Maverick, his companion J. W. Smith, and the women in the house all denied having any involvement. The Centralists, still suspicious, searched the yard. Alejandro Vidal "in the house next door," Maverick reported, "owned that he had shot his guns, saying he shot at some of the Americans on the point, on the opposite side of the river. This was a lie but . . . no more was said." The Mexican officer, convinced by this Bexariño's explanation, left. Maverick and his American companions knew his Tejano neighbor had lied and saved their lives. "If he had declined answering at all, they would have been fully convinced it was we, and certainly if a soldier would have said this. . . they would have shot us instantly. It was certainly a fine specimen of Centralism. Damn such a government."

NOVEMBER 12

The next morning, Colonel Ugartechea called on Maverick to see if he could determine what had happened the night before. The Americans pleaded with the officer to let them leave town. "He reports that the General can't suffer us to go out of his custody; but they promise ample protection,"

Maverick wrote. Down the street, the entire incident nearly led to blows as Centralist soldiers gave conflicting accounts and theories as to what might have caused the incident. Eventually Ugartechea intervened. "The times don't allow brother officers to quarrel," the colonel ordered. He also said their American guests should be allowed to shoot any intruders who bothered them, but they were still not free to go. "If the like insult is offered again," Ugartechea declared, "tell them to shoot down the rascals but they cannot be permitted to leave town."

Time was working against the Texians. While the Centralists showed no sign of collapse, the volunteers besieging them grew restless. Austin had already prohibited liquor in his army but had siphoned away his best troops to ride with Fannin to the south and west of Béxar. What remained in camp were the rowdies and the loafers, growing bored with their adventure. Some began to melt away from the army, going home or off to other pursuits. Austin knew that idleness might undo everything gained in the last six weeks and issued orders to tighten up his army. There were other issues as well, as the various commanders did not seem to know how to coordinate their actions. Colonel Burleson, commanding at the Old Mill, had sent out his own detachments to the west of Béxar, but most of his men had become lost or separated; they returned tired, hungry, and confused.

NOVEMBER 13

Burleson, perhaps chastened by his commander's orders to restore discipline in the Texian ranks, distracted his volunteers by firing upon the Centralist positions. "Report of a cannon heard early this morning," wrote Maverick, "and at about 10 o'clock twenty guns fired in answer to five or ten from the Mill, commenced by the Americans." Texian riders

For as much as the interest of the Country the success of the Campaign and the Safety and Honor of the Army require that order and discipline should be observed as far as it is possible to do so.

It is ordered that no one pass the guard lines at any time without written permission from the Commander in Chief.

It is also ordered that each company in camp be paraded at the Sound of the trumpet morning and evening, the roll called and the number present reported to the proper officer.

The Commander in Chief has no higher ambition than the interest of the Country and the Safety and honor of the Army and expects every officer in the line to use his influence and utmost exertions to preserve order and regularity and to prevent shooting without leave.

Head Quarters [at Concepción] – Novr. 12th 1835
S. F. Austin

also traded shots with Mexican cavalry near the Alamo and the eastern edge of town. Despite the noise and dust, the posturing and shooting accomplished nothing.

Sam Houston, working with the Convention at San Felipe, continued to try to manage Austin's command from afar. The government named him general in chief of the forces to be raised in Texas. Therefore, he worked to dismantle the army at Béxar, fall back to Goliad and Gonzales with a force sufficient to hold that line against enemy probes, and send the rest of the army home for the winter. Houston suggested leaving Cos undisturbed in Béxar. "When the Artillery, is in readiness, march to the combat with sufficient force and at once reduce San Antonio!" he wrote in a letter to Fannin. "Remember one Maxim, it is better to do well, late; than never!" The siege of Béxar had been a mistake, Houston argued. "The army without means ought never to have passed the Guadalupe without the proper munitions of war to reduce San Antonio," he continued. "Therefore the error cannot be in falling back to an eligible position." Houston had other plans as well. Fannin would be his new inspector general of the army, tasked with equipping and organizing the proposed Army of Texas. Houston would lure away Austin's better officers to serve as the cadre of his command.

NOVEMBER 14

The siege ground on. While a half dozen rounds of artillery arced from the Texian positions near the Old Mill toward the Alamo, General Austin relocated his headquarters north of town near Burleson's command. He also took the opportunity to update the government on the progress of his campaign. "Captain Travis has taken three hundred head of horses, that were sent out of Bejar to Loredo — They are poor horses; and were taken about forty miles from this place," Austin reported. "The enemy is closely shut up in Bejar, and more and more discouraged every day." Beyond rounding up some undernourished nags and burning gunpowder to make some noise, the Texian army was accomplishing little. Even so, Austin remained optimistic. "All we need is preseverance, and re-inforcements to keep up the army," he continued. "I entreat the Convention to hurry on re-inforcements with all possible dispatch. There is very little prospect that the enemy will get any aid from the interior."

NOVEMBER 15

Both the Centralists and the Texians continued to fumble around, each trying to discern the other's intentions. That morning, Texian artillery opened up again, this time with greater effect. "Shot as if by an experienced gunner," noted Maverick as cannon balls ricocheted through town. "The fourth shot entering the fort took a soldier's leg off. One shot supposed to be aimed at the Church . . . in the middle of town, hit in a treetop on the bank of the river and fell into the water, one hundred yards from us or less." The projectiles made him nervous as they whizzed by his position. "One hit the corner of Don Fernando Rodrigues' stone house." The Centralists did not return fire.

Meanwhile, Mexican cavalry patrolled to the west and south, hoping to discover and destroy Austin's cavalry under Travis and Fannin. The crossings of Leon Creek and the Medina River were searched by both sides. The Centralists hoped to intercept Travis and his purloined horses; Fannin hoped to discover the truth behind rumors of Mexican reinforcements. Both commands ended their searches disappointed. Travis returned to Austin's camp unmolested, having sent the captured horses east toward Gonzales.

There was other good news for Austin: reinforcements were on their way. At Goliad, Captain Phillip Dimmit welcomed the company of New Orleans Greys that stopped at his post on their way from the coast to Béxar. "They appear to be animated with the enthusiasm of Patriot Soldiers, devoting themselves to the cause of liberty and of Texas," Dimmit wrote, "and they wish for an opportunity only to demonstrate to the world, the strength and purity of the zeal they feel, in espousing a struggle for the freedom of their countrymen; a struggle imposed by the acts of tyranny, and the ambition of their author."

Within the works at Béxar, Maverick watched the inner workings of the Centralist garrison. For the first time, he noted, a flag was flying over that post. He also watched his neighbor, Señor Vidal, gruesomely

Looking over the Nixon house (with gable roof), we see Maverick's angle of view of the Old Mill camp 1,400 yards away (circled left) and the Alamo ("the fort") 550 yards away (circled right).

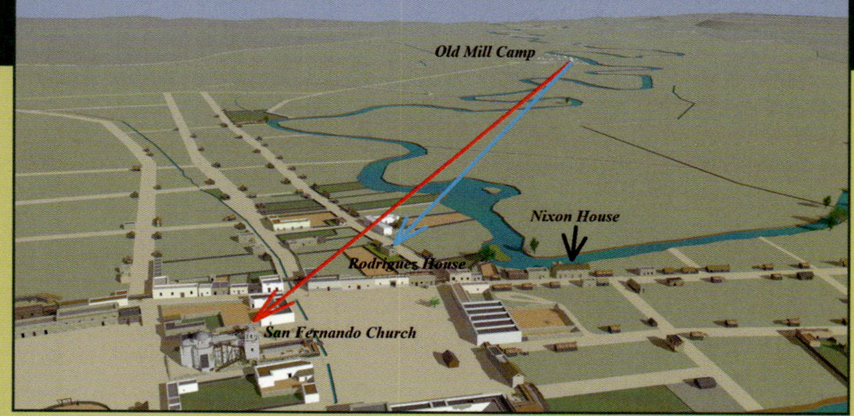

Looking north over the plazas, we see the trajectory of cannon shots from the Old Mill battery to the town. The red arrow shows the one that would have hit the church 1,585 yards away. The blue arrow shows how easily a shot aimed at the church could hit the Fernando Rodrigues house. Maverick, in the Nixon house, had a front row seat, if a risky one.

amputate a wounded soldado's leg with a carpenter's saw. "His operation was singular and savage," Maverick wrote. "He (the man) died at sunset."

NOVEMBER 16

The next morning erupted in yet another artillery barrage from the Texian camp. "Firing commenced a few minutes after at the fort again and after a while at the church near us (where there is a constant lookout kept and where there is a battery etc.)," Maverick noted. "The balls fired at the town fell short a hundred yards or so, one falling at the picket's cannon (No. 2) in the second street, and one knocking down a woman's hen house

— dreadful!" Still trying to find a way out of the Mexican fortifications, Maverick managed to send word to his friend Ben Milam with news that he was under house arrest and trapped. He also hinted that he might be able to escape Béxar and serve as a guide to the Federalist army.

As the cannon smoke drifted away from the Federalist camp at the Old Mill, Travis wrote the report of his successful horse raid, erasing the stain of his earlier failure that had led to his resignation ten days before from his own command. As a volunteer officer in Captain Andrew Briscoe's company, though, he had regained his honor. When his commanding officer had given up the hunt and headed back to the camp at the Old Mill,

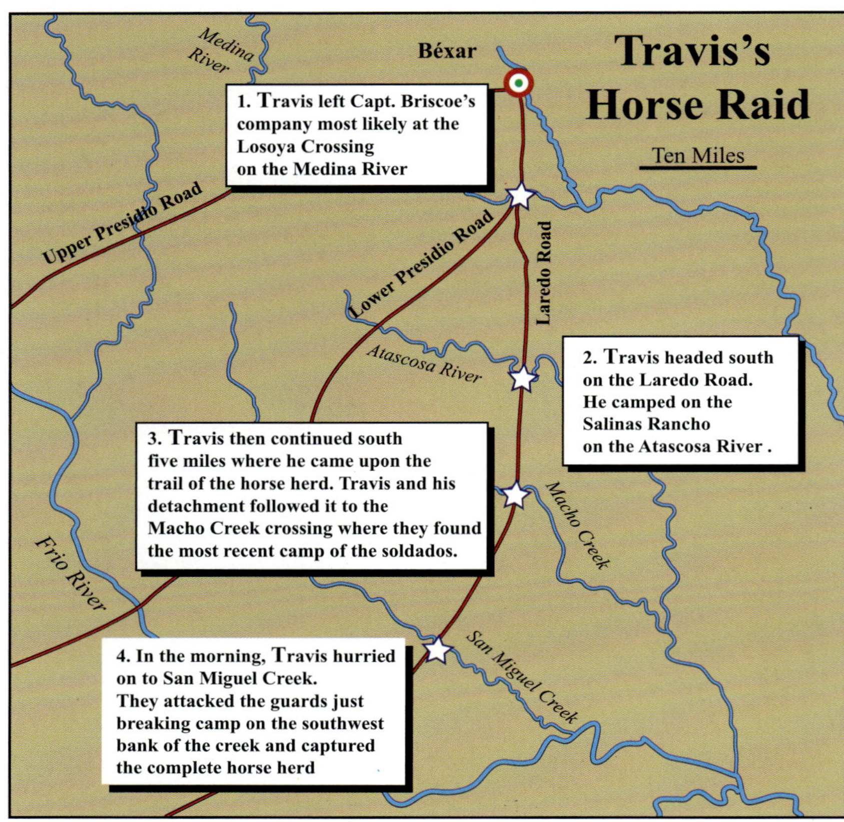

Travis and a twelve-man detachment had persisted. His tenacity had paid off. "On the morning of the 10th, at daybreak I marched to attack the enemy with all speed. I found them encamped in the very advantageous position amidst some oaks on the west bank of the San Miguel about 70 miles from St. Antonio," Travis wrote. "Seeing two of their men out collecting the horses, I ordered my men to charge into their camp on horseback, with a view to divide them as I supposed their force to be superior in numbers to our own." Putting spurs to flanks, Travis and his riders galloped into the Centralist camp and scattered the sleepy *soldados*, who had no idea the enemy was nearby. "They surrendered with out the fire of a gun," Travis crowed. "Two of them escaped — we took five prisoners, six muskets, two swords & 300 head of gentle Spanish horses including ten mules."

NOVEMBER 17

The next day was quiet. The Texians did not shell the Mexicans, and both armies kept their cavalry close. "Not a sound," noted Maverick. "The wind hardly blows. All gayety again in town. Officers riding about on their pampered and mettlesome steeds." News had arrived that General Santa Anna had landed on the Texas coast to come to the garrison's rescue, lightening the mood. The *soldados* figured their ordeal would be over in three or four days. Reinforcements arrived in the vicinity of Béxar, but they were Texians. Captain David Harmon Garner brought in a small militia company from East Texas near Sabine Pass.

Although Austin welcomed the newcomers to his army, their arrival aggravated the need to find food for the Federalist Army of Texas. Ripe corn surrounded the town, but only a few landowners had agreed to help support the besieging army; most others had insisted on cash rather than paper promises from a so-far-nonexistent government. Austin was careful on which corn could be brought in. Since he had no way to pay for the grain, he depended on the owners' generosity. Fields on the east side of the San Antonio River, north and south of the Alamo, were owned mostly by descendants of mission Indian converts who were very willing to help the insurgents. Wealthy Béxareños owned the fields west of the river, and they would settle only for cash.

NOVEMBER 18

The stalemate at Béxar appeared to be breaking. Texians had learned that many of the mounted troops in the garrison were patrolling toward the Rio Grande to bring up supplies and reinforcements. The Centralists, too, felt vulnerable with part of their forces away, and they beefed up security in the town amid rumors that Austin would soon storm Béxar. "From the very uncommon caution observed last night for the first time (and in the afternoon) in challenging citizens as they passed [the home of Don Ramón] Musquis' corner, and (what they never did before) making them tell what business they were upon etc., it is my opinion that some news came in during yesterday afternoon about the Americans' design of making an attack," observed Maverick. Potrero Street, going east from Plaza de las Islas to the Alameda, was the only street entrance not formally barricaded, as it was the main thoroughfare between the plazas and the Alamo. The entrance had now become a checkpoint, worsening the tension and inconvenience for the Béxareños trapped in the town.

The Centralist fears had a basis in fact. Austin, with his health finally improving, had become quite enthusiastic about the situation and possibilities. He wrote to the Consultation to express his views and

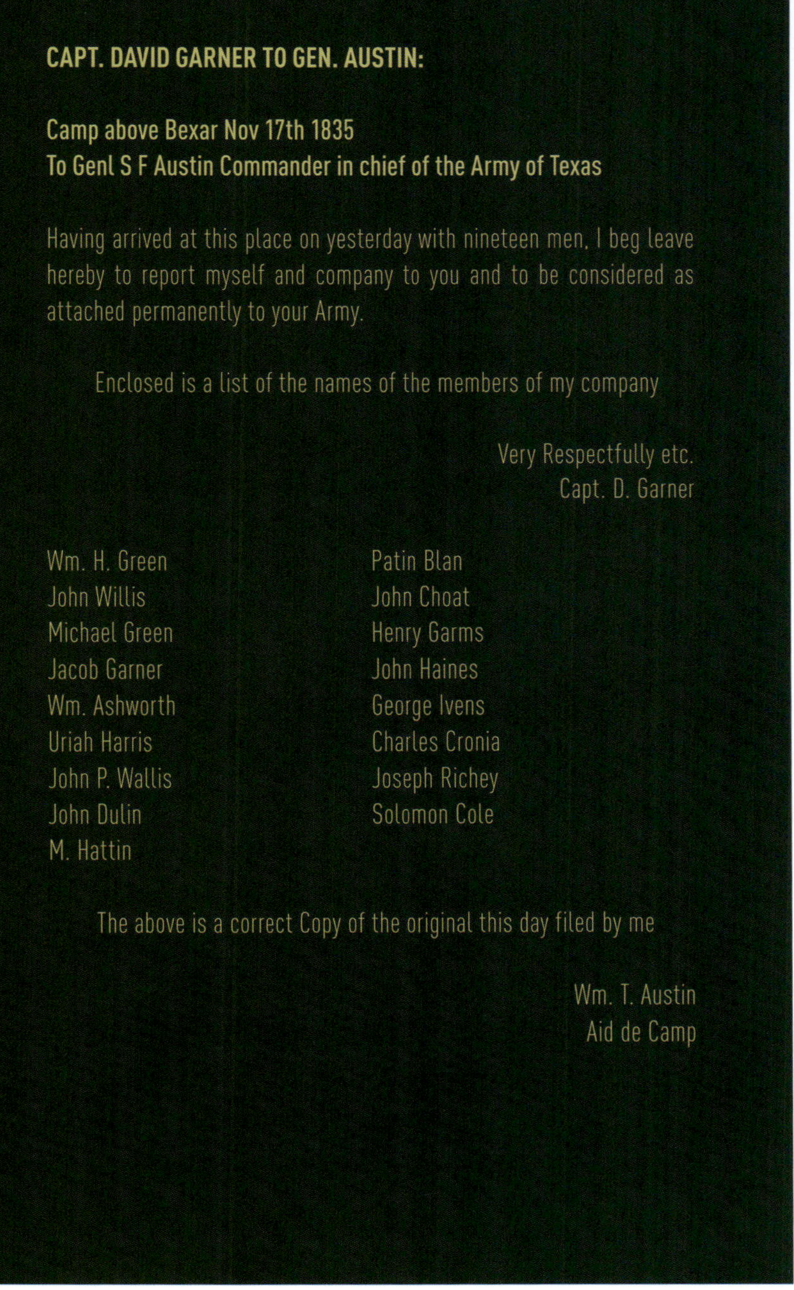

CAPT. DAVID GARNER TO GEN. AUSTIN:

Camp above Bexar Nov 17th 1835
To Genl S F Austin Commander in chief of the Army of Texas

Having arrived at this place on yesterday with nineteen men, I beg leave hereby to report myself and company to you and to be considered as attached permanently to your Army.

Enclosed is a list of the names of the members of my company

Very Respectfully etc.
Capt. D. Garner

Wm. H. Green   Patin Blan
John Willis   John Choat
Michael Green   Henry Garms
Jacob Garner   John Haines
Wm. Ashworth   George Ivens
Uriah Harris   Charles Cronia
John P. Wallis   Joseph Richey
John Dulin   Solomon Cole
M. Hattin

The above is a correct Copy of the original this day filed by me

Wm. T. Austin
Aid de Camp

The "Musquis' corner," referred to by Maverick, is the entrance to Potrero Street at the northeast corner of Plaza de las Islas. The house on the right behind the carreta (ox cart) is owned by Don Ramón Músquiz, the past alcalde (mayor) of Béxar, hence Maverick's reference. As explained, Maverick is in the gable-roofed house on the left side of Potrero Street 200 feet beyond the sandbag barricade and has a good view of activities at this new checkpoint.

plans. "The enemy are shut up within the walls and fortifications of Bexar, parties of our volunteers go around the town daily, and within cannon shot," he wrote. Some of these men had managed to scavenge nearly two dozen spent Mexican cannonballs, to be loaded into Texian guns and shot back at the enemy. Austin had met with his officers, who had agreed that the time for an assault was close, "so soon as the orleans Greys get up from Goliad; and Burlisons detachment returns." The Centralist works, Austin argued, were too extended to be held successfully. Morale in Béxar had also plummeted. "The troops inside are also very much discouraged and begin to consider the contest as hopeless, cut off as they are from resources with a wilderness in the rear, which has been burnt nearly all the way to rio Grande on all the roads."

Moses Austin Bryan, privy to his uncle's plans, wrote to his father and mother. "There are about 6 hundred men in camp, a sufficient force to take Bexar if we had the necessary tools. It will be attacked in a day or two at all hazards as the corn is getting scares and it seams that there is no hopes of the cannon coming soon." The absence of Colonel Ugartechea and the Mexican cavalry bedeviled Texian planning. If he should return

— perhaps even with reinforcements — it might swing the issue in the Centralists' favor. The attack also needed to happen soon or the Texian army might simply call it quits and head home. "Some days agoe I thought the army would be broke up as they were all tiard of waiting for the cannon and hearing no news from the colony and desertion more or less every day," Bryan wrote. There seemed to be a new burst of enthusiasm, but few believed it would last long. "Now everybody is in good spirits and reinforcements expected . . . Bexar must fall in a few days or it will not fall at all."

Austin believed he could carry the Centralist works in one great rush. Perhaps, he hoped, this could be avoided, and the enemy would collapse for lack of supplies. The next few days would be telling. Two sizable infantry companies of the Battalion of New Orleans Greys were on their way — one on the Nacogdoches Road and the other at Goliad. They might decide the issue. Either way, Austin, who had suffered for weeks from dysentery, was growing weary of his task and needed some relief from the tension. Even though his health was improving, nothing seemed easy. "Uncle is better," admitted Bryan, "and tired enough of commanding militia."

Francis W. Johnson, one of Austin's key officers, was not optimistic about the Texians' chances. He presented the current problem clearly to his friend Robert McAlpin Williamson, a delegate from Mina at the Consultation in San Felipe. "The Town and Garrison is strongly fortified, much stronger than you could imagine, and they are hourly engaged in fortifying and strengthening the place — we can do nothing without battering Cannon," he wrote. "The pieces we have are too small though we will make the best use of them possible, but for them we have but few balls which we are now trying to remedy by collecting all the copper & bells about the old missions and casting it into ball for the pieces we have here."

A rider on a lathered horse rode in later that afternoon and put the entire issue to rest. Austin would no longer lead the Federalist Army of Texas. A new executive authority and council had formed and needed Austin to serve as a commissioner to the United States, where he would drum up support and funding for the insurrection. "I can only say that I am ready at all times to serve Texas in any station where it is considered I can be useful," the general responded. "Some prudence will be necessary to keep this army together should I leave at once. I therefore cannot at this time say when I can be in San Felipe." Austin's decision had been made for him. "God, Liberty, and Federation," he signed his reply. The next few days would be telling indeed.

10 DIRT BATTERY AND REINFORCEMENTS

NOVEMBER 19, 1835

Probably relieved to have some clarity to his purpose at last, Austin kept his new assignment as commissioner to the United States under wraps for the time being and focused on advancing and, with luck, concluding the siege. Cos had made it clear that the Centralist army would remain behind the well-fortified walls of the town and the Alamo, so it remained for the besieging army to breach those walls and root out the defending *soldados*. The principal tool for the task, the long-awaited 18-pounder cannon, remained somewhere in the vastness of Texas. Austin would have to make do with what he had, and he ordered his lighter guns closer to the enemy.

Another sugar mill, owned by José António de la Garza, an enterprising Béxareño, sat on the same side of the river as the Texian camps at the Zambrano Mill but was 700 yards downstream and much closer to town. At this location, a meander of the river loops to the south, providing a cul-de-sac usable as a cannon position fewer than 800 yards from the town plazas and 440 yards from the Alamo's northwest corner.[1] Austin figured that the Texians could construct a battery position as an earthen fort, with the river protecting it on three sides. He ordered his men to make the attempt.

The news spread quickly. Before work had even begun, Maverick recorded, "The Americans said to be erecting a battery one half [mile] this side of the mill, a little above La Garza's sugar mill." Maverick had heard rumors — perhaps deliberately leaked by Austin to worry Cos — and he also had a clear view from the back of the Nixon house. The Mexicans fired a single gun at the Texian camp that day, but little else transpired. (See map below.)

NOVEMBER 20

Overnight, a blue norther swept across Béxar, and temperatures plummeted. "This day the worst norther we have had," noted Maverick. "Thermometer 42 degrees with rain and wind." Both armies suffered as the siege continued. The Texians fired a couple of rounds from their cannons at the Mexican garrison that morning, but with little effect. Couriers arrived in Béxar with news of the fall of Fort Lipantitlán on the Nueces, but it caused little stir as the day ended quietly. Discipline, never strong with the Texian volunteers, continued to deteriorate. "After dark an American came into edge of town, enquiring for Gen'l Austin's camp," Maverick wrote. "He was seized by the picket guard and carried to the jail of the Plazas." A second Texian lay drunk and passed out on the edge of town. Before the Centralists could drag him into their lines, a sympathetic Béxareño had given him a horse, and the inebriated hotspur rode off into the night.

That night, The Texians broke ground on their artillery battery. When finished, Austin's gunners would have a 400-yard shot to hit the Alamo, and twice that distance to lob shots into the heart of Béxar. Maverick could see the work under way. "The Americans are raising a battery or something not far from La Garza's sugar mill," he wrote, "one half mile this side of the Molina [mill] where Austin is."

NOVEMBER 21

The next morning brought yet another cold, bleak, rainy day; temperatures hovered a little above freezing. At Béxar, shivering *soldados* patrolled

Location of the sugar mills above Béxar. The Federalist camp is north of the Zambrano mill, commonly called the "Old Mill," and the battery being considered by the Texians will be in the loop of the river 670 yards downstream, below José António de la Garza's mill. The red lines indicate Maverick's view of the mill and battery from town.

outside of their fortifications to see how many *gringos barrachos* (drunk Texians) might still turn up. "They found an American by the roadside sleeping (or drunk)," reported Maverick. "He woke up and said he was their friend (in bad Spanish). However, one of the soldiers shot a ball through him, but still speaking, another shot and killed him." The Centralist stripped the dead man of his clothes and weapon, seized his horse tied nearby, and took them back into town in hopes of selling the items. Officers debated the fate of the other Texian prisoner who remained anxiously waiting in a cell in the town jail. Perhaps he too should be shot as a rebel, they reasoned.

Despite the drunk Texians littering the roadsides, Austin grew increasingly enthusiastic about attacking Béxar. As the artillery earthwork went up a quarter mile from the Centralists' fortifications, the Federalist Army's general hoped to order the attack for the next morning. Austin alerted all his officers. If they could get the dirt battery completed quickly, despite the brutal weather, his army would have a sturdy staging area just 400 yards from the northern edge of town and the same distance to the walls of the Alamo from which to launch the assault. Austin's aide-de-camp, William T. Austin, was impressed by the new enthusiasm among the volunteers. "During the day the prospects in camp appeared decidedly encouraging; every man appeared firm and anxious for the conflict," he wrote. "In the evening the volunteers were all paraded and inspected, and reviewed by the commander-in-chief, when he made a few remarks appropriate to the occasion." After the necessary orders and arrangements were made with the army, word went out that the attack would occur before dawn the next day.

As Austin's command grew bold, the first of the New Orleans Greys arrived to elevate their morale further. During the cold and windy afternoon of November 21, Captain Robert C. Morris rode into the Old Mill camp at the head of the Second Company of New Orleans Greys. His company consisted of First Lieutenant William G. Cooke and sixty-eight uniformed men. They had left La Bahía on November 15 after an exuberant Captain Dimmitt had secured mounts for them — unbroken mustangs from the local Tejanos — which the Greys had mastered despite some aches and pains. Dimmitt had praised the Greys for "devoting themselves to the cause of liberty and of Texas" and suggested that they "wish for an opportunity only to demonstrate to the world, the strength and purity of the zeal they feel."

The Greys brought with them even more hopeful news. A 12-pounder gunade trundled into camp as well, and while it was not as powerful as the much-anticipated 18-pounder, it was a battering cannon all the same. The newcomers had brought two from New Orleans to Velasco on the Texas coast, where they left one, shepherding the other up the Brazos River twenty-five miles to Brazoria. There they disembarked and marched overland to La Bahía, 115 miles west, laboriously dragging the cannon with them by hand. This cannon made the Greys doubly welcome in General Austin's army. They set up camp near the Old Mill, tired but eager for what might come.

Sometime after nightfall, the First Company of Greys also arrived. Captain Thomas H. Breece and his fifty soldiers left New Orleans within days of Morris' company, but instead of travelling by way of the Gulf, they had taken the steamer *Washita* up the Mississippi and Red rivers and had disembarked at Alexandria, Louisiana. From there, they marched west on the Old Spanish Trail seventy-six miles to Gaines' Ferry, where they crossed the Sabine River into Mexican Texas. As the New Orleans Greys shambled toward a settlement, their quartermaster rode ahead and warned the inhabitants that the volunteers were on their way. "Then all hands had to go to work," German immigrant and recent volunteer Herman Ehrenberg noted, "grinding corn, baking bread, brewing tea and coffee, slaughtering the oxen, and whatever else was necessary." They were first welcomed on the road between the ferry and San Augustine by an adoring delegation of local women who presented the Greys with an azure-blue silk flag designed for them and boldly decorated with the words "First Company of Texan Volunteers from New Orleans." The American colonists then hosted a grand dinner in San Augustine, followed soon after by an even bigger feed in Nacogdoches featuring roast bear and champagne. The Texian settlers also provided horses for at least two-thirds of the company to ease the 280 miles remaining down El Camino Real to San Antonio de Béxar.

After this arduous trek, Mag Stiff, one of the Greys, found his first Béxar night to be anything but comfortable. "I arrived at what is called the 'old mill' on the San Antone River . . . from one to two miles above the Town of 'Bexar,' " he wrote. "I arrived during a heavy rain and passed a very disagreeable night — not having the benefit of fire, and but one Blanket — without shelter." His plight was typical of that of most of his comrades, who also shivered without shelter or proper clothing.

The arrival of the First Company, New Orleans Greys, also solved the mystery of the Texians killed and captured in Béxar the previous day. They were both members of this command who had become separated and lost in the unfamiliar country. The volunteers located the corpse of their slain companion, "having received two shots passing through his body-entering on his left side," remembered Stiff. "His horse and Pistols were missing — also his coat." Their other comrade, a Mr. Vose, had left the Gonzales Road crossing of Cibolo Creek, but "he took the left-hand rode and instead of going to the Texian Camp," Stiff reported, "and found him self standing by the walls of the Alamo where he found that he was in the wrong [pew]." The resourceful American posed as an itinerate laborer to avoid a hasty execution. "He then enquired of Genl. Cos where Austins Colony was, Cos answered that perhaps he was mistaken, that it was Austins Camp he was looking for, he said not, that he was a poor man looking for work, and would work for him (Cos) as soon as any body else if he could get paid for it." The Mexican officers asked if Vose was Catholic and whether he could roll cigars. When the American answered yes to both inquiries, the Centralists decided not to shoot him on the spot and instead hauled him to jail where he might prove useful rolling smokes.

The reinforcements would certainly provide an important boost in the coming fight. The distant sounds of shovels and axes welcomed the New Orleans Greys as Captain James Cheshire and Dr. James Grant directed their crews as they dug trenches and piled up earth. That night, a triangular fortification took form with two 40-foot earthen breastworks — one facing the Alamo, the other the town plazas. The planned assault would surely come the next day, as planned. Austin retired to his quarters.

At 1 a.m., Austin's aides awakened him to meet an unexpected visitor. Lieutenant Colonel Philip Sublett, commander of the second division of the army, brought bad news. "On receipt of your general order announcing that an attack would be made by storm in the morning, I have ascertained the disposition of the officers and men of my division and believe it to be my duty to report that a majority of them are opposed to the measure and are unwilling to attempt it," he reported. "I concur in opinion with them." Austin could not believe what he was hearing. Half of his army would simply not attack. Austin sent for Colonel Burleson, who commanded the first division, to get his views. "This officer accordingly reported that the feeling generally in his division in relation to the contemplated attack

UNITED STATES
MEXICO
Nacogdoches
FORT JESUP
San Augustine
Alexandria
1st Company (Morris)
Steamboat Washita
Bastrop
San Felipe
Béxar
New Orleans
Gonzales
Brazoria
2nd Company (Breece)
Victoria
Schooner Columbia
Goliad
PRESIDIO DEL RIO GRANDE
Laredo
Monclova
March of the New Orleans Greys
Two Hundred Miles
Matamoros

corresponded with that reported by Colonel Sublett in relation to the second division," reported Austin's aide, William T. Austin, "but stated that he was willing to make the attack and lead on as many of his division as would follow him."

The news stunned General Austin. Although perturbed and embarrassed, Austin "determined to persevere in the attack, in the event that a sufficient force could be obtained for the purpose to justify it," his aide continued. After ordering his staff to count heads and see who would still make the attack, they came back with fewer than 100, augmented by the still enthusiastic New Orleans Greys. Austin looked for the cause of this mutiny and discovered that the petty bickering and jealousy among his officers had undermined his plan. Austin canceled the attack.

NOVEMBER 22

The frosty sunrise brought with it a day of frustrations. "The Grays were greeted the next morning by the sound of cannon firing in the Alamo and by reveille in our own camp," noted Herman Ehrenberg, a member of the First Company. "As these sounds were subsiding, the autumn sun that was just rising above the serene eastern horizon bathed the bustling camp of the backwoodsmen in its brilliant rays." Austin, in his quarters, organized these enthusiastic newcomers into a third division composed of their two robust companies, numbering 120 men. Soon after, however, Austin lost one of his most reliable officers. "Capt. J. W. Fannin having represented to me that the absolute necessity of returning home, I have granted to him an honorable discharge," the general wrote, "and have to say that he has uniformly discharged his duty as a soldier and as an officer." Fannin headed back toward the settlements then took the opportunity to join Sam Houston's staff.

Austin's enthusiasm of the last two days cratered. His old maladies returned. "My health has been very bad since I left the Cibolo, more than a month ago, and I have been unable to attend personally to the duties of my station with that activity which the service required," he complained in a letter to his brother-in-law James F. Perry. Austin took the blame for his army's loss of nerve. "I begin to doubt whether much more can be done here, than to leave a force in winter quarters at the missions below town, say 250 men, until the necessary regular force and guns and other supplies, come out." Austin, against his better judgement, was yielding to Houston's plan. He would head back to the states: "I shall leave as many as will stay in winter quarters and go to the U. S. under the appointment they have given me as commissioner," he penned. "So far as my own wishes and feelings are concerned, I much prefer an appointment out of Texas, then in it." Austin had been a reluctant general but had seen no alternative. "I accepted the appointment I now hold here, because I could not do otherwise, I never sought it, nor wished for it — my constitution is too much worn out and too feeble for the exposure and hardships and activity of a winters campaign, destitute of everything like comforts," he explained. "I have done the best I could."

His army, he believed, had fatal flaws. "This army has always been composed of discordant materials, and is without proper organization," he continued. "The volunteer sistem will not do for such a service." Austin recognized that his proper place should have been in helping to organize a government and not in the field. "I could have been of more use in the convention than here — and I can be of service to Texas by going to the U. S. and I wish to go there," he added, with a hint of self-pity. "How I envy a poor and obscure man in his quiet cottage, free from care and trouble and faction."

With no action at hand, the newcomers from New Orleans explored their new surroundings. Ehrenberg wandered about the Texian camp. "On our left flowed the warm waters of the San Antonio River," he noted. "Although its source was just a few miles away, it nevertheless had a depth of about six to eight feet at our camp and a width of eighteen to twenty yards. Already a considerable stream, its waters flowed down toward the enemy's camp, forming a large peninsula along the way." He noted that the Texian camp lay on the upper outside bank of the river's bend, while downstream stood "the venerable old city of San Antonio." The timber along the river veiled the Centralists' positions from view, while "between us and the city a corn field, now bare, stretched out for an English mile along the river."

A greater curiosity lay across the river. "Opposite the corn field, on the river's left bank, which was bare of any trees, stood the chief fortress of the former province of Texas, the aforementioned Alamo," Ehrenberg wrote. "It was about three quarters of an English mile from our camp and was separated from the city only by the river."

Having scouted out the enemy positions, Ehrenberg roamed among his allies in "the camp of the Texas colonists." Their bivouac lay bordered by cornfields on the side nearer the river, and prairie beyond, "dotted with mesquite thickets and with large clusters of a variety of huge cactus plants." The Texian horses and cattle grazed undisturbed on the high grass. As the volunteer ambled along the edges of the cornfield, "millions of blackbirds would fly up together like dark black clouds in the air," he wrote. "The huge flocks would circle a few times and then settle to the earth again nearby in search of food on the ground."

Ehrenberg also strolled over to where the volunteers butchered. "Flocks of vultures, several different species of them, hunted about on this killing field for their food," he observed. "Plenty of food was available too, and so the vultures would sit with their wings spread out and their gaping beaks on the bare branches of the nearby pecan trees and warm themselves in the bright rays of the sun." Wolves and coyotes also lurked about nearby, carrying off the heads and hides of the slaughtered beeves as trophies, "as if they too belonged to our army, and like us, they calmly ate their breakfast."

Having noted the local wildlife, he ambled over to the parade ground to watch the Texian volunteers form up. "The roll of the drums echoed through our camp and the individual companies, which had erected their tents and shelters here and there in no particular order or disorder, assembled individually for the roll call," Ehrenberg wrote. "Any one of these companies of freedom fighters could be selected for description . . . to give an accurate picture of the kind of army we were." He liked their pluck, even if they seemed to be haphazard soldiers. "Against the courage and rifles of these men," he concluded, "the discipline and even the vastly superior numbers of the enemy could accomplish nothing."

These Texians were certainly amusing. Huge hunks of meat roasted slowly on spits over campfires. "Soon a small rank of only partially clothed warriors was standing in front of their sergeant who, with the muster roll in his hand, was awaiting the arrival of the others," Ehrenberg observed. "Those present were not holding a rifle but instead a nice wooden spit bedecked with a flavorful roast in one hand and the famous bowie knife in the other." Many of the volunteers eschewed roll call altogether in favor of minding their fires. "Several men did not even show up for roll call because their roasting meat had reached a critical stage and they could not leave it to an uncertain fate, or because the imminent boil-over of the coffee did not permit them to join our ranks," Ehrenberg continued. Some of the volunteers simply refused to get out of bed. "Sometimes the loud

Looking south-southwest over the Old Mill camp toward the Alamo and Bexar in the direction Ehrenberg describes. The dirt fort, built overnight, stands in the loop of the river near José António de la Garza's sugar mill.

voice of a backwoodsman would be heard emanating from under the wool blankets in a tent, which was greeted by a loud outburst of laughter in the company," the observer wrote. "The sergeant, although somewhat annoyed, let it go by as an ordinary event." As the volunteers heard their names, they simply returned to their previous pursuits, not waiting to be dismissed. "The last man to remain standing at roll call was carrying a steaming coffee pot in his hand."

Ehrenberg, recently arrived from Germany, wondered what sort of soldiers these men would make. He also puzzled over the Greys, who, despite appearing warlike, also behaved like schoolboys on a lark. At least the Texians paid "attention to form, and if there were no pressing matters to keep them away, numbers of their men did show up when called," he noted. "We never had roll call in the morning."

True to their independent nature, several Greys continued their roaming and decided to head over to an earthwork where a pair of cannons were firing. The jaunt was risky; the onlookers had to cover several hundred yards under enemy fire. "The enemy's artillery was being handled much better than ours," Ehrenberg wrote. "But this fact provided us with a great deal of amusement, since the grape shot put many of our men to the test as they ran across the field." The curious sightseers, having made it to cover, enjoyed the show. "They were pounding the old Alamo with these guns so that from time to time one could really see different pieces of the old walls come tumbling down," Ehrenberg wrote. "We had no orders and no other reason to be out there than to get a better look at the imposing sight of the Alamo from that position and to join in the cheering when the stonework came crashing down from the old walls or from the now dilapidated and deserted church."

The Centralist gunners inside the Alamo were not amused and focused their fire on the Texian position. "Such a volume of grape shot went whizzing past us and raining down on us that we had to take cover for a few minutes behind a pecan tree," Ehrenberg remembered. "After positioning ourselves there, we looked at each other and laughed that we were now standing eight men deep behind a single tree." As the Mexican cannister shredded their only cover, onlookers in the battery and back in camp "laughed loudly at us with every load that struck our tree and made the dry branches come raining down on our heads."

The nosy soldiers scrambled over the ramparts and into the relative safety of the battery. "Inside the little fort there was a lot of activity," Ehrenberg continued. "Everybody was standing around the cannon and by turns one of us and then another had the pleasure of giving the old walls of the Alamo a wallop." Of course, the troops began wagering on who could place the best shot. "Each marksman had to say in advance what part he intended to demolish, and then the men would wager for him or against him."

The gambling soon grew serious. One trooper bet "one hundred fine rifle balls against your twenty that I'll strike between the third and fourth windows of the barracks!" He missed "and had to spend the whole next day pouring rifle balls." The competitions continued until one volunteer wagered a brace of pistols that he would hit the mark. He, too, missed. "Well, to give you a chance to get even, friend, I think I'll fire once too," offered one of the Texians. "And if this boy doesn't hit his mark — then, friend, you can have your pistols back." The frontiersman and some of the Greys loaded the piece, and the gunner took his aim. "With one eye closed, as if he were aiming his rifle, his face showed how intently he was

TOP LEFT: *The north wall of the Alamo with its very active artillery, looking from the direction of the Old Mill. Battery No. 1 is one cannon firing "en barbette" (over the top of the low wall). No. 2 is a battery of three cannon firing through embrasures. No. 3 is only one cannon firing north with another aimed west toward town, both through embrasures. The five cannons pointing north have a good shot at the Old Mill camp 1,000 yards just east-of-north and now at the Dirt Battery a mere 440 yards northwest.*

TOP RIGHT: *The "imposing sight of the Alamo" from the Dirt Battery. Their view is of the northwest corner of the fort with the trees of the Alameda beyond towering above the walls.*

RIGHT: *The two wings of the "Dirt Fort" breastworks allow cannon to be fired at the Alamo and the town. Our view is looking south.*

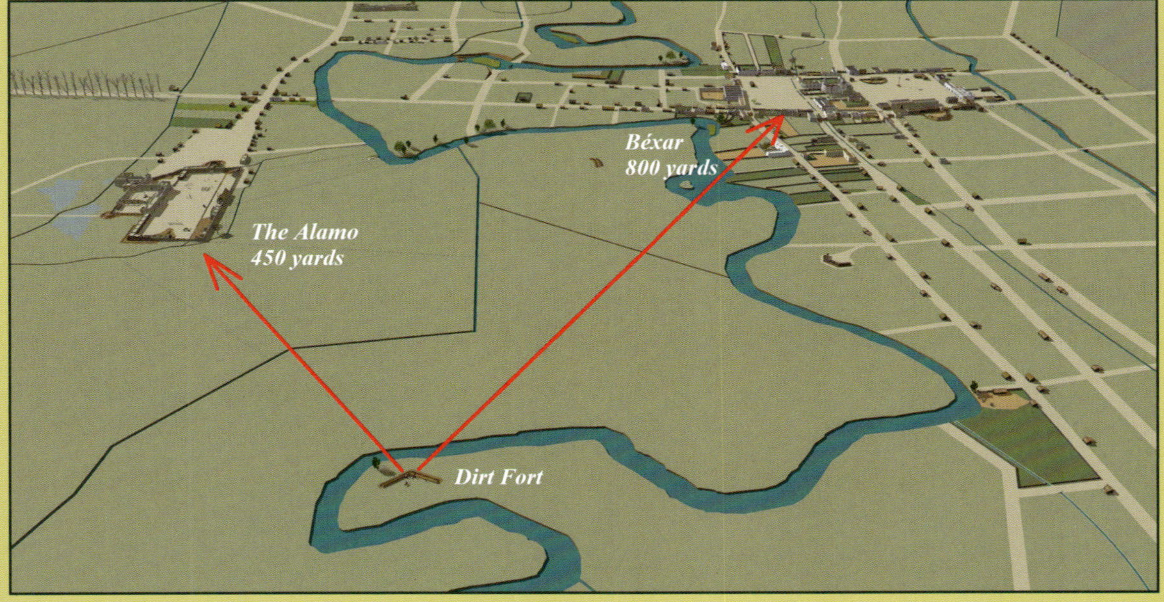

Béxar
1835
Zambrano Mill
One Half Mile
De la Garza Mill
Main Acéquia
San Pedro Creek
Acéquia Street
Soledad Street
Alamo Acéquia
Alamo
Upper Presidio Road
Foot Bridge
Alazan Creek
Plaza de Armas
(Military Plaza)
Plaza de los Islas
(Civic Plaza)
ford
Powder House
Laredo Road
San Antonio River
Missions Road
La Bahia Road
Gonzales Road

making some mathematical calculations while his right hand described in the air a lot of geometric figures," Ehrenberg observed. "Finally, he was finished. Once more he looked the cannon over quickly. Then he took the slow match to light the fuse and, propelled by the powerful charge of powder, the destructive ball flew to its mark. The crashing fall of the stones told us, even before the smoke had cleared, that he had hit his target. But when the smoke had dissipated, we looked in vain for the third and fourth window." The Texians and the Greys were ecstatic. "As if with a single voice, we all cheered 'hurrah!' for old Deaf Smith, as we called him, for he was the bravest Texan who ever raced across the prairie," Ehrenberg remembered.[2]

While these amateur artillerists played against the gunners at the Alamo, other Centralists moved stealthily toward their position; soon bullets went whizzing overhead, ending the celebration. "While we were concentrating on the destruction of the Alamo, several shots rang out from the high grass and brush on the opposite bank of the river, making it inadvisable for us to look out over the earthen breastworks," Ehrenberg wrote. The Greys still in camp bounded out to counter the threat; after a short firefight, the enemy *soldados* retreated.

In Béxar, Maverick noted the increase in the warlike tempo. "One hundred guns at least fired through the day; say seventy from the Alamo and a cannon placed on W. side of the river, and thirty by the Americans," he jotted. There was other news. His fellow prisoner, John W. Smith, has completed a map of the Mexican defenses and had smuggled it to the Texians. "This Mr. Smith was a surveyor by profession," noted William T. Austin, "and had been held in duress by the enemy since the commencement of the difficulties; during the time he availed himself of opportunities to make said map, which was forwarded to the place of destination in good time to be very useful on this occasion."

CHANGE OF COMMAND

11

NOVEMBER 23, 1835

The norther tightened its icy grip on the two armies. Arctic wind slashed like a saber, killing most activity in Béxar and freezing water in sheets "thick as a dinner plate," wrote one soldier. The Texians managed enough energy to fire off five cannon shots in the morning just to let General Cos know they still kicked, but even that didn't warm them. All lay quiet for the rest of the day as both sides struggled against the numbing cold.

Meanwhile, in Columbia-on-the-Brazos, William Hall dashed out a letter with frozen fingers to General Austin, apprising the commander of his search for the 18-pounder — a fruitless search thus far. But even if the cannon were located, it was anyone's guess on when it could make it to Béxar with such frigid temperatures and such muddy roads blocking the route.

NOVEMBER 24

The next day dawned a bit warmer. A weak sun peeped through the cloud cover. The Texians warmed themselves this afternoon, exchanging pleasantries with Ugartechea and his Mexican reinforcements brought up from Laredo to aid Cos. "Some two or three hundred discharges of muskets, now and then the crack of a rifle is heard," Sam Maverick recorded in his diary. "In the midst of the firing the Americans fired two cannon at the fort (over it) and one at the church here in town." A few Mexican soldiers were killed or wounded, but none on the Texian side. The *soldados'* muskets and poor powder scored no hits, and Texian rifles had a far deadlier range.

But amid the intermittent crack of rifle and cannon, a much larger drama unfolded. Austin ordered a general parade of the men to share a bombshell of his own: he was leaving them. The convention had appointed him commissioner to the United States to drum up much-needed support for the Texian cause, forcing him to leave his role as commander-in-chief.

How the mighty had fallen! Just two months before, William B. Travis had told Austin he was the only hope of revolutionary Texas. "Texas can be wielded by you and you alone; and her destiny is now completely in our hands — I have every confidence that you will guide us safely through all perils." Indeed, Austin's unanimous election to commander–in-chief of the army was the only thing that had kept it intact as it teetered on the brink of disintegration back in October. Each militia refused to serve under any commander other than its own captain. But all eventually agreed on Austin to lead them. Now, just six and a half weeks later, the Father of Texas was largely abandoned by the Army of Texas. Most of his officers shunned him and questioned his military leadership capabilities. But even so, he still had enough supporters amid the rank and file that he grew concerned that his leaving "might produce some unpleasant dissatisfaction in the army …" Hence the parade and his personal speech to the gathered volunteers. William T. Austin described what followed:

"He announced his determination to accept the appointment of commissioner to the United States and withdraw from the army. He clearly explained the importance of continuing the siege of San Antonio, and urged upon them therefore the necessity

of their remaining and organizing anew instantly. After concluding his address, the adjutant-general was ordered to call upon the troops to volunteer to remain before San Antonio and to organize at once for that purpose, when four hundred and five promptly turned out and pledged themselves to remain. The election being ordered to take place immediately for commander-in-chief, General Edward Burleson was elected without opposition, none having been allowed to vote but those who were pledged to remain."

Austin's parting orders spoke of the importance of maintaining the fort at Goliad and recommended that the army reinforce the place when the siege of Béxar ended. He also sounded an ominous word of warning about preparations in Mexico for a springtime invasion by Santa Anna at the head of 10,000 men. This information he gleaned from letters intercepted from Lipantitlán, a Mexican garrison to the southeast captured by some of the Texians stationed at the Goliad fort. He also took a moment to write an affidavit applauding the services of a young friend and protégé of the past fourteen years:

> *This is to certify that Juan N. Seguín of Béxar presented himself to . . . and offered his services as a volunteer in the defense of the rights and liberties of Texas.*
>
> *I gave him the appointment of Captain of a volunteer company of native Mexicans which he had raised. This company although not a full one was very efficient in the cause. It intercepted two expresses from the interior to Genl Cos which were of the highest importance, and Cap Seguín and his men were at all times ready and willing to go on any service they were ordered. They uniformly acquitted themselves to their credit as patriots and soldiers.*

Austin took his leave the next day — another cold one — amid surprising displays of emotion. Despite the negative judgment of some politically opposed officers, many of the volunteers still respected him as a man and statesman, shaking hands with him amidst tears and silences choked with profound emotion. And so the Father of Texas began his long journey to drum up money and supplies so his successors could ride to victory at the head of an army he alone had saved.

Sadder still, it began to look as if his early departure was a result of sabotage. According to William T. Austin, W. H. Wharton, a so-called friend and confidant of the general, had been leaking plans from headquarters to the other officers and soldiers, portraying Austin's military plans as foolhardy. This unconscionable backstabbing helped turn the army gradually against its beloved commander and set Austin up for his fall from grace. Wharton also happened to be friends with Sam Houston, and in William Austin's mind, Wharton was deliberately sabotaging the army's leader so that "the laurels might be reserved for General Houston, who was electioneering at San Felipe for an appointment to the command of the Texas army." It seemed that Houston's political skullduggery had crippled Austin from the beginning. William T. Austin went so far as to accuse Houston of writing letters to all his friends in the army to discourage General Austin from assaulting San Antonio, reasoning that the Texian army was far too small for such an attempt and that an attack would prove disastrous. So Houston's friends, believing him wiser about military matters than Austin, did as he advised and prevented the army from launching an attack on Béxar. William Austin bitterly believed that if Houston hadn't deliberately played dirty politics, "General Austin would have captured San Antonio with but trifling loss of life." Austin would now be the heroic leader of a victorious army, not an ex-general demoted to ambassador.

Meanwhile, the newly elected Edward Burleson assumed command of an army in desperate need of supplies. Col. Thomas J. Rusk vividly painted the army's dire straits in a desperate plea to Lieutenant Governor Robinson:

> *We are out of provisions We need Clothing Shoes and Amunition And without Cannon and Mortars Scaling the walls would be the death of very many worthy men. The enemy will be very shortly reinforced by Large numbers — we must be reinforced ourselves unless the Country are willing to see this Army cut off . . . We have suffered much for the last few days with cold I am now half frozen while I write.*

The 450 soldiers remaining in "the People's Army" pulled their coats tighter, built their fires higher, and settled in for the long wait — waiting for supplies, waiting for reinforcements, waiting for some kind of plan.

12

THE GRASS FIGHT

Deaf Smith shattered the morning stillness of the following day with news of 150 Centralist soldiers just five miles west of town. Mexican deserters had predicted a convoy bringing food, supplies, and army payroll to General Cos any day now. This seemed to be that promised relief. Whatever their purpose, they needed to be swiftly dealt with. Reports painted Cos' men as hungry, destitute, and on the verge of surrender. The Texians couldn't allow the enemy to regain hope.

Colonel Burleson quickly ordered James Bowie to take thirty-five to forty cavalry and attack the convoy before it reached town. As Bowie's cavalry departed, Burleson ordered 100 infantrymen under Colonel William H. Jack west toward San Pedro Creek. They would make sure all possible routes to Béxar were cut off. Burleson himself rode alongside Jack's men. They came to the cold waters of the San Pedro, plunged in, and forded the wide, deep creek "with the greatest cheerfulness," in Jack's possibly sarcastic words. Slogging through icy water in 30-degree temperatures probably produced warm and colorful language but no real cheer. As soon as the Texians finished crossing, one of the scouts "reported there was firing ahead, between our cavalry under command of Colo Bowie, and a party of the enemy," Jack later said.

The Texians marched double time now over treacherous terrain, over gullies and washes, through oak and elm groves, and around thorny mesquite thickets, hungry to join the fray. Over the next half hour of struggling through nature's obstacle course, a rumor began to spread among the men that the convoy wasn't carrying supplies. Instead, Mexican saddlebags became swollen with money — pay for the besieged Mexican soldiers, they decided. The march now became a hunt for treasure— a just reward, in their minds, for fighting without compensation in the cause of Texas. "Visions of suddenly acquired wealth floated before each Texan's eyes," Creed Taylor remembered.

But the treasure hungry Texians had no idea that this wasn't a pay party. It was a grass party.

Cos "found it expedient to send out foraging parties under cover of night, to cut and bring in grass for his horses." The convoy of 150 consisted not of reinforcements but of cavalry from the Alamo, foraging for desperately needed horse fodder.

Meanwhile, Bowie and his cavalry fought it out with a force three times their size —typical odds for Bowie, a man with a history of fighting vastly superior forces and always somehow coming out on top.

When the Mexicans first saw Bowie's forces coming for them, they took the initiative and charged in all their superior numbers while the Texians tried to cross a dried creek bed. A firefight erupted at the creek bank."After two or three fires Col Bowie threw his men under cover of the creek & kept up the fight. The enemy charged him with over three times his number but were immediately repulsed with considerable loss…" Bowie and his men must have had flashbacks to Concepción, for the odds were nearly the same. The Texians were also fortunate that they had the high ground and were shooting"at an angle of about 45 degrees down"at the foraging party. They were only fifteen feet apart."The fight was brief but sharp," according

Colonel Jack's infantry marches double time 1.2 miles from camp to the ford on San Pedro Creek, along with Colonel Burleson's horsemen. From there they hear the gunfire from Bowie's battle with the Centralist cavalry (probable location).

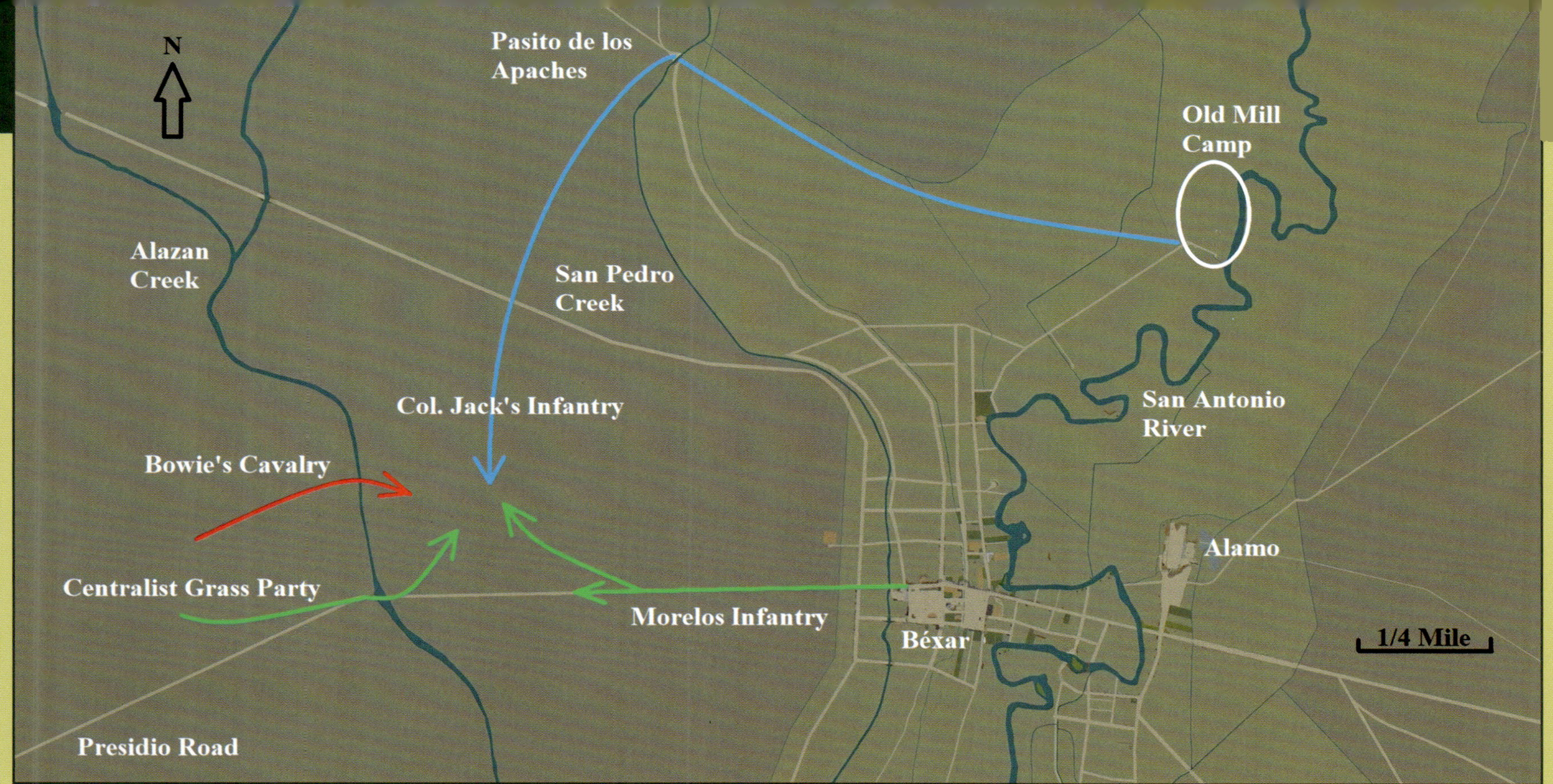

A heated battle ensues between Bowie's and Jack's men and the Morelos infantrymen supported by the Grass Party.

to Creed Taylor. The enemy "fled helter-skelter and in great confusion, every fellow for himself to escape the fury of these 'diablos encarnados' [devils incarnate] as they called the Texans. The coveted packtrain was in our possession. Our only casualties in the fight were two wounded and one man missing. It was said that this man became so frightened or excited during the melee that he actually ran away on foot at breakneck speed, and never finally halted until he reached the settlements."

Cos scrambled to salvage what he could from the debacle. Hearing the battle from the Plaza de Armas, he ordered fifty infantrymen from the Morelos Battalion out to reinforce the Grass Party. They marched west on the Presidio Road, preceded by an artillery crew with a 6-pounder.

Burleson reported:

"The main body of our force came up very briskly and came in contact with the reinforcements and a very warm engagement took place between the main body of our army and the reinforcements."

But just as Burleson and Jack's force neared the scene, about fifty Mexicans who had pulled away from the Grass Party ambushed them. "We were saluted from the distance of forty to Sixty Yards by a tremendous discharge of musketry along our whole line from an unexpected and undiscovered foe," Jack recalled. The Texians had inadvertently marched right between the retreating Grass Party and their reinforcements from town. None of the Texians could see the Grass Party participants because of "a little eminence" in the land between the two groups and a mesquite thicket. The ambush threw all into confusion. Someone shouted an order to lie down; another shouted for them to retreat. No one knew who ordered a retreat, but it wasn't Burleson. Colonel Rusk instead ordered the men to

"charge on them and rout them." With only fifteen men by his side, he barreled straight into the teeth of the hidden enemy. Rusk later said:

"In the charge we got in some forty yards of where the grass party were lying concealed on our right and the reinforcement gathered to our left. The grass party then opened a fire on us, which was repeated before we could discover where they were… our men charged on them and routed them from the ditch, killing and wounding several of them. They ran entirely off the field and I do not believe that they again joined in the fight. Our forces were by this time scattered over about one hundred acres of ground, and in small parties, every man fighting pretty much on his own hook.

Colonel Bowie and his cavalry thundered across Alazan Creek to their aid and, according to Burleson, "charged the Enimy and drove them back about three hundred yards toward town."

Then the Morelos infantry finally showed up with the cannon. The fight was far from over, according to Rusk.

We got in about eighty yards of the cannon, when it was discharged on us with grape and cannister and ran back a short distance, where they halted and fired again. They then attempted a charge with I think about a hundred and fifty cavalry on about forty of our men who were occupying a little eminence on the field to prevent the enemy bringing their cannon to that point, which would have given them an advantage. The cavalry came up at a beautiful charge until they got within about one hundred yards, when they broke their ranks and fell back. They twice repeated this attempt at a charge but failed to get any nearer us than about one hundred yards. About this time the Morales [Morelos] Battalion was brought up to drive our men from the eminence.

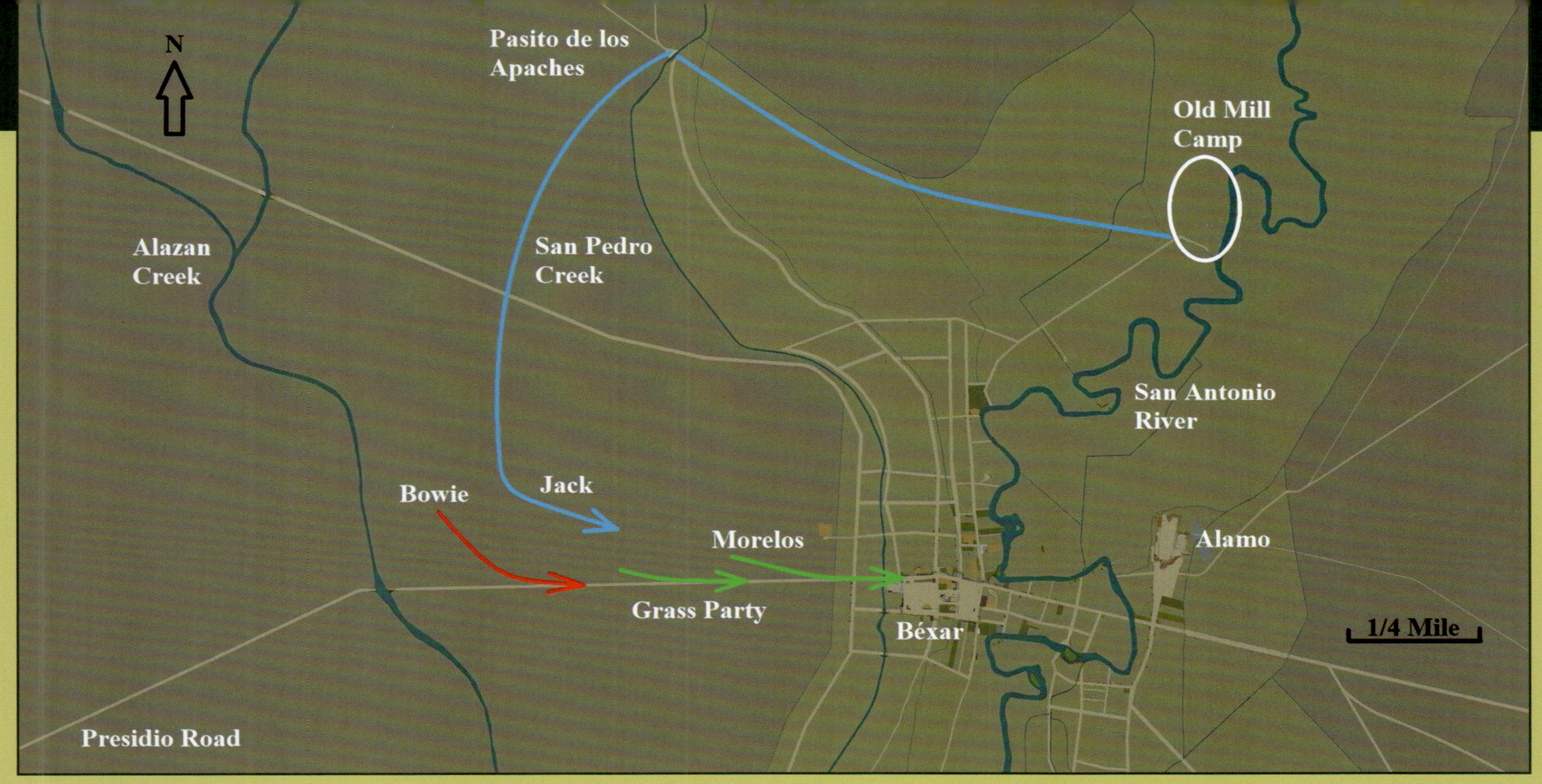

Bowie and Jack pursue as the Grass Party and the Morelos infantry retire to the town, sans grass.

Even in the rush and roar of battle, Rusk couldn't help but admire this renowned Mexican infantry battalion that "advanced with great coolness and bravery under a destructive fire from our men, preserving all the time strict order and exhibiting no confusion."

They got up in about twenty yards of our position; all our guns and pistols had been fired off and we had no time to reload and must have tried the butts of our guns against their bayonets but for the fact that some of our men who were fighting in a different place hearing the steady fire . . . at that point attempted to come to them and in coming across the field ran nearly upon the enemy's cannon. The Mexicans took it for granted that it was an attempt to take their cannon and ordered the Morales Battalion to reinforce the cannon. They soon after retreated until they came under cover of the guns of the town.

Back and forth the battle went, with each side taking turns in ascendant. Curious scenes flickered in fire and black-powder smoke like photographs. "A Mr. Murphy felled by a musket ball in the head - When asked if he was hurt, he replied, 'No,' felt his forehead and the back and saw blood on his hands. "Blood threw & threw by gad" he roared and then reloaded. A Texian sat behind baby mesquites, loading his gun, when a whistling charge of cannister shredded the trees before him but missed him completely. "A Mexican officer charged alone, bravely, wildly into the midst of the Texians," one Federalist wrote, "and was blown off his horse by his admirers."

But soon enough the brave Centralists had enough of the Texian ferocity and began a slow retreat into town, firing their cannon at intervals to keep their enemies at a healthy distance. After three cannonades, Cos's forces were ensconced within the safety of Béxar — without the grass they fought so hard to keep. The Texians were not happy about the outcome, either. "Our chagrin and disgust knew no bounds when we found that instead of silver coin, the packs contained nothing more than grass which was intended for the starving horses of Cos's cavalry inside the walls of Béxar," Creed Taylor bemoaned.

Three Mexican soldiers were killed and several wounded, and according to Sam Maverick (still in Centralist captivity), the wounded later reported "that every kindness was offered and done to them by the Americans. By their request they were left by the Americans covered up with their blankets and grass." No Texians appeared seriously wounded, and the army confiscated twenty or thirty of the Mexican mules. The men mockingly dubbed the battle "the Grass Fight" almost immediately.

As ridiculous as some of the disappointed treasure-seekers seemed to find the battle, it still brilliantly displayed the cool courage of both sides and kept Cos's army from getting the necessary feed for their mules and horses. The besieged sank deeper and deeper into discouragement, while the Texians' morale soared. But the buoyancy faded soon enough as the siege continued unabated, and no reinforcements or supplies arrived. Both sides sank back into a funk of frustration, hunger, and boredom.

13

THE ARMY DISINTEGRATES

NOVEMBER 27, 1835

The Grass Fight farce had settled nothing, and the aftermath proved anticlimactic. The day after the dustup, James Bowie left Béxar under previous orders from Austin to oversee the fortifications at the Presidio La Bahía. Austin, fearing the siege would fail, wanted to make sure he had strong positions at Goliad and Gonzales where he could make a stand. Bowie had proven his worth on many occasions, and the now-resigned Austin had trusted him with this important task. Bowie would see to it even if his old war chief had moved on.

In town, Sam Maverick and his fellow detainee John W. Smith enjoyed a windfall. In the confusion of the Grass Fight, one of the *soldados* had captured a Texian horse with all its rigging as well as three pistols. Smith bought this booty for forty-six dollars.

NOVEMBER 28

The siege continued while the weather improved. The Texians tried their luck again, this time against a foraging party on Salado Creek. The Centralists, however, gave them the slip and made it back to Béxar undamaged. There were the usual random shots from the guns in the Dirt Battery against the Alamo, but they accomplished nothing. After a lackluster day, a flurry of gunfire near midnight pointed to a potential assault at last against the Mexico positions, but it proved to be nothing more than jittery sentries on Soledad Street. "The picket guard," Maverick wrote, "reported (falsely) that they saw the Americans coming in with a great many ladders to scale the walls. Poh! No need of ladders."

NOVEMBER 29

The rhythms of the siege continued, but new currents swirled through camp. While the periodic thumping of cannon echoed across the San Antonio River Valley, a dispatch addressed to Robert C. Morris, an officer in the Second Company, New Orleans Greys, arrived in camp. Sam Houston, staffing what he hoped would be the principal army of Texas, wanted the young Louisianan to accept a commission as a regular. Morris declined. "There are now here 225 men, nearly all from the U. S. who on no consideration will enter into any service connected with the Regular Army, the name of which is a perfect Bugbear to them," he responded. Besides, Morris continued, if an attack on Béxar were planned, he would lead his men and others on a campaign to capture Matamoros in sympathy with Federalist uprisings in Mexico. If his men were denied action and glory, he would not be able to hold them in Texas. "Should this not be undertaken," Morris warned Houston, "they will return home direct from hence." "Matamoras fever" was once again rippling through the ranks, and such a swashbuckling adventure in Mexico seemed far more enticing than being in the regular army. The New Orleans Greys, who had hurried to Texas only to have their enthusiasm squandered by inaction, proved particularly interested.

NOVEMBER 30

Meanwhile, 150 miles east of Béxar, a road-weary Austin and his nephew Moses Austin Bryan reached San Felipe de Austin. The boy dashed off a letter to his parents letting them know of their safe arrival and that his uncle no longer commanded the army at Béxar, but the youth remained unclear as to what Austin's next move might be. "If he is not vested with the power to attaching Texas to the U. S. but only to borrow money," Bryan wrote, "I think he won't go." Meanwhile, Austin composed an update for the new Texas government on the state of affairs at Béxar. "Col. Edward Burleson was elected by the volunteers comprising the army to succeed me in the chief command," Austin explained. "I have the satisfaction to say that the patriotism which drew together the gallant volunteers now in service before Bexar and at Goliad is unabated. They left all the comforts and endearments of home to defend their constitutional rights and the Republican principles of the Federal sistem and constitution of 1824, and the vested rights of Texas under the law of 7th May of that year." The Texians were Mexican Federalists, Austin claimed, but should Mexico continue the path of despotism, they would shift their allegiance. "The volunteer army will," Austin claimed, "do their duty to their country — to the cause of Liberty and themselves, as honor, patriotism, and the first law of nature may require."

This resolve would soon be tested. Bryan relayed news that President Antonio López de Santa Anna was raising a 10,000-man army to squash the Texas insurgency. "Perhaps they will be here next Spring," he warned.

DECEMBER 1

In Béxar, General Cos finally agreed to release Americans Sam Maverick, John W. Smith, and A. H. Holmes from their house arrest on the condition that they leave Texas. The men agreed, left town, and moved downriver, away from the Texian camps to the ranch of José Ángel Navarro on Leon Creek nine miles southwest of town. Almost immediately the Americans made plans to join the volunteers at the Old Mill.

DECEMBER 2

The next morning, the trio passed wide around Béxar while an artillery duel rumbled in the background. Lieutenant Colonel José Maria Mendoza, the Centralist officer who bravely led the Morelos Battalion at the Battle of Concepción and again in the Grass Fight, had his leg mangled in the exchange as the Americans made their way into the Texian camps. The three men reported to Colonel Burleson with their assessment on how best to carry the Mexican positions. "Smith and myself urge an assault," Maverick wrote later. "After a great many objections being urged and answered by our offering to head the divisions, it is finally agreed to make the attack." The plan was simple and systematic: the Texians would capture three houses, all the same distance from the plazas: the Veramendi home, the De la Garza house, and the Cadena house. Smith's familiarity with the town and Cos' fortifications, as well as the detailed map he had forwarded several days before, provided the blueprint for the attack. To prove the merit of their plan, Smith and Maverick would serve as guides, leading the Texians into combat. The proposed plan was immediately approved by Burleson and a council of his officers, and each man in turn studied Smith's map.

There was merit, and danger, in Smith's plan. The three houses were all built of stone, and each stood about a block from the plazas. These homes were believed to be unoccupied by Centralist troops and would serve as strongholds and springboards for an assault on the plazas. There would also be challenges, as the three streets leading down from the north end of town —Soledad, Acéquia, and Flores — all had barricaded cannon emplacements at the plaza entrances. These emplacements could sweep the streets, and they covered the approaches to the targeted houses.

Smith, though, also noted the weaknesses of the Centralist positions. The breastworks at the end of all three streets were only six feet high.

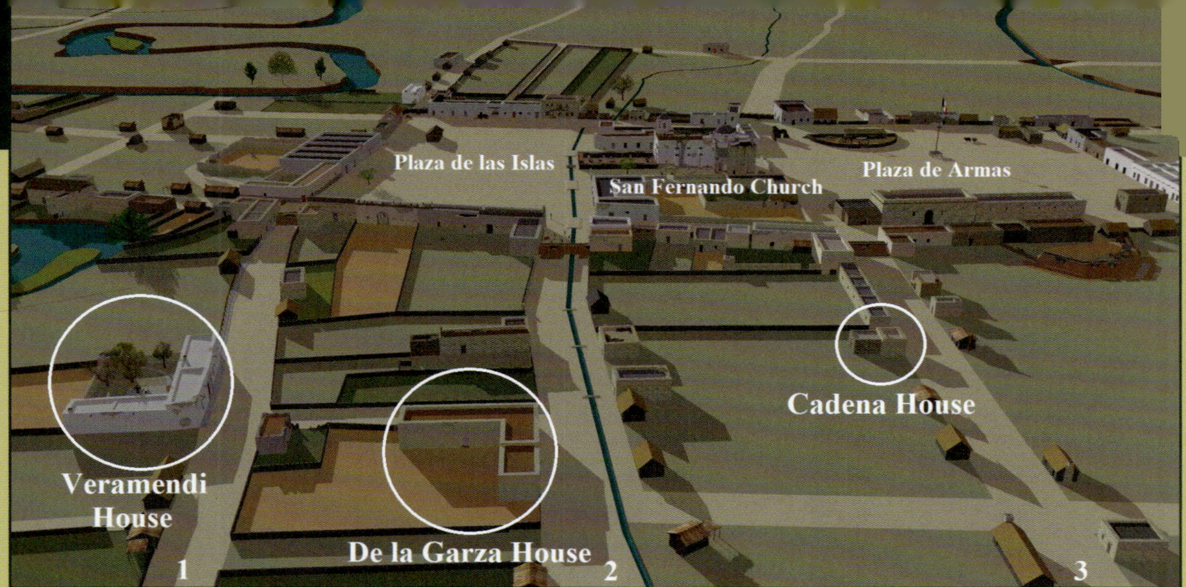

Looking south over the three streets leading to the plazas: (1) Soledad, (2) Acéquia, and (3) Flores. The Veramendi house, the José Antônio de la Garza house, and the Cadena house are the targets to be captured and used as springboards for attacking the plazas. Earthen and palisade barricades can be seen at the plaza end of each street.[1]

Capturing nearby houses and firing down on them from rooftops would make the positions untenable. The Texians would have to take their chances as they dashed down those deadly streets to gain the tactical advantage. Burleson would attack on December 4.

While Burleson's command puzzled through the best way to upend the Centralist positions at Béxar, Austin spent the day in San Felipe doing his best to help the provisional government understand where events in Texas were headed. Dispatches taken by Tejanos from a Centralist courier near Béxar made the immediacy of the situation quite clear. "This approaching storm is of a serious nature," Austin wrote. The leadership was playing with fire by trying to make the conflict about anything more than Mexican Federalism. "Should the Govt. succeed in giving to this war a national character as they are attempting, Texas will have to contend against the whole nation united against her," Austin warned. "That such a character will be given to it is probable — in fact it is almost certain, for the reason that the declaration made by the General Consultation tends fully as much to independence as to adhesion to the Constitution of 1824." The Texian government, in effect, had gone too far. A complete secession from Mexico would bring down the wrath of the entire nation upon Texas and serve to unite Federalists and Centralists in a common cause.

Austin woke up the next morning still worrying about the direction the conflict had taken. He wrote to Don Carlos Barrett, a close friend who had been elected to the General Council on November 14 as a representative from Mina. "The character of the struggle in which Texas is engaged, is now clearly developed; it evidently is one of life or death, 'to be, or not to be,' " Austin wrote. "It is no longer a mere question of the forms of political institutions; it is one of self-preservation." Mexico would not stop until Texas was vacated by every American settler. "Texas is menaced with a war of extermination; the government of Mexico has so proclaimed it," he lamented. The Texians no longer had a government within the Mexican pollical establishment, and the Decree of October 3 converting states into bureaucratic and administrative departments answering only to the central government had made it clear that Texas, as it existed, would be dissolved into some new creation. "The people now understand their situation, and consequently are much better prepared to elect public agents to provide against such a danger, than they were at the time of the last election," Austin observed. "By the decree of the 3rd of October last . . . no such thing as a state exists, not even in name." This was, in Austin's estimation, the work of one man: Antonio López de Santa Anna.

Back in Béxar, the highly anticipated assault — now invigorated by Smith and Maverick's plan of attack — fell apart. "Doubtless from similar causes to those which paralyzed the efforts of General Austin on a previous occasion," confided William T. Austin. The troops had been prepared for an attack at dawn, but just after midnight Captain Major C. Morris reported disturbing news. "The guard had observed a man go from our encampment to the Alamo," reported Captain William G. Cooke of the New Orleans Greys, "and after hailing the Centinel on the walls was admitted. Morris and Cooke reported this to Burleson, who, fearing their plan had been compromised, called off the attack. "This created great dissatisfaction in camp," noted Cooke. Recriminations rippled through the ranks, and men searched for a scapegoat. The blame at first rested on a free man of color, Hendrick Arnold, but he returned to camp that day after being on a hunt. Since no one else turned up missing, the incident of the compromised plan was dismissed as jumpy sentries mistaking loose livestock for a deserting Texian. Maverick laid the blame on the Texian leaders. Colonels Alexander Somervell and William Houston Jack simply were not prepared to face the fire of battle.

The army shattered. "There was a general breaking up," recorded Maverick. "Another faux pas is made: the volunteers curse the officers and 250 or 300 set off for home. All day we get more and more dejected. The spectacle becomes appalling." The cohesion of the Texian force, never strong, dissolved. Burleson did what he could to keep the men in the ranks "and begged them not all to go," Maverick continued. A number headed for La Bahia in hopes of finding shelter and leadership worthy of their sacrifice. Burleson, yielding to events, prepared orders for a general retreat.

Colonel Francis W. Johnson disagreed. "An evacuation, without striking a blow, would be fatal to the campaign, and expose our Mexican friends in and around San Antonio de Béxar to the ravages of the enemy, perhaps drive them from their homes," he argued. Johnson also believes that going into winter quarters somewhere else, even Goliad, would break up the army, which was the last hope for Texas. Cos would take advantage of the dissolution of the army and march directly into the settlements. Burleson, while sympathetic to Johnson's arguments, issued his orders for a retreat.

The men who had stayed firm while watching scores of their comrades simply quit the field felt betrayed. "This order was received with great indignation by the soldiers, particularly by the New Orleans Greys, who were very active in what follows," noted Dr. Joseph E. Field. Mag Stiff, one of the Greys, was also annoyed but followed orders. "We took up the line of march but proceeded only as far as the Col's tent where we were ordered to halt," he remembered. A Mexican deserter, Jesús Cuéllar, an officer in the Mexican cavalry and ardent Federalist, arrived and told the Texians that now was the time to strike, "and said we could take the town with much ease." Johnson could not believe the good fortune. "He reported the defenses of the town weak, and that the place could be taken easily." Deaf Smith was suspicious, but Captain Cooke heard the same thing as Johnson. "He stated that the Mexican troops were in a destitute condition and would soon surrender if we would attack the town, offering to act as our guide."

Burleson halted his army.

Colonel Johnson suggested to Colonel Ben Milam that he should call for volunteers — that "now is the time." Milam and another officer, Frank Johnson, after an animated and heated conversation, seemed to reach a conclusion and headed for Burleson's quarters while most of the army that remained gathered around. "Suddenly, the flap of General Burleson's tent was thrown back and a man stepped boldly out and forward," observed Creed Taylor. It was Milam. His gaze raked over the confused and angry mob around him. The Texian officer drew a line on the ground with the stock of his rifle and waved his slouch hat in the air. "Boys! Who'll go with Ben Milam into Bexar?" Milam bellowed "The quick commingled responses, 'I will,' were almost deafening," reported Taylor. "Well, if you are going with me," Milam hollered, "get on this side." Johnson could not believe that this

rump of the once powerful army seemed determined to take their chances. "After a respectable number had formed in line," he observed, "they were requested by Milam to assemble, at the Old Mill, at dark."

The remaining Texians scurried to make ready for their bold attack. "Much activity now prevailed in camp, and the remainder of the evening, and until far into the night, was spent in preliminary organization, polishing guns, distributing rations and ammunition," remembered Taylor. "In fact, but few of us slept any that night. The excitement was too tense, at last we were 'going into town.' "

Maverick, swept up in the bravado and zeal that now animated the Texians, worried they would be too few. "The men fall into ranks to see if we are strong enough," he noted. "The mere fragment of the seven hundred, say two hundred & fifty, volunteer to make the attack next morning." Fewer than a third of Austin's once-robust Army of the People — his Federal Army of Texas — remained to face the decision of dawn. Texian officer parceled the men into two divisions and made plans to rush the Mexican defenses at first light. The officers also dropped one objective, the Cadena house on Flores Street, from the plan.

Milam commanded the First Division, with Major Robert Morris as second in command. It was tasked with moving down Acéquia Street and taking the house of Don José António de la Garza, just 120 yards from Plaza de las Islas. This division consisted of the companies of Captains John Crane, George English, William Landrum, Thomas Llewellyn, William Patton, and John York. Sam Maverick and Hendrick Arnold would guide them. Accompanying them would be Nidland Franks, who would lead 15 artillerymen bringing along two cannons: the stubby 12-pounder gunade that arrived with the New Orleans Greys two weeks ago and the brass 6-pounder captured by Bowie at Concepción.

Colonel Francis W. Johnson commanded the Second Division, with Colonel William T. Austin and Dr. James Grant sharing second-in-command duties. Company captains were Thomas Alley, Thomas H. Breece, William G. Cooke, Peter J. Duncan, H. H. Edwards, J. W. Peacock, James G. Swisher, and Plácido Benavides with his company of twenty-six Tejanos from Victoria augmented by more than a dozen additional Béxareños. Deaf Smith and John W. Smith would guide this column. They would be accompanied by the Mexican deserter, Lieutenant "Comanche" Cuellar. Johnson would move his division down Soledad Street along the river and capture the Veramendi house, a mere 100 yards from the plaza. Both companies of New Orleans Greys were in Johnson's division.

As for the federal cavalry, Captain Juan N. Seguín's company of Tejanos remained, and he gathered all of the Texian mounted units under his direction. These included the companies of John S. Roberts, James Cheshire, and Robert Coleman. They would circle the town, watching for Centralist reinforcements said to be on their way from Laredo, 600 men strong. They would also forage for food to feed the fight.

Lieutenant Colonel James Clinton Neill received orders to take a third cannon and crew, supported by a company of thirty infantrymen under the command of John S. Roberts, and make a feigned attack against the Alamo as a diversion. They were to cross the river at the upper ford one-half mile above the Old Mill and then proceed downriver toward the Alamo a mile below and set up within range of the north wall. Neill would initiate the advance on Béxar by pounding the Alamo and drawing attention his direction while the army rushed into town. With luck, Milam and Johnson could sneak into town unnoticed and occupy the two designated houses.

Starting at midnight, the various commands sorted themselves out at the Old Mill. Burleson remained in position in command of the reserves.

He would reinforce whichever column achieved success or cover the retreat in case of disaster.

Then the wind shifted, and the anxious men felt the temperature plumet as yet another bitter-cold norther swept over the San Antonio Valley. "It blew some of the tents and huts over and sent the embers of the fires swirling away, but we lay peacefully under our blankets dreaming about the events of the coming day," noted Herman Ehrenberg. "It was exactly two o'clock when the night watches were relieved. Then they went from tent to tent waking up the sleeping men as quietly as possible. The men started up from their dreams but dropped off again just as quickly when the icy breath of the wind rushed over their warm limbs."

One reluctant Texian tried to beg off from the coming attack. "'I wouldn't mind going with you fellows, but I have no gun. My horse fell with me yesterday and broke the stock of my rifle,'" Creed Taylor recorded him saying. "'We'll take you along to cut bullet patchin,' roared Johnson and for years afterward that man went by the name of 'Bullet Patchin.'"

Word spread from tent to tent that the hour was at hand. "Soon we were all standing in ranks with our faithful rifles on our shoulders, but still wrapped in our blankets, awaiting the signal to move out," Ehrenberg remembered. Neill's diversionary force splashed across the ford and away into the darkness while the rest of the army shivered. "Consequently, we still had to wait a while," Ehrenberg wrote. "During this time, since no fires had been made yet, we froze terribly and looked forward impatiently to beginning our march." To break the tension, Major Morris stepped forward and called roll. Dozens who had answered Milam's challenge had melted away in the darkness. "Many heroic thoughts had disappeared, and the weak courage of some men that the evening before had glowed warmly in their hearts had been blown away by the cold wind like the embers of the fires," Ehrenberg observed. Those that remained steeled themselves for the fight. "Our motto was: 'The fewer we are, all the greater is our fame.'"[2]

The seriousness of the undertaking fell upon them all. "Long before dawn of the day, every volunteer was ready, anxious for the fray; but as they armed, formed, and fell into line for marching, a marked decrease in the levity was observed," noted Creed Taylor. "They all felt, and knew, that great danger confronted them, and that they must do some tall fighting to achieve victory over such a well-armed and strongly fortified enemy."

Volunteer Henry Dance noted the changed mood of his otherwise lighthearted companions: "Everything still as death."

14

WITH MILAM INTO BÉXAR

At 3 a.m., Colonel Neill's artillery and Captain Roberts' cavalry splashed across the river at the upper ford and moved silently down toward the Alamo. Directing his gunners to set their piece to good advantage, Neill steadied his detachment for the work ahead.

Meanwhile, the Mexican sentries atop the walls of the Alamo kept their routines. From his position across the river, Herman Ehrenberg could hear the *soldados* on their beats. Unconcerned, the numerous enemy sentinels on the Alamo were calling out their *"centinela alerta*!" into the night, he remembered. "Besides their long, drawn-out words, and the howling of the wind, there was not the slightest sound to be heard."

Having shivered in place for hours, the Texians finally began moving toward Béxar, the punishing wind and the numbing cold forgotten. "Soon we did not notice anymore the harsh wind blowing," continued Ehrenberg. "Instead, we were warm from running and from the anticipation of facing the enemy very, very soon." The volunteers began casting off their blankets on either side of their column as breathless men whispered the password for the day, "Béxar," through the ranks. "Everyone realized the seriousness of the situation and the desperate fight ahead," agreed Creed Taylor, "and yet not one of them ever doubted but that they would win victory over the fearful odds."

At 5 a.m., a cannon shot broke through the sound of men rustling through the dry cornstalks outside Béxar. "The peal of Neill's cannon told he was at his post of duty," observed Taylor. Ehrenberg agreed, writing, "A roaring sound different from that of the vicious northwester told us

that our friends were doing their duty and attacking the Alamo." The men began shuffling toward their jumping-off positions.

The Alamo garrison responded with alacrity as they tried to determine where the attack was coming from. "Instantly, we heard the roll of enemy drums and their bugles blared in colorful confusion over the drums," Ehrenberg wrote. "From the fort a constant roar of cannon went thundering toward the plaza," the German continued. "With their little cannons our people were boldly challenging the whole enemy army."

Jesús Cuéllar, the Mexican lieutenant, studied the Alamo 800 yards away across the river, a mere shadow on the horizon. A second flash from Neill's cannon followed by the sound of the blast two seconds later convinced him that the diversion was working. Signal rockets streaked skyward as the Alamo garrison summoned help from the troops just across the river. "We can be sure that the way is clear, for those shiny artificial stars are calling a part of the forces out of the city for assistance at the Alamo," the lieutenant declared. "We have to hurry now so that we can reach the city in ten minutes." The Texians began their advance in earnest, the buildings of Béxar shrouded in an early morning mist. As they scuttled past the De la Garza sugar mill on the left, Nidland Franks' artillerymen dragged the two guns up from the Dirt Fort to join the rush toward the northern edge of Béxar.

As the Texians approached the Centralist position, Cuéllar urged caution. "Do you see the forward outpost there at the fire?" he questioned. "Let them run away unmolested. Our shooting at them would only kill a few, [but] would bring the rest of the troops down on our heads." Once the sentries had fled, the Texians should chase close behind, "so that we reach the city square as soon as they do." The insurgents, picking up their pace, rushed toward the startled pickets. "We were already within twenty paces of the fire when the sentries first noticed us," Ehrenberg recalled. "Without making the slightest noise, they fled — some of them even without their muskets." Having gained the edge of town, the two Texian divisions could see the two streets they would use to pour into the town between the rows of dark, grass-roofed *jacales*.

The Texians divided. Colonel Francis Johnson's column turned left onto Soledad Street and started south near an old lime kiln.[1] Soledad, parallel to the river for 700 yards, led to the northeast corner of Plaza de las Islas. Milam led his division another block west and turned down Acéquia Street, which leads to the northwest corner of the same plaza. The only objective for this initial rush was to capture the Veramendi and De la Garza houses one block before the plaza while avoiding the cannon blasts of grape and canister that probably would come up the middle of the streets. Darkness and the morning haze covered the troops' movement. Taylor, with Milam's first division, remembered his war chief's command: "Forward, boys! We're going into town!"

The open streets rattled the Texians, who braced for that first blast of cannister from the Mexican cannon. Ehrenberg, with the New Orleans Greys in Johnson's second division, passed down Soledad Street, but the column abandoned the street, veered left, and passed through the yards and over the fences of the small houses along the way. "It was a good thing we did too, for we had hardly come within two hundred paces of our objective, when the first load of grape shot from the enemy's cannons went sweeping down the street," Ehrenberg recalled.

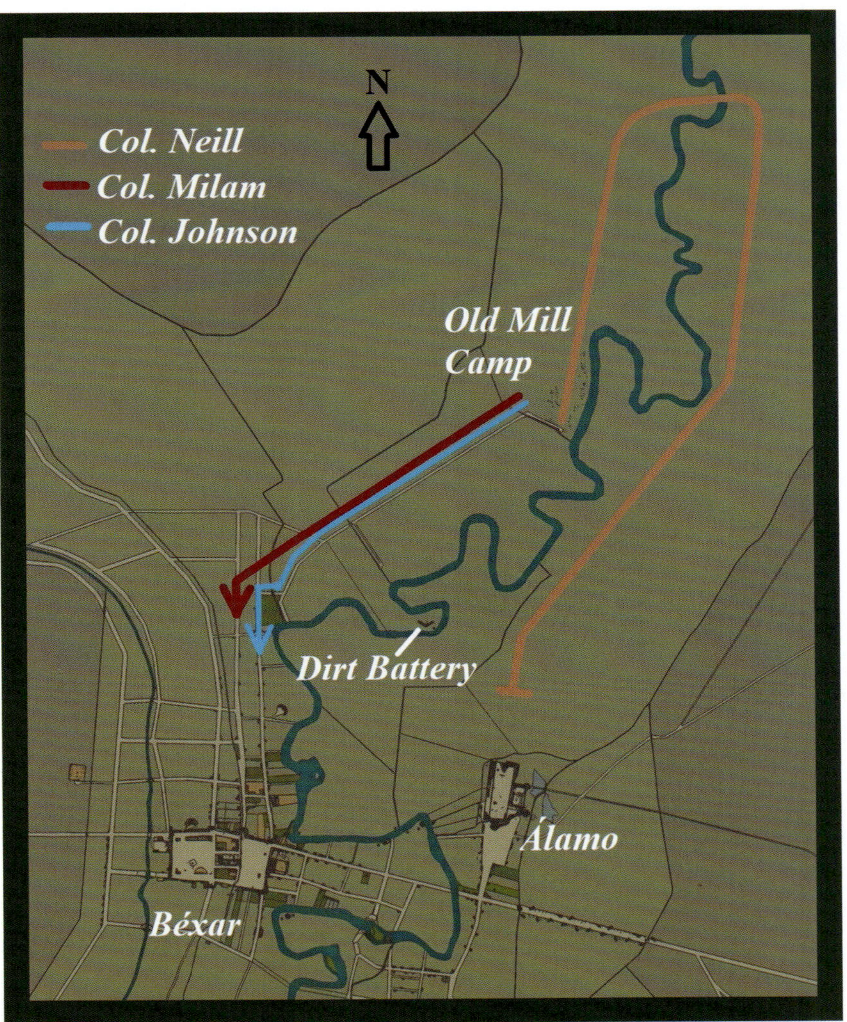

Routes of the attacking columns of Colonel Milam and Colonel Francis Johnson as well as the diversionary column of Colonel Neill.

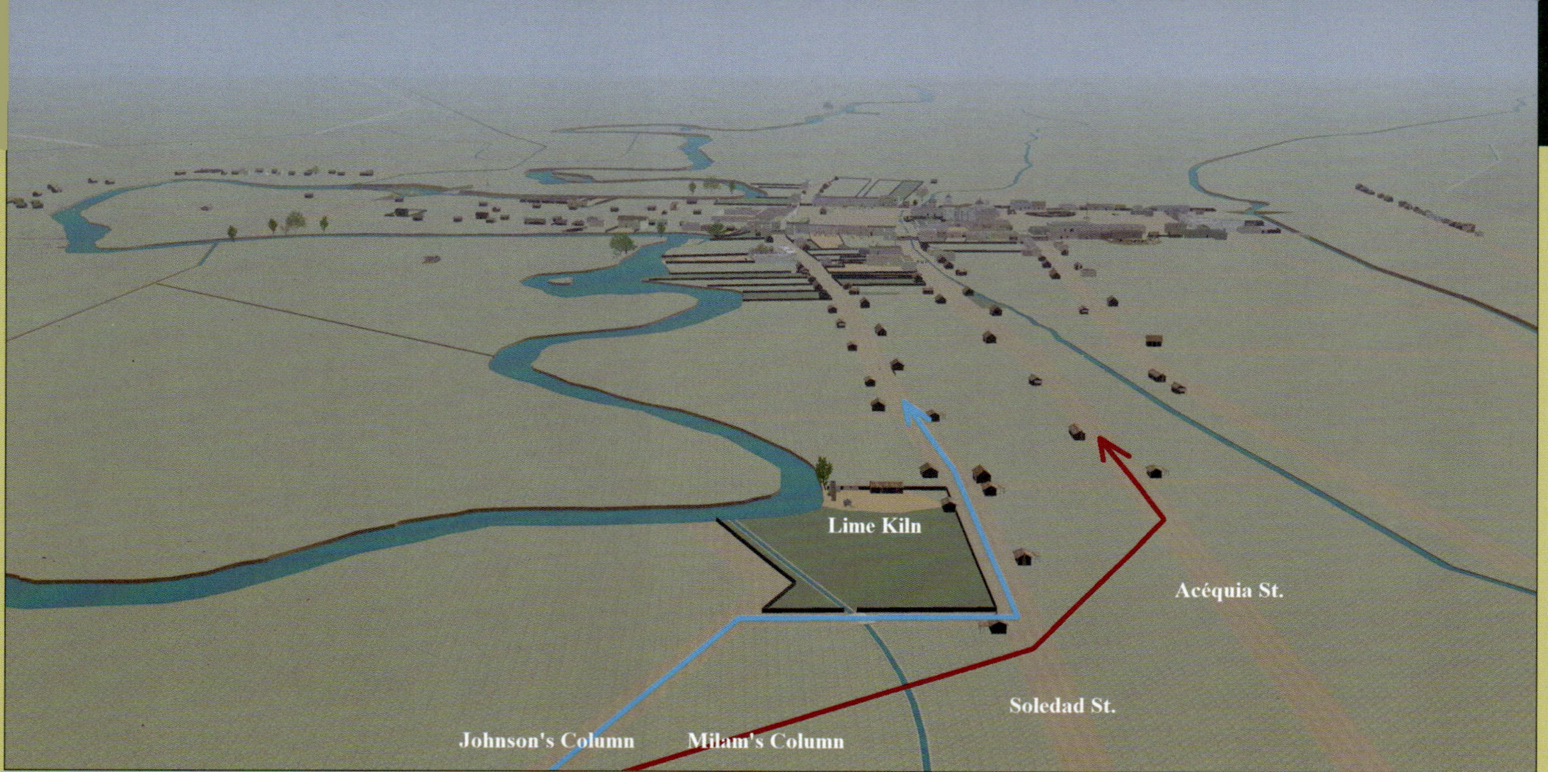

Looking south toward town. Johnson's division (blue line) turns down Soledad Street, and Milam's (red line) turns down Acéquia Street.

Likewise, Johnson's column could see the cannon barricade in the distance and abandoned Acéquia Street as well in favor of the sheltering houses to either side. As the Texians worked their way through the gloom toward the Veramendi house, the Centralist pickets opened fire. "One of them was immediately shot down by Deaf Smith," Captain Cooke noted. The Centralists, used to the occasional artillery exchange and inured to false alarms, were now alerted to the presence of the Texians in town — and close by — and they struggled to recover from the surprise as drummers beat the alarm. The groggy *soldados*, suddenly alert, sought cover and looked for the source of danger.

The Centralists began shooting at the figures moving about in the shadows. "From the moment the enemy were sighted," reported Mexican General Vicente Filisola, "they were fired upon by those who were defending the portholes and the houses." As the Texian attack developed, though, the defenders learned the shortcomings of their fortifications. The only lines of fire were straight ahead. None of the Centralist officers had thought to provide flanking fire positions to enfilade any approaching enemy. "There was a lack of foresight in not setting up the parapets in such a manner that they could be of mutual protection, and thus the defense of each one of them was reduced exclusively to the front and nothing more," Filisola lamented. "With this situation the attackers with little effort could avoid the shots."

Texian volunteers could not believe their luck. "The streets along which we approached were swept by Cos' artillery, planted in the barricades at the plaza," observed Taylor. "They had been trained to sweep only the center of the streets, and a man on the sidewalk on either side was in little danger of being hit by a cannon shot."

Colonel Johnson's division made it to the stoutly constructed Veramendi house as planned. This stylish home belonged to the family of the late Don Juan Martín de Veramendi, James Bowie's father-in-law. Now it would become a Texian citadel. Johnson's men piled into the back courtyard, its six-foot stone walls on the east and south sides serving as natural defenses. While some men spread out there, others continued into the back of the house itself through the *zaguán*, a covered passageway going through the building to the large double doors of the front entrance. The home was occupied, and as the Texians came through the back, startled Mexican defenders scrambled out through doors and window.[2]

Colonel Milam's division reached their objective, the De la Garza house, at nearly the same time as Johnson's men captured the Veramendi house. The cannon behind the barricade at the end of Acéquia Street had fired at the Texians, but also without effect. Milam's men piled in behind

the building and forced their way in. This stout stone house sat just forty yards west of the Veramendi house and connected to it by a narrow cross street called Veramendi Alley. The De la Garza place also faces Plaza de las Islas about 120 yards to the south. From here, Nidland Franks' cannon crews could put the heart of the Centralist defenses under their guns.

The two Texian columns represented a cross section of the insurgents opposing the Centralists. The men in the De la Garza house were largely Texian colonists from the United States. The volunteers in the Veramendi house were from a variety of backgrounds and included newcomers to Texas mixed with men with deep roots in the region. The combined companies of New Orleans Greys were the most organized and had some

Johnson's division faces a barricade (circled) with a cannon port at the far end of Soledad Street, perhaps preparing to fire a load of grape-and-canister up the street. The two divisions continue into town.

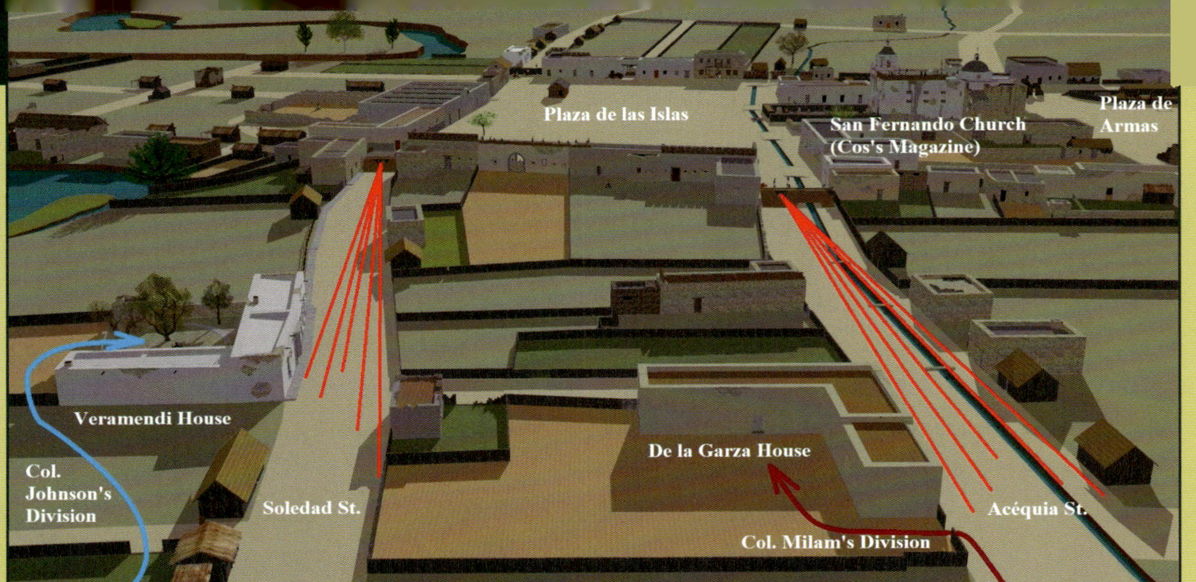

Plaza de las Islas
San Fernando Church (Cos's Magazine)
Plaza de Armas
Veramendi House
Col. Johnson's Division
Soledad St.
De la Garza House
Acéquia St.
Col. Milam's Division

LEFT: *Looking south toward the plazas. The red lines represent the grape and canister blasts raking the streets north from the portholes in the earth-and-palisade barricades as the two divisions of Federalists avoid the streets and take protected approaches to their destinations. In addition to breaching the plazas, the goal is to capture Cos's gunpowder stored in San Fernando Church.*

BOTTOM LEFT: *The José António de la Garza house on Veramendi Alley, which leads from Soledad to Acéquia Street.*

BELOW: *The Veramendi house, often referred to as the Veramendi Palace, with its large double doors.*

Centralist cannon emplacement at the southwest corner of the Alamo pounds the Veramendi house 600 yards away.

rudimentary training, but the units had existed only for a month and were far from seasoned. Young men from different parts of the U.S. and Europe, like Herman Ehrenberg, filled its ranks for the most part. By law, they had come into Mexican Texas illegally, looking for adventure. With them, however, were men who clearly had a stake in the battle's outcome. Plácido Benavides and his company of Federalist Tejanos were fighting to defend their rights and the Constitution of 1824 — and for their homes. Besides this mixed band of Tejano patriots and New Orleans swashbucklers, there was a handful of American frontiersmen armed with flintlock long rifles, highly accurate at 200 yards.

Colonel Johnson distributed this mixed crew behind the walls of the back yard as well as inside the house. He soon learned that he was in a crossfire, with rounds coming in from the Alamo on his left and from the plaza at his front. The first shot in the Texian attack had rung out two hours before, but as the sun rose, the Centralists had sorted out what was happening. "At seven o'clock, a heavy cannonading from the town was seconded by a well-directed fire from the Alamo," Johnson wrote, "which for a time prevented the possibility of covering our lines, or effecting a safe communication between the two divisions." The troops remained snug within the Veramendi house despite the shelling. "The houses of all wealthy Mexicans are literally little fortresses," concluded Ehrenberg.

In the growing light, Johnson's men studied the town's layout. Most of the New Orleans Greys had never been in a Spanish Colonial town before and seemed quite surprised by what they saw. "In astonishment we gazed at the dark outlines of the blocks of houses that we saw around us," Ehrenberg wrote. "We had never seen buildings of this type before. All of them were only one story high and built literally in the shape of a long box."

Johnson's men, under fire for hours, took stock of the enemy positions. "Even though it was still dark as night when we got there, a murderous fire from the enemy's muskets soon revealed his position to us," Ehrenberg noted. "The whole plaza was one blazing firing line, with the enemy firing in one continuous but irregular volley, and interspersed among the musket fire were the loud booms from all the Mexicans' cannons. Twelve to sixteen of their six-pounders were firing on the little fort occupied by us."

The Centralists' artillery did have the Texians in a crossfire. Three or four cannons in the Alamo faced toward town from the west wall. While two on the Plaza de las Islas were aimed up Soledad and Acéquia streets, three more pointed from a redoubt on the north side of Plaza de Armas, easily repositioned to fire at the captured houses. There may have been a light cannon or perhaps a small wall gun mounted in the bell tower or on the roof of San Fernando Church that could have thrown shots at either

house as well. Despite the impressive numbers, the pieces are light — perhaps two 6-pounders and five 4-pounders. These small-caliber cannon would do little against the heavy stone walls of the Veramindi and De la Garza houses.[4]

The Texians nearest the river submitted to the pounding. "One of their cannons was within eighty paces of our position and it was doing its part by planting a nice long-range six-pound ball against the wall at the lower end of our house that ran parallel to the plaza — and at the very moment when we were right behind that wall!" recalled Ehrenberg. This cannon, firing from the emplacement behind the barricade at the end of Soledad Street, had a clear shot at the south side of the house and courtyard just 100 yards away.

The situation at the home of Don José Antonio de la Garza was little better. Owned by a wealthy Béxareño like Don Juan Martín de Veramendi, this structure too resembled a small fortress. It needed to be. Back in 1818, de la Garza became the first person to coin money in Texas and continued to do so up until the Centralist invasion.[5] Like many other Béxareños who did not wish to be forced into service by Cos, de la Garza had removed his family to his *rancho* fifteen miles south of town. Now his home in town was a Texian stronghold.

DeWitt colonist Richard Chisholm brought his company down Acéquia Street trying to reinforce the De la Garza house and found themselves dodging artillery. "Our course lay along a ditch about four or five feet deep, and more than half full of water," Chisholm wrote. "The command was given to fall in the ditch, which was obeyed. Every man jumped into it, up to his hips, in water as cold as ice." Fire from the Alamo and San Fernando Church plowed up the ground around the Texians as they sloshed up the *acéquia* to cover. As soon as they got the chance,

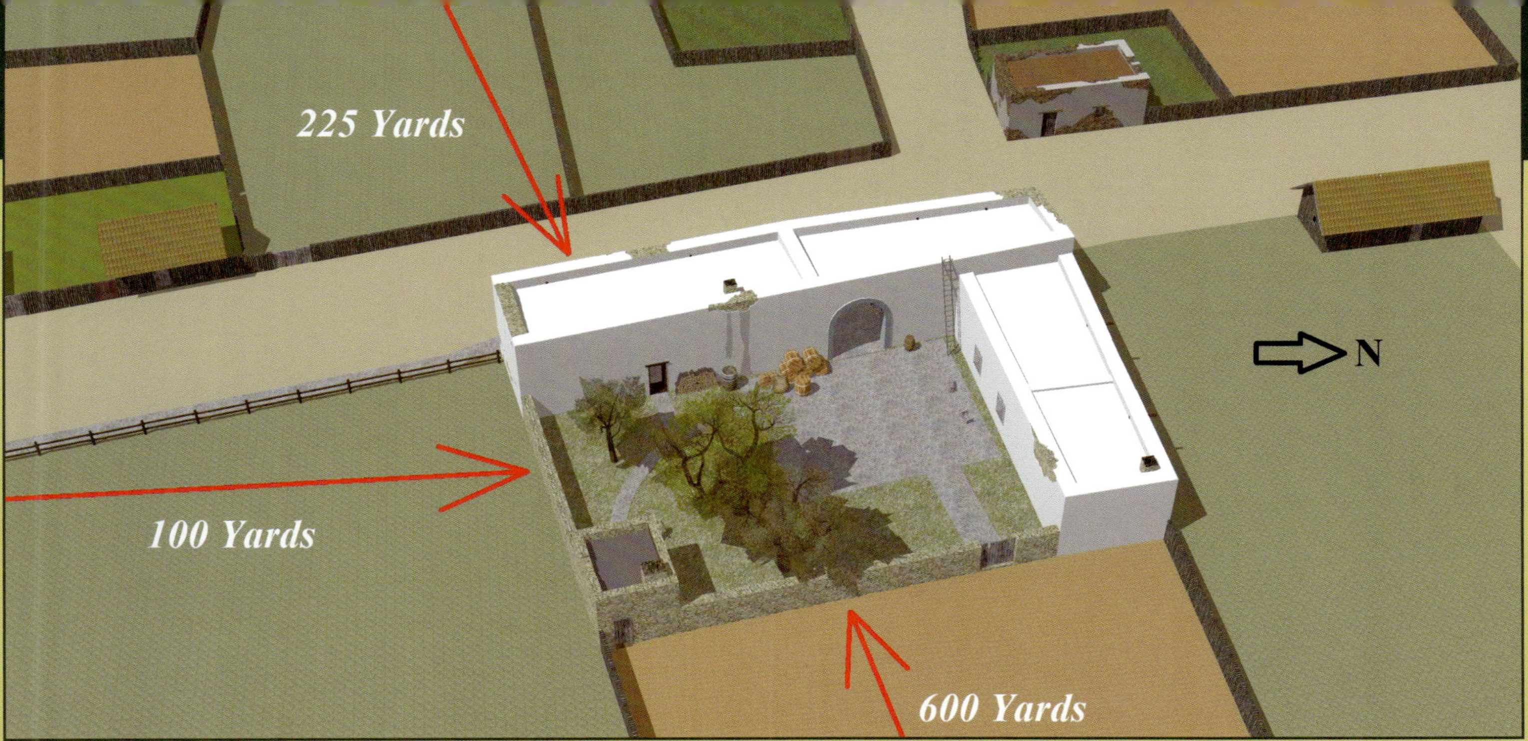

TOP: *A cannon crossfire batters the Veramendi house, with fire from the battery at the end of the street 100 yards south, from the three-gun redoubt (El Fortín de Santa Anna) on the north edge of Plaza de Armas 225 yards west, and from at least three cannon at the Alamo 600 yards east.*

LEFT: *Looking south at the buildings Ehrenberg describes, there are four stone houses between Soledad and Acéquia streets. Their occupants are (left to right) Maria Menchaca, Padre Refúgio de la Garza (parish priest of San Fernando Church), and Manuel Yturri, who lives in the last two buildings making up the right half of the block and owned by Francisco de Arocha.[3] The arched passageway through the priest's house is like that of the Veramendi house and has been barricaded by Cos' soldiers with a stone wall higher than a man and with a firing step behind it to allow fusiliers to shoot over the top. The rooftops have loopholed adobe parapets at the ends close to the streets, and soldiers are rapidly placing sandbags in between to provide further protection for firing positions.*

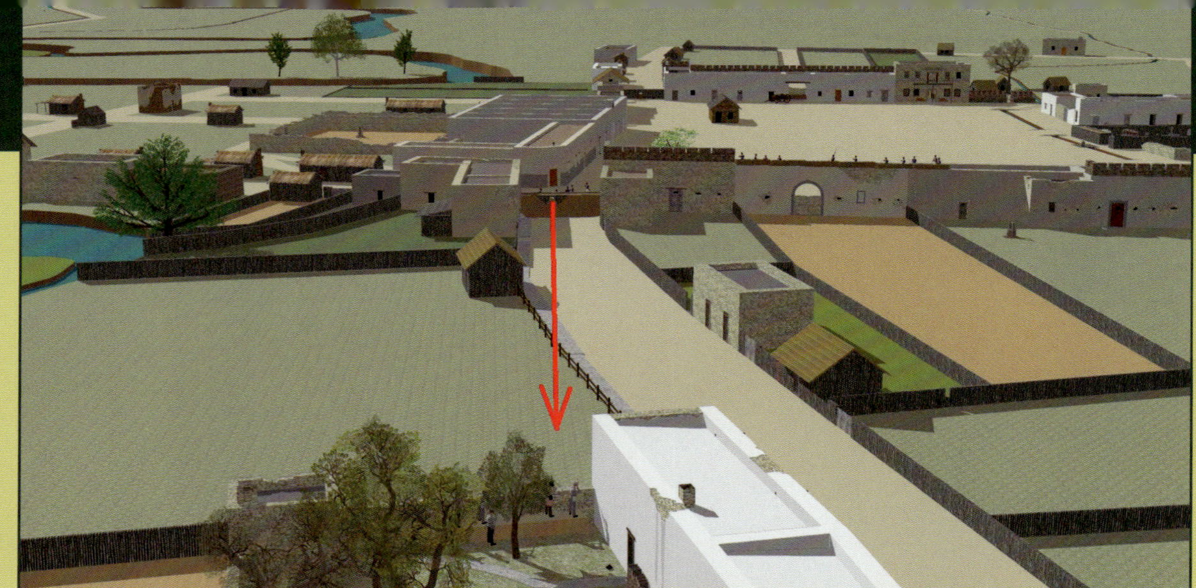

TOP: The Federalists can be seen at the bottom of the picture behind the south wall of the Veramendi courtyard as Centralist cannoneers behind the barricade at the end of Soledad Street fire 6-pound balls at their position.

RIGHT: The 6-pounder on the plaza aimed up Soledad Street at the south wall and yard of the Veramendi house.

Looking south along Acéquia Street, another breastwork and cannon emplacement can be seen blocking this entrance to the plaza. An irrigation ditch (an acéquia, hence the street's name) flows toward the plaza along the west side of the street. It was dug by hand in the 1720s to supply the newly established Presídio de Béxar (now the Plaza de Armas) with drinking water. The acéquia originates behind a dam on San Pedro Creek 1.5 miles north-northwest just below its springs and empties into the San Antonio River 2 miles south of town. Along the way, it irrigates Tejano farms known as labores.

Chisholm and the others scrambled out of the *acéquia* and ran across the street to the warmth and safety of the De la Garza house.

Unlike the Veramendi place, the yard of the De la Garza house was not surrounded by a wall. It was covered by stout outbuildings, though, and protected from artillery and musket fire from both the plaza to the south and the three-gun redoubt to the southwest. In the confusion of the attack, the Centralists were only aware of the insurgents in the Veramendi house and applied all their firepower in that direction, the artillery rounds passing over and beyond Milam's men.

Mexican *soldados* soon discovered that there were enemies closer at hand. "The enemy's fire increased as we drew nearer the plaza where the buildings were stronger and more compact, all of them being of stone or adobe with flat roofs, and a wall projecting around and about four feet above the surface of the roof," wrote Creed Taylor. "These walls were manned by Mexican troops who kept up a brisk fire upon us." Even so, the *soldados'* aim was not true. Poor weapons and inadequate training led many of the Centralist troops to fire wide of the mark. "If they had been trained marksmen, armed with any other gun," noted Taylor, "few of us would have escaped death."

In terms of small arms, the Centralists were outgunned. "Those Mexican soldiers would load, thrust their guns over the crest of the low wall and send a constant shower of balls in our direction, with harmless effect," observed Taylor. "On their part it was a matter of self-preservation, since no sooner did a head appear above the walls than it served as a target for a dozen hunting rifles, and there was always another dead Mexican." Armed with old surplus East India Brown Bess muskets, the Mexican line infantry had a range of only seventy yards, while the American frontier hunting rifles were accurate at 200 yards. Many of the volunteers so equipped used them to good effect.[6]

On Soledad Street, Mexican musketry and artillery also pinned down Johnson's men. "As the balls whistled over our heads, they sang a unique morning song — in countless tones from the treble down to the bass, like the notes of the Aeolian harp," quipped Ehrenberg. "We had never seen such shooting before." Having heard that the flat roof on the Veramendi house had a parapet around the edges that might serve as a covered firing position, some of the men decided to scramble up the ladder from the courtyard and see if they could return fire. These "parapets," though, extended only one or two feet above the roof. Too late the eager marksmen learned of their error and fell flat to the roof, hoping they could lie flatter than the few stones along the edge of the roof. "Even those men directly behind the wall were not safe since the snipers on the church, which towered over all the buildings in the city, had a good view of our roof too," Ehrenberg observed.

Centralist sharpshooters on the roof of San Fernando Church spied the Texians as they clambered atop the Veramendi house and opened fire. This time, the *soldados* brought British-made Baker rifles to the fight. The 200-yard shots were tricky, but soon the Mexican marksmen began to strike home. "It was a hot berth, for the enemy poured a deadly fire upon us, killing and wounding several," noted one defender. Pinned flat, the Texians had trouble retuning fire. The strong north wind also made loading their weapons difficult. Learning of their plight, Deaf Smith climbed up to lend a hand. "As he raised himself up," the soldier continued, "he received a ball in the shoulder which disabled him." The legendary scout, stricken, lay wounded and exposed. His comrades used hatchets and blades to carve a hole in the roof, and they lowered him down to safety. The others atop the house followed. "Shortly after dawn the snipers who had climbed up there had to climb down again and quickly," Ehrenberg quipped. "They had the pleasure of being laughed at for their agility."

Trapped in their miniature fortress, Johnson's men made the best of their situation. They slaughtered a bull tied to a tree in the courtyard and started cooking bloody beef for breakfast. Other delectables turned up to round out the meal. "In the house we found a few barrels of wheat flour from Missouri that had been opened," Ehrenberg reported, "and a little leftover sugar, coffee, and chocolate."

Fed and under cover, Johnson's men turned to other issues. Where were Milam's men? Had his division captured the De la Garza house? "We assumed they were nearby, but no one could say exactly where they were," Ehrenberg wrote. "We found out only through an unfortunate incident. On our right and a little behind us there rose from time-to-time little clouds of smoke from several stone buildings like ours." Johnson's men watched the action to the northwest and concluded that what they were seeing was Milam's men firing.

The men at the De la Garza house were not sure if Johnson's men had cleared the Veramendi house, and some Texian bullets flew into Johnson's position. "One of their rifle balls struck a Mississippian named Moore, but it ricocheted off of two dollars [coins] that he had in his vest pocket," Ehrenberg continued. Blessing his luck, the stunned volunteer sought cover from the friendly fire. A companion was not as lucky. "A second rifle ball cut down another man, the tall Mississippian," wrote Ehrenberg. "It ripped a part of his brain from his skull and splattered it over the big

TOP: *Angles of cannon fire at the Veramendi house (A) and De la Garza house (B) from the Alamo, the street batteries on Plaza de las Islas, a small gun in the church bell tower, and the three-gun redoubt on the north side of Plaza de Armas.*

LEFT: *Centralist troops firing from the roofs of houses on the north side of the plaza and from the entrance hall of Padre Garza's house, its back entrance barricaded by a stone wall and earthen firing step.*

courtyard and on those of us who were standing around him. His large limbs twitched convulsively for several more hours in the clotting blood that ran from the wound. It showed us newcomers to this handiwork the body's struggle with the ebbing life force."

The friendly fire threatened to make Johnson's position untenable. A German, Wilhelm Thomas, was firing at Centralists in the plaza, but a Texian bullet flew in from his right, crippling him. "The wounded man, driven by a powerful force, wheeled around involuntarily as a gust of wind blew past him, and a stream of blood gushed from his sleeve," observed the Ehrenberg. "As pale as white marble, he looked around in surprise, clapped his left hand on his shoulder, and said apprehensively that he must be wounded but that he was feeling no pain. The terrible pain did not come until later, for his shattered shoulder bone later caused the surgeons more concern than the wounds of all the other injured men put together."

A handful of Johnson's men determined to contact Milam's troops and stop the inadvertent fratricide. "Several men immediately volunteered," Ehrenberg remembered, "to hop over there and straighten those people out."

The mission was fraught. It was a 65-yard dash from the Veramendi front door to De la Garza's entrance, across wide-open Soledad Street, and then west on Veramendi Alley protected only by four-foot cedar post fences. One man tried and was badly wounded by bullets from the houses on the plaza. Others followed. "Running across the street was extremely dangerous, for as soon as the enemy caught sight of us, which happened after a few seconds, they would fire at least thirty copper and lead 'apples of paradise' at us," recalled the German, Ehrenberg. Some of the runners made it through, and the Texian divisions were once again in contact.

Johnson's men, having solved the friendly fire issue, improved their position as well as they could. Soldiers knocked a hole in the northern wall of the Veramindi house, allowing men to pass in and out of the dwelling without being exposed on Soledad Street. Others knocked loopholes on the southern face to get a better angle on the Centralists in their plaza fortifications just eighty yards away.

The enemy cannon in that position, as well as those in the Alamo, had pounded Johnson's position. The Texians decided it was time to quiet the closer of those hazards. Marksmen aimed their rifles through the loopholes and began felling Mexican gunners as they passed ever so briefly behind the open cannon embrasure. "It became now the main object of

New Orleans Greys and other volunteers on the roof of the Veramendi house.

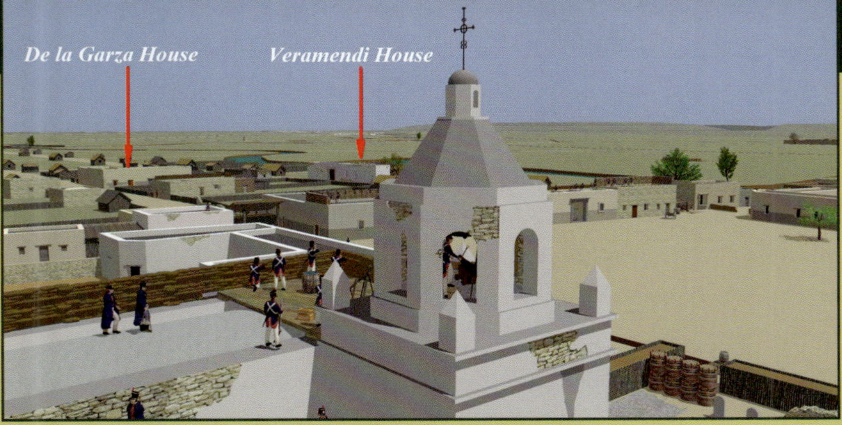

A view from San Fernando shows the Veramendi house in relation to the De la Garza house. The plaza to the right is 100 yards from the Veramendi home.

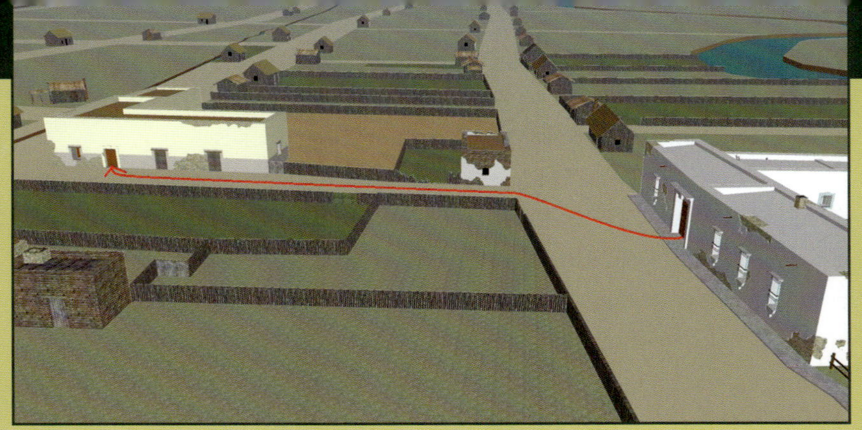

Coordinating the efforts of the Federalist attack columns meant crossing the bullet-swept ground between the two positions.

our attention, and after a short while it fell silent since the backwoodsmen and the Grays," Ehrenberg noted, "were cutting down every bluecoat that approached that cannon. Consequently, it could not be loaded, much less aimed at us."

On Acéquia Street at the other end of Veramendi Alley, Nidland Franks brought his Texian cannon into action. His fifteen-man artillery command positioned the bronze Concepción 6-pounder and the 12-pound gunade in the open, ready to blast apart the Centralists' position at the plaza end of the street just 120 yards away. It was a foolhardy mission. The enemy gunners beat the Texians to the first shot and dismounted the larger gun. Soldados atop nearby buildings picked up the challenge and began to

cut down the crewmen. Soon three wounded and writhing Texians lay at the feet of Virginia-born Lieutenant William Ridgeway Carey, while two others were sprawled nearby, dead. Those who could still do so abandoned the remaining cannon and took cover inside the De la Garza house as enemy bullets cut them down as they scurried. "I thought & still think that nothing but fate saved me," remembered Carey. "We only had four killed and thirteen wounded."

Only Carey and two other Texians remained. Still, he was determined to finish this artillery duel. "I loaded and fired the gun assisted by two more instead of ten and escaped only slightly wounded," the Virginian wrote. "A ball passed through my hat and cut the flesh to the scull bone and my clothes received many shots." But his aim was true. A 6-pound ball from his cannon flew through the open embrasure of the enemy barricade, smashing the Mexican gun. His three-man crew next turned their gun toward Centralists firing from the cover of some houses.

Watching from the Veramendi house, Ehrenberg applauded the gun crew's work. "Our shiny long six-pounder was playing real havoc with a row of houses standing across from us," he wrote. "But we had to be very sparing with our cannon balls since we did not have a great many of them." Colonel Johnson was less impressed. "In consequence of the twelve pounder having been dismounted, and the want of proper cover for the other gun, little execution was done by our artillery, during the day," he reported. "We were, therefore, reduced to a close and well directed fire from our rifles, which, notwithstanding the advantageous position of the enemy, obliged them to slacken their fire, and several times to abandon their artillery, within the range of our shot."

The morning passed, and the battle fell into a stalemate. Soon water was running short for the Texians. Neither of their positions had a well. "All the water running through town was commanded by the enemy's guns," explained Texian Henry Dance. At the Veramendi house, runners who made the 100-yard dash to the San Antonio River drew steady fire from *soldados* on the opposite bank. "We would dip our containers into the water and race back through a rain of enemy rifle balls to our friends," Ehrenberg observed. "This exercise became too dangerous, however, for more and more bluecoats took a position opposite this point on the river." Thirsty Texians bought water off their more daring comrades, but the risk sparked inflation. "Soon the price of water had increased to three or four dollars a bucket, until finally no one wanted to take the risk of dipping water from that crystalline stream even for a higher sum."

María Jesusa de García, a Bexareña who had been swept up in the Veramendi house when the Texians had captured the place, offered to fetch the water herself. "As a woman, she said, she had nothing to fear," Ehrenberg wrote. "She insisted on doing it, and smiled in saying that we did not know the Mexican male very well who loves the fair sex." Another Texian, Mag Stiff, watched the plucky women move toward the river. "She got the water and on her return to the house . . . was shot through the arm by the Mexicans and did not reach our station. We did not get the water until night."

Thirsty and exhausted by the violence of the day, the men of Johnson's command dug in to await events. They dug a trench inside both walls of the courtyard and piled the earth against them as reinforcement against cannonballs. The dirt also formed a firing step to allow them to shoot over the six-foot wall. With their position thus improved, they waited.

With the energy of the day spent and night coming on, Johnson planned his next move. A stone building closer to the Plaza de las Islas had commanded the right flank of the Veramendi house and had caused problems all day. "The enemy had been shooting with considerable zeal through the spaces between the barred windows of that building," Ehrenberg remembered, "and, owing to our proximity to the building, their fire gave us no particular pleasure." The Texians needed to capture that position.

There would be other benefits as well. Capturing that structure would put the insurgents in a position to fire with effect on San Fernando Church and make life difficult for the *soldados* on the plaza. Captain Thomas H. Breece volunteered to lead the Second Company, New Orleans Greys, in the task. His troops leapt out of the windows of the Veramendi house and rushed in the darkness with wrecking bars, ready to break a hole in

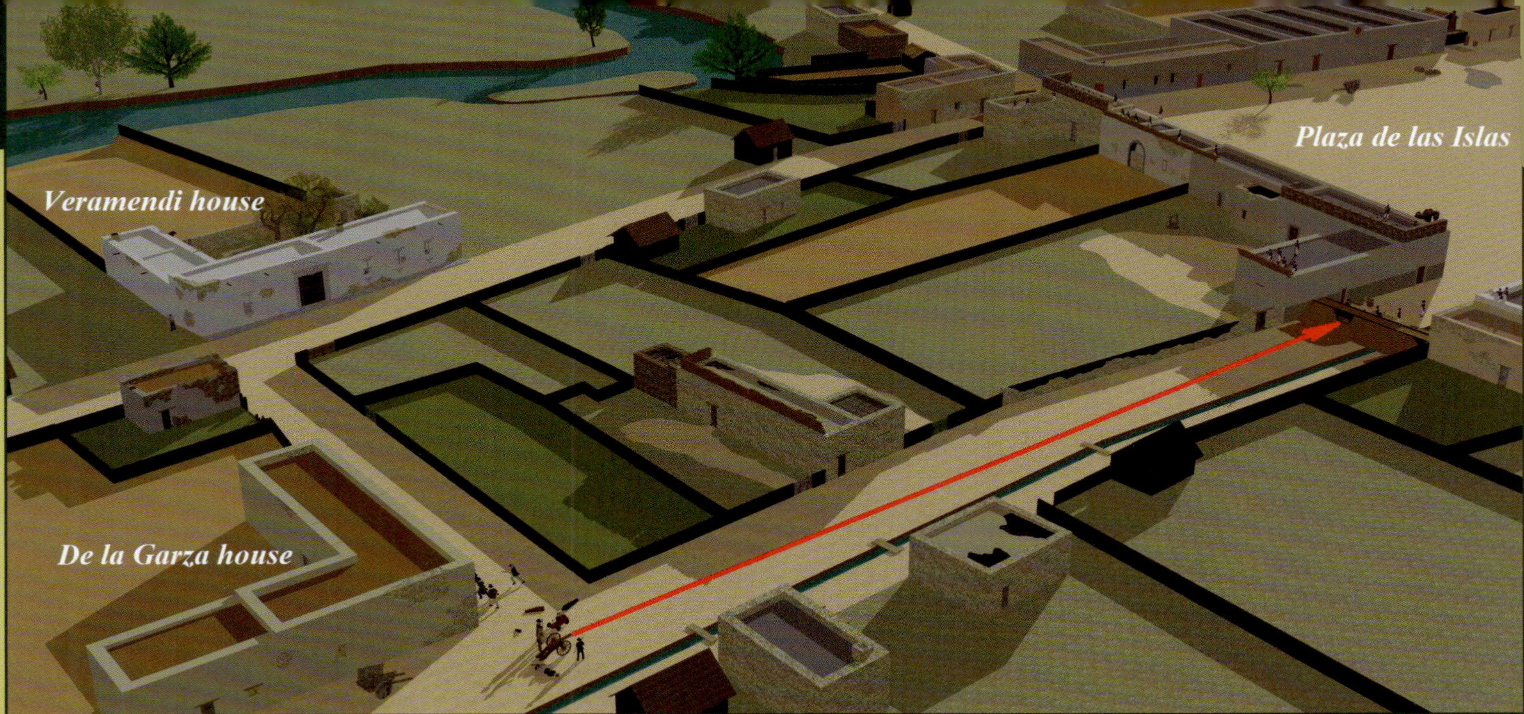

Lieutenant Carey's "lucky shot" (red line) at the cannon port at the end of Acéquia Street.

the stone walls of the building. They arrived too late to be first. A squad of volunteers calling themselves the Mississippi Greys had beat them to the target, and together the Texians began hammering away at the wall. "Hardly ten minutes had passed before the first stone broke loose and fell down inside the building," Ehrenberg wrote.

The eager volunteers thrust their muskets into the opening and fired blindly at whatever might be inside. "The dreadful screams of women and children from inside told us that the building was full of people who were now screaming pitifully for mercy," Ehrenberg continued. "Immediately our deadly fire ceased, but the attack on the walls continued, and soon the Mississippians had broken out a virtual door." Women and children stumbled out of the opening, followed by men. "They told the people that we had no intention of waging war against the Mexican people, and that the Mexicans need not be concerned about their property," the German remembered. "Having said this, they gave the Mexicans permission to leave. The captured men did not wait around to hear it a second time but

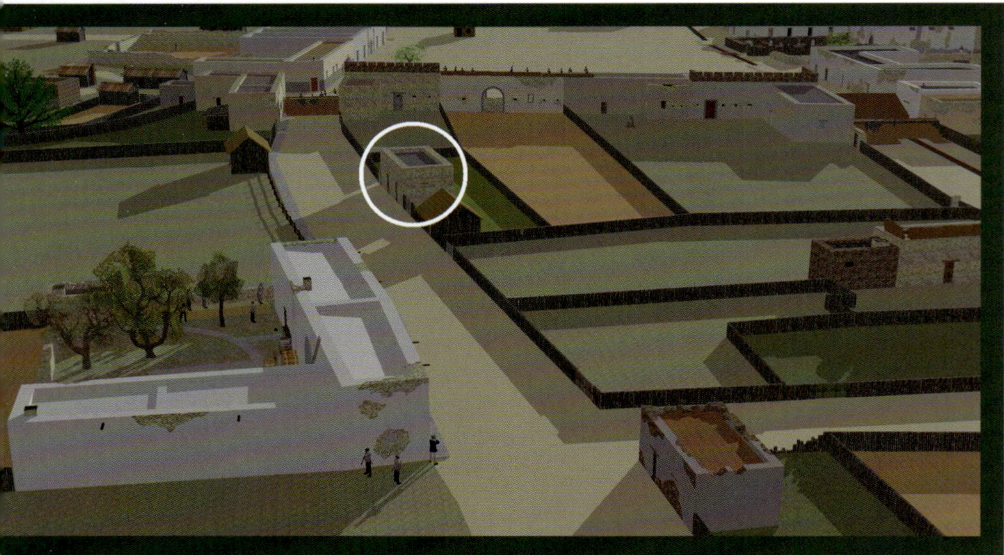

The house circled is the probable goal of the men in the Veramendi house.
It belongs to Fernando Rodriguez and is a perfect steppingstone toward the plaza.

took off full speed." Johnson's division advanced in the darkness, closer to the heart of Béxar.

As the darkness deepened, Henry Dance and six or seven others received orders to make the mile run back to camp to get cannon balls and supplies — "a very hazardous undertaking," according to Dance. They climbed out through the hole in the north end of the Veramendi house and hurried up Soledad Street. Alert *soldados* across the river heard the Texians and opened fire. "The musket balls came after us as soon as we were out of cover of our position as far as they could reach," Dance recalled, "and a crossfire of grape from the Alamo the whole route."

Once back at the old mill, the squad of volunteers loaded up. Not only did they grab ammunition and powder, but they also gathered meat, milk, and bread before making the dangerous trek back to town. They also

brought in reinforcements — about forty fresh and eager muskets to add to the battle.

The Centralists were waiting. "They seemed determined to Rake us off the face of the earth with canister and grape," Dance wrote. "We went through all with only a few cuts with splinters [and] portions of Rock . . . falling into our faces at every discharge of the cannon."

With supplies and ammunition shepherded safely to the Veramendi house and more troops at hand, the battle for the day shuddered to a close. The hungry soldiers feasted on the new groceries, adding them to the beef from the slaughtered Veramendi bull as well as an unlucky neighborhood rooster. Then they counted the day's cost. Colonel Francis Johnson took a tally. "Our loss during this day was one private killed, one colonel and one first lieutenant severely wounded," he wrote. "One colonel slightly, three privates dangerously, six severely and three slightly wounded." One man killed and twelve wounded at this end of the fight, he noted. Who knew what the next day's score would be?

Under the cover of night, the Texians tried to improve their positions. One squad of men in the Veramendi house filled sandbags for barricades while others worked outside preparing defenses and communication lines between the two Texian positions. "During the whole of the night, the two divisions were occupied in strengthening their positions, opening trenches, and effecting a safe communication, although exposed to a heavy cross-fire from the enemy, which slackened towards morning," wrote Colonel Francis "Frank" Johnson. "I may remark that the want of proper tools rendered this undertaking doubly arduous." Morning revealed a trench crossing Soledad Street from the north end of the Veramendi house to the front door of the De la Garza house. They also dug a trench to the river for safe access to water. Meanwhile, Milam's men were also busy. "With the lull of the guns and under cover of darkness we made considerable advance, erected a few barricades in exposed places," remembered Creed Taylor.

Another squad saw to the critical task of recovering the Texian artillery, still lying in the road on Acéquia Street. These men reclaimed their abandoned 6-pounder and moved it to the Veramendi yard, where its crew would be better protected while enjoying a clear shot at the Mexican fortifications at the south end of the street. The Texians also hauled over the dismounted tube of the 12-pound gunade. "During the night our long twelve-pounder had been brought," Ehrenberg wrote. "Immediately we began constructing a fortification with an opening for firing it." The men in the Veramendi yard helped the artillerymen finish mounting both cannons behind the south wall, positioning the bronze 6-pounder on its field carriage to fire through a quickly made cannon port in the stone wall, while the dismounted 12-pounder gunade tube was simply laid across the broken wall.

One fact remained certain: the Texians were now committed to this attack. The Centralists would contest any advance — or retreat. For Johnson and Milam, it would be either victory or disaster. The decisive point in the campaign had finally arrived.

15

ADVANCING TOWARD THE PLAZAS

At sunup, the Centralists saw the Texian improvements and did their best to make life miserable for the insurgents. The *soldados* "opened through loop-holes, a very brisk fire of small-arms on our whole line, followed by a steady cannonading from the town, in front, and the Alamo on the left flank," reported Colonel Johnson. The men in Colonel Milam's division were catching fire as well. "During the night, the enemy had not been idle," Creed Taylor wrote, "and when the fight began . . . it seemed that Cos had assembled his entire force in front of Milam's division."

The Texian artillery drew attention as well. Centralist sharpshooters in the San Fernando Church bell tower resumed their precision work, this time against the volunteers in the Veramendi yard as they finished mounting both cannon. John Ingram, a 27-year-old Kentuckian, watched as the Texians brought their guns into action. "Captain [Almeron] Dickinson sighted it for the cupola of the church and another man took a long pole and touched it off." While the shot did not end the snipers' harassment, it did reveal that the Centralists could not keep shooting from the church without a response from the Texian cannon.

While Johnson's men were fed and ready for the day's action, the men in Milam's command cast about for rations. They had not sent a party back to camp, nor did they have captured livestock. As a result, the men on the western end of the Texian line woke up with growling stomachs. "When we went into action on the morning of the fifth, each man was supposed to carry two days supply of rations, but by morning of the second day there

was not a morsel in my (York's) company, and every man was ravenously hungry," Taylor noted, "fighting all the day and working hard all the night gave us a ravenous appetite." Around midmorning, Texian quartermaster Captain William G. Cooke was heartily welcomed when he arrived at the De la Garza house with food. "While the air seemed filled with flying missiles, and the smoke from the enemy's guns hung in dense clouds over the old town, he sent forward an abundant supply of nicely barbecued beef," Taylor continued. "This was issued to the men while they stood or crouched under cover of fences, walls of houses, etc., and was devoured with a relish."

While Milam's and Johnson's men had been actively engaged against the Centralists, the men in Colonel Burleson's reserve at the Old Mill sat idle. "Those who had refused to go into the assault — had nothing to do but loaf around the camp and watch us do the fighting," Taylor fumed. Cooke organized these vagabonds and set up a system of supply. Men drove in cattle from the nearby prairie while others chopped wood, dug cook pits, tended the fires, slaughtered beeves, and roasted the meat. "It was thus during the entire siege, and no man went hungry as long as he was within reach of the quartermaster," Taylor boasted. "The captain became a favorite with the men who fought at Béxar."

While the Texian camp came to life and the men in Béxar fought for their lives, Burleson slipped into town to assess the situation. What he discovered troubled him. Taking the plazas would be far more difficult than capturing the first two houses. Desperate, he and Milam penned a dispatch to the Texian provisional government to bring officials up to date on events and pressure them into sending munitions, supplies, and reinforcements. A band of enthusiastic volunteers might have gone with Old Ben Milam into Béxar, but now both he and Burleson doubted they could finish the job without help. Perhaps the Texians had been rash.

Still, the Texians fought on. Late in the day, Milam's men sallied from the De la Garza house and captured a house across Acéquia Street — possibly the Pedro Martinez house about 100 feet away — and thus moved slightly closer to the plazas. Colonel Johnson reported that "a detachment of Captain Crane's company, under Lieutenant W. McDonald, followed by others, gallantly possessed themselves under a severe fire, of the house to the right, and in advance of the first division, which considerably extended our line." Meanwhile, the guns of the Veramendi house roared. "The rest of the army was occupied in returning the enemy's fire and strengthening our trenches, which enabled our artillery to do some execution, and complete a safe communication from right to left," he continued.

The day sputtered to a close with little progress made on either side. The Centralists had not dislodged the pesky insurgents, nor had the Texian Federalists advanced appreciably. Both forces, spent from two hard days, passed the night nervously. The Texians continued to dig in while counting their losses. Three more volunteers had been badly hit, while two others were bandaged and back on the line. By the following morning, all the captured houses were connected by trenches to allow traffic and communications among them. This was accomplished despite the harassment of cannonading from the Alamo and the batteries at the end of both streets, which had continued all night.

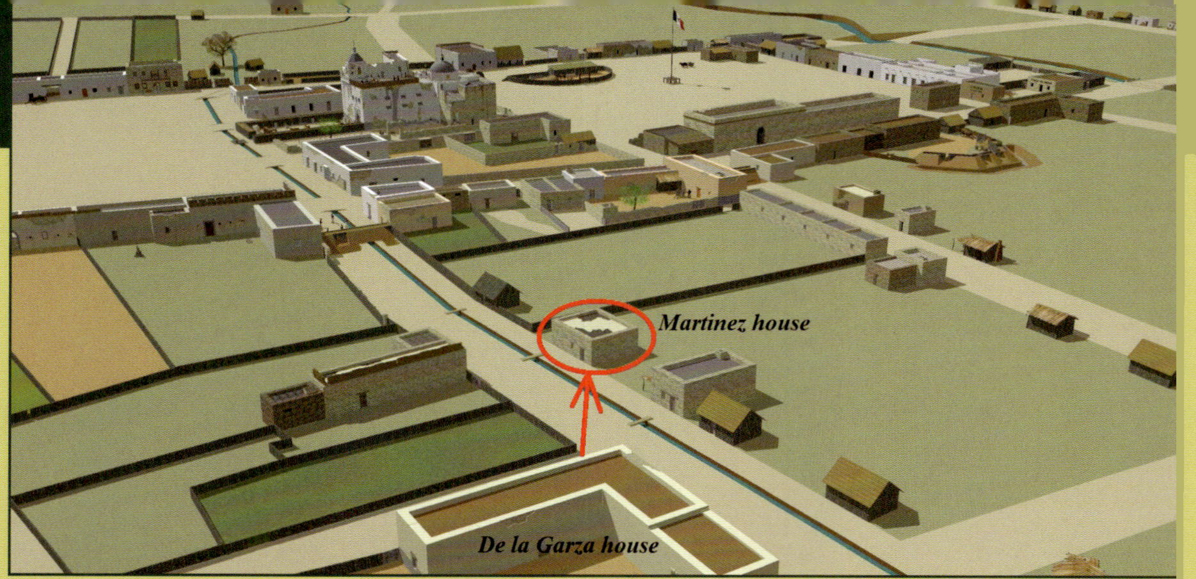

Martinez house
De la Garza house

TOP: Lieutenant McDonald captures a "house to the right and in advance of the first division." This would have been across Acéquia Street and possibly was the Pedro Martinez house, moving Texian forces closer to the plazas as well as giving them easier access to the acéquia for drinking water.

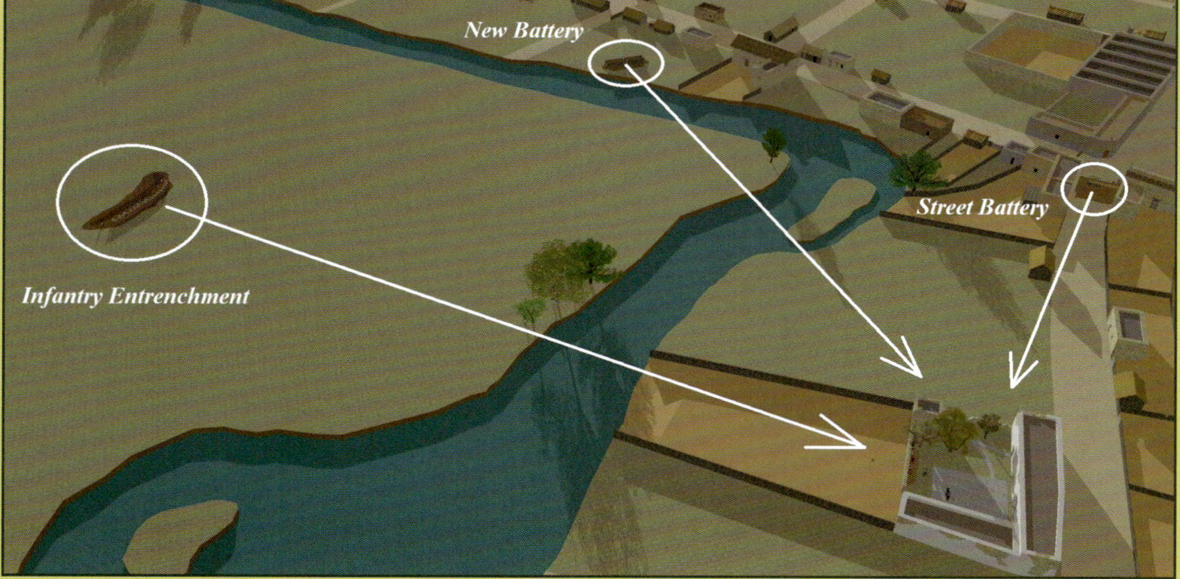

New Battery
Street Battery
Infantry Entrenchment

BOTTOM: The infantry entrenchment and the two cannon batteries pound at the walls of the Veramendi garden.

Mexican infantry entrenchment and Alamo compound over the Veramendi roof.

DECEMBER 7

The Centralists had been busy overnight. Colonel Johnson looked out from the Veramendi house to discover the enemy had strengthened its positions across the San Antonio River. "At daylight," he reported, "it was discovered that the enemy had, during the night previous, opened a trench on the Alamo side of the river, and on the left flank, as well as strengthening their battery on the cross-street leading to the Alamo." This last position, probably on Potrero Street, would bring additional weight against the stone walls of the little Texian fortress. Muskets blazed away from the new earthworks, as did artillery. The Texians responded with long rifles that eventually drove the Centralists under cover and away from their cannon. By noon, the exchange had ended, but clearly the battle was far from over.

With this new threat neutralized for the moment, Johnson focused his men on silencing the snipers atop San Fernando Church. "We watched the twelve-pounder with pure pleasure as it hurled its thunderbolts through the firing slot and with a thundering war whoop launched a roaring attack on the old tower from where the enemy had pestered us considerably," Ehrenberg crowed. "Already by the third shot, fired by a Braunschweiger by the name of [Wilhelm] Langenheim, a part of the cupola collapsed. That was a warning for the enemy to abandon that position or to take the consequences."[1]

It also discouraged onlookers. Béxareños had joined the Centralist sharpshooters in the bell tower to watch the sport of shooting at the Texians. A Texian later learned that some of those civilians came to regret their choices. "The gunner was ordered to direct a 12 lb. shot at the crowd in the steeple," this soldier reported. "He did so and struck the Arch overhead." The debris struck down several of the locals. "A Second Shot was fired and the ball carried away half its bulk in the upper side of the first hole from which time there was no more looking out from that position."

The morning had been deadly, and more bloody work was coming. Having cleared the bell tower, and "in order to spare the venerable old ruin, we halted our firing after that shot and directed all of our cannons on a few buildings that we planned to take very shortly," Ehrenberg wrote. The Centralists, though, had done serious harm to Johnson's command. Losses among the Texian artillery crew had been heavy, with most of the gunners out of action and nursing dangerous wounds. "The tall Braunschweiger, as we called him," Ehrenberg continued, "a handsome six-foot tall man, remained oddly enough unscathed, although he was constantly fully exposed to the musket balls of the bluecoats as he went about loading and firing the cannon."

While Johnson's guns pounded nearby houses, Milam's men in the de la Garza house prepared to make another rush. Henry Wax Karnes, one of the standouts of the Battle of Concepción, studied the Mexican defenses and searched for a way forward. The fortified houses facing on the plaza were 120 yards away, but Mexican soldiers have moved beyond those dwellings and positioned themselves along the back fences, just sixty yards distant. Between the fences and Karnes' position directly in front sat the stone house of Manuel Menchaca, a mere thirty-five yards away and within easy musket range. To Karnes' amazement, Centralist *soldados* now occupied the building and the roof. The enemy was advancing. "Our only hope lay in getting possession of the building, although its flat roof, and those of the building adjoining, swarmed with Mexican soldiers," wrote Taylor.

Karnes decided. "Boys, load your guns and be ready," he told the volunteers. "I am going to break open that door." While the others looked on, stunned, he grabbed a crowbar. "I want you to pour a steady hot fire into those fellows on the roof and hold their attention until I can reach the door," he said, "and when I break it in I want you boys to make a clean dash for that house." When one of the men balked, Karnes grew emphatic. "It's that house or retreat! You men do as I tell you!" Chastened, the soldiers loaded their rifles and prepared for the coming terror.

Karnes bolted across the street. He climbed over the first fence as the Texians fired at the soldiers on the roof and drove the soldados to cover. Clearing a second fence, Karnes made it to the Menchaca house and swung his crowbar, intent on smashing in the door. As ordered, his men surged forward and arrived just as the door gave way. The insurgents burst into the house, screaming wildly as the enemy soldiers piled out the back door. The *soldados* on top abandoned the roof and retreated to the safety of a fence twenty yards beyond the house, where they regained their composure and opened on the Texians. Karnes and the men returned fire out the back door and window, but they soon came to a conclusion: the fence must be burned, and soon.

Back in the De la Garza house, Colonel Milam was elated. Seeing that Karnes' bold move had gone well, and needing to confer with Colonel Johnson, he jumped into the trench and crossed to the Veramendi house, climbing in through the hole in the north end. He passed through the long room to the *zaguan* of the main entrance and stepped out into the back yard. The late-afternoon shadow of the building filled the yard as he walked across to the south wall and into the sunlight to confer with Johnson. What must the next move be? "Milam carried a small field glass," remembered Taylor. "With this glass, and while standing in the . . . yard of the building, Milam was viewing the Mexican stronghold on the plaza."

Hidden in the branches of a tall tree, Centralist sniper Felix de la Garza — the best shot in the Mexican army and a half brother of Colonel Juan Almonte — saw the movement in the Veramendi yard, aimed his Baker rifle, and squeezed the trigger. "At this moment a shot rang out and Milam fell, the ball piercing his head," Taylor continued. The Texians scrambled to find the assailant. "One of those present in the yard called attention to the fact that at the report of the shot he saw a white puff of smoke arising from the branches of a large cypress tree that stood on the margin of the river." Texian rifles turned east toward the river and shredded the branches of the tree with bullets. "The corpse of the daring sharpshooter crashed down through the branches," Taylor wrote, "and rolled into the river."

The men who went "with old Ben Milam into San Antonio" were devastated by the news of their courageous leader's sudden death. Milam had clearly been the spirit behind the attack on Béxar. Johnson announced his death as "an irreparable loss at so critical a moment." Henry Dance feared the Texians army might come unraveled at the news. "The tremendous fire of the Mexicans would have been alarming had it not been for the composed continence of Milam and Johnson and several Brave captains," he wrote. Now one of those stalwarts lay wrapped in a bloody blanket while his men dug a hasty grave in the yard of the Veramendi house.

The battle now fell to Johnson to win. "At a meeting of the officers at 7 o'clock, I was invested with the chief command," he wrote. He advanced Major Robert C. Morris of the New Orleans Greys to be his second. Those men knew instinctively that the fight needed to be concluded boldly, and swiftly, if the Texians were to emerge from the trap into which they had stumbled.

Morris devised a plan. At 10 p.m., he assembled four companies of volunteers: the men of Captains Thomas Llewellyn, George English, John Crane, and William Landrum's commands. They would move toward the southwest and storm the Ángel and José António Navarro house on the northeast corner of the Plaza de Armas. With this accomplished, the Texians would have a lodgment in the center of the Centralists' fortifications, with the ability to sweep both plazas with rifle fire. It would also separate the enemy's Morelos Battalion, quartered in the century-old cuartel on the north side of Plaza de Armas, from Zambrano Row — a line of connected stone houses along the east side of North Flores Street perpendicular to the fortified plaza. This second barracks stretched north from a narrow alley separating it from the Navarro house. If Morris' men could succeed in this bold stroke, the enemy infantry would be split and the Texians fortified with impressive fields of fire.

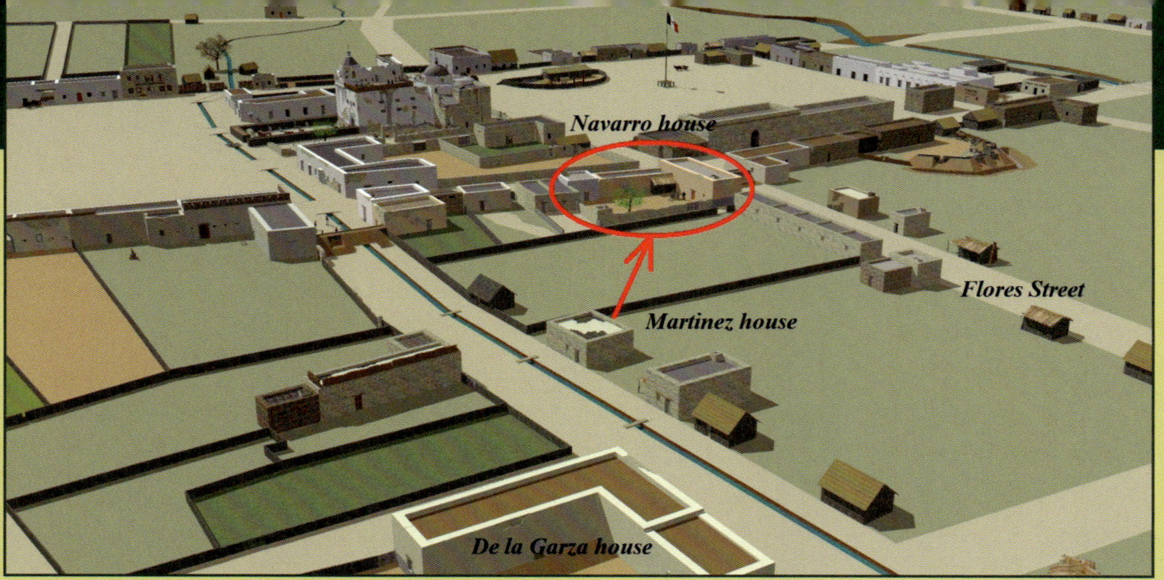

TOP: *Looking southwest over the De la Garza house. Four companies led by Major Robert C. Morris assault the Navarro house.*

BOTTOM: *Looking southwest over the Navarro house into the enemy's fortress.*

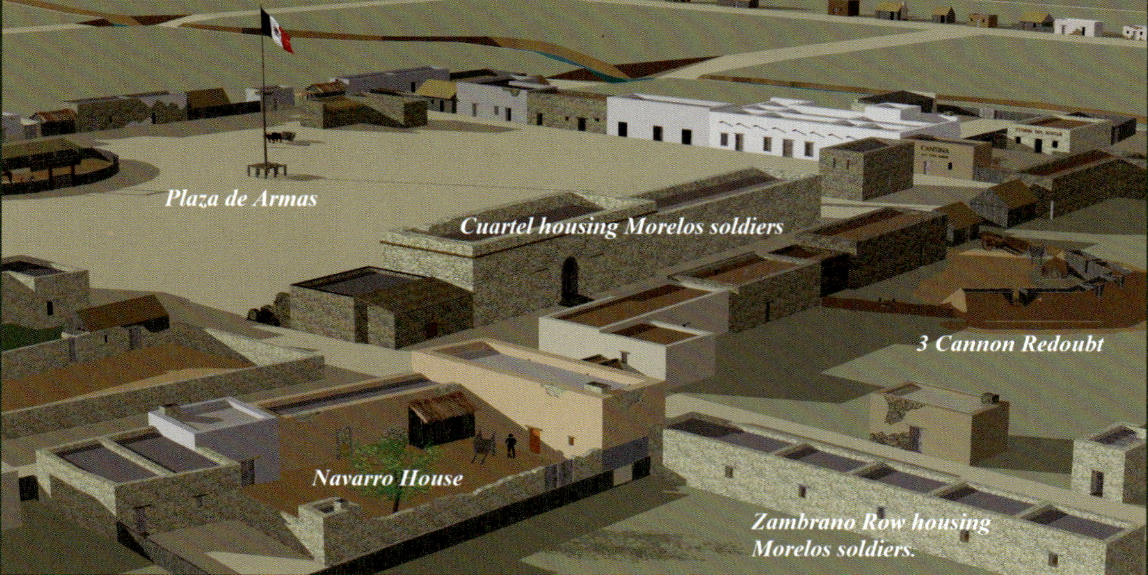

The attack would launch from the recently captured Martinez house. A cold north wind howled through the house as Morris assembled his assault column. Once in position, the volunteers hurried out the back door, clambered over and around several fences, and rushed toward the Navarro house. The Mexican soldiers inside, huddled around a fireplace to keep warm, were taken completely by surprise as the Texians broke in. Most bolted for the exits, but a few slow movers promptly surrendered. This swift coup unhinged the Centralist position in one bold move. Now Morris deployed his men to defend against the inevitable counterattack.

Centralist attempts to undo the damage were lackluster. A few enterprising *soldados* made it to the roof of the Navarro house, chipped open a hole, and fired into the interior. Texian marksmen took up the challenge and outshot their assailants, who quickly quit the game.

Realizing that the Federalist insurgents now had the ability to sweep the Plaza de Armas with rifle fire, most of the Morelos Battalion fell back in the darkness, moving their cannon and equipment to the Plaza de las Islas. Only the three cannon and crews in the redoubt outside the north buildings of the plaza remained behind, as did the *soldados* cut off and trapped in Zambrano Row.

At nearly the same time, Karnes and the men in the newly captured Menchaca house made their move. Fearing the rain that the cold front must surely bring, the Texians hustled to the fence south of their position and set it ablaze, both to deny the enemy cover and to open better fields of fire. The flames spread. "The enemy," reported General Filisola, "succeeded in setting fire to a wooden fence located at the back of one of the houses that they were fighting and which served as a parapet for our men." The fire also consumed the fence behind a house fronting the north side of the Plaza de las Islas, reducing the number of fighting positions even

further. "It was then necessary to abandon those enclosures [the yards] and limit the defense to the walls of the houses themselves by knocking holes through which to push the guns and fire very directly and," Filisola observed, "not very effectively." This act of arson had further compromised the Centralists' position. The entire attack had come at the loss of two Texians slightly wounded.

DECEMBER 8

The morning dawned cold and wet as Morris' men finished the work begun the night before. The Texians inside the Navarro house surged across the alley and broke open the south end of Zambrano Row. Reinforced by a

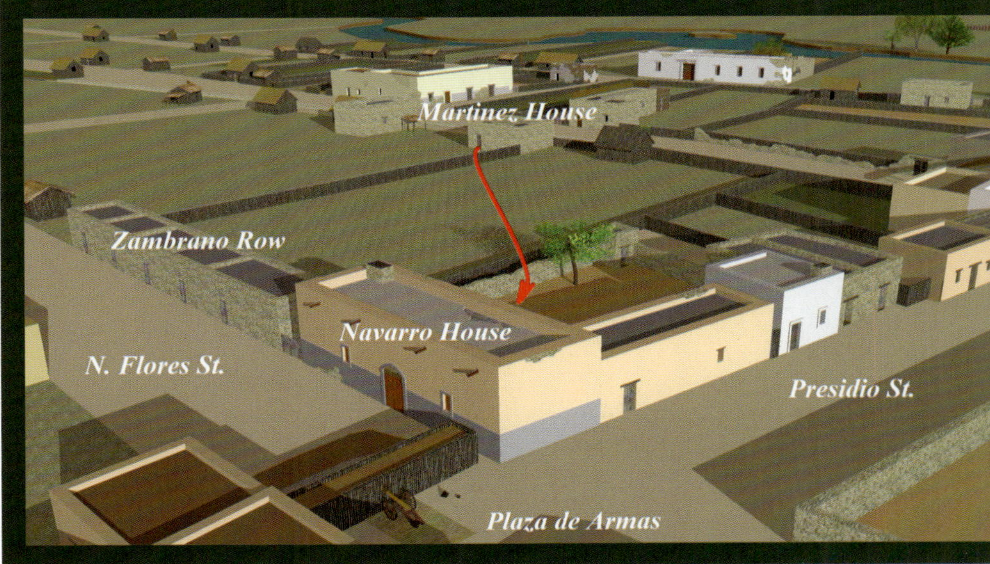

Looking northeast at the Navarro house and Zambrano Row, Major Morris' assault route is marked in red.

TOP: *The Navarro house with Zambrano Row across the alley to the north.*

BOTTOM: *Captain Morris' men from the Navarro house capture Zambrano Row under fire from the three-cannon redoubt, El Fortín de Santa Anna.*

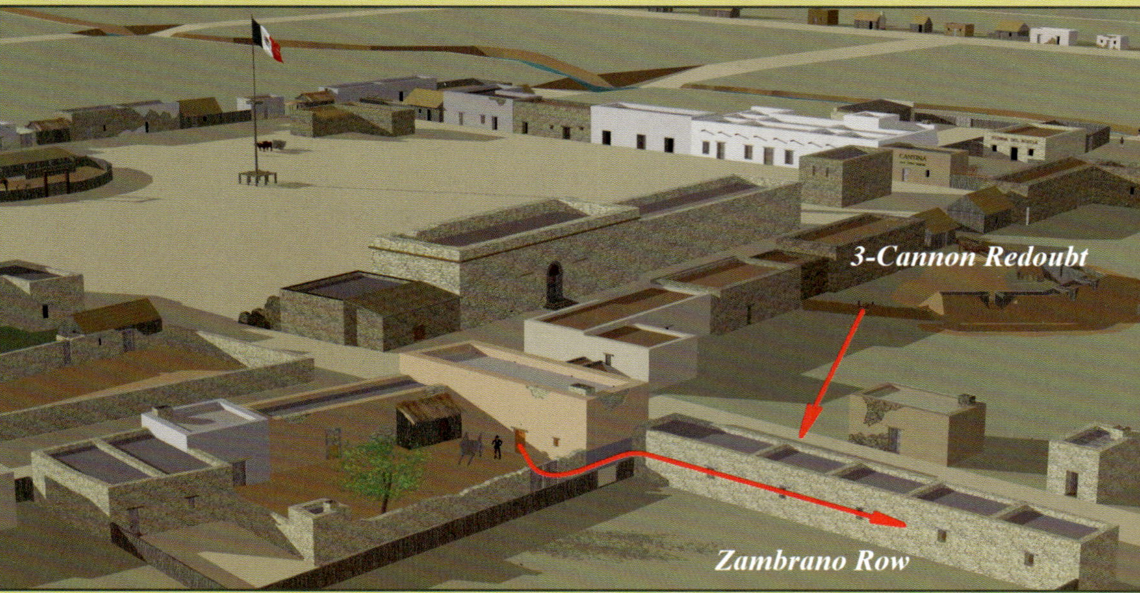

detachment of Greys, the Federalists fired into the southernmost room, driving out the men of the Morelos Battalion. The houses in this row all opened to the west onto Flores Street, and there were no connecting doors between them. The only alternative for Morris' men was to break through the stone or adobe partition walls and conquer each room one by one.

Advancing steadily, the Texians cleared each room in close combat. "They began to make holes in the walls that separated them from our men," reported General Filisola. "The latter were doing the same thing, and there was the example of one and the same wall serving as a shield to combatants on both sides." The Centralist forces concentrated their fire on this close-order battle as they tried to swat away the insurgents. "A heavy fire of artillery and small-arms was opened on this position by the enemy, who disputed every inch of ground," reported Colonel Johnson. Eventually, the Mexican defenders could hold no longer, and the survivors of this close-quarters gun battle quit the building. Meanwhile, another detachment of Texians under Lieutenant John Porter Gill arrived to strengthen the Texian position.

The Mexican gunners in the redoubt sixty yards to the west pounded Zambrano Row, now solely occupied by Federalist forces, but the stout stone walls withstood the hammering. The crewmen of the 4-pounder cannon in the redoubt, Fortín de Santa Anna, meanwhile made good targets. Texian rifles firing from the newly gained vantage point kept the enemy crews pinned. Wounded artillerymen soon littered the redoubt.

But help for the Centralists was on the way, and that same dawn brought what was, at least on the surface, good news for the beleaguered Centralists: the long-awaited reinforcements had finally arrived. Colonel Ugartechea and 173 soldiers, including cavalry and artillery, led the way. Behind them followed 454 newly conscripted men, rounded up and driven in by Lieutenant Colonel José Juan Sánchez-Navarro, adjutant inspector in the Mexican Army. Many of the newcomers were in shackles, having been "recruited" from local jails from Saltillo to Laredo. The Centralist officers could hear the battle raging in town from several miles away and believed that the Texians must certainly have seen their arrival. Perhaps the mere appearance of the relieving force would drive the insurgents away.

Staying off the main roads, Ugartechea had successfully led his command past the Federal scouting companies and even Juan Seguín's hawk-eyed company of Tejanos. "We entered town by the trail to cadet Flores' house and from there to the plaza where we were greeted with rifle fire, acclamations and ringing of bells by 300 valiant souls who had for 55 days been preparing breastworks day and night without regard for distinction of rank," reported Sánchez-Navarro. He realized, however, that his band of reinforcements were not crack troops. "What poor support

The unmistakable signal of "no quarter" hangs from San Fernando Church.

Cos ordered a flag of "no quarter" flown from the Alamo as well.

we offered!" he added. Some of the convict troops had been dragooned as enemies of the state by Santa Anna after his sacking of Zacatecas the previous May.

The celebrations in the plaza bewildered the Texians. Henry Dance feared "it appeared we were to be swept off by a general charge by the Cavalry infantry and lancers playing more music than I ever heard." Ehrenberg was less concerned by the swarm of new *soldados* appearing on the south end of the plazas. "We knew that we had little to fear from them," he wrote, "since most of them were compelled to serve in the army because of murder or robbery convictions or for having participated in the uprising that swept over all of Mexico a short while back against the usurper, Santa Anna. They were chained together in pairs."

Cos was also surprised by their arrival. He believed he had the battle well in hand, and the arrival of the newcomers complicated his calculations. "At the time my few soldiers were fighting . . . inch by inch over the Plaza," he reported. The arrival of reinforcements, especially such as these, "did not help, as we could not utilize them . . . due to the fact they lacked training, were tired from a twenty-three-league march to the city, and they only aggravated matters by increasing the consumption of provisions of which there was an absolute lack." The officers in Béxar assembled the troops to see what they could make of them and assigned then to where they might do the most good — or the least harm.

Sánchez-Navarro rode toward the sound of the guns to learn what he had marched into. "I then found myself alone in the main square without even a mounted aid and there I would have remained if my friend el señor captain Don Andres Videgaray had not given me shelter in his lodging," he recalled, "which is on the plaza facing the church." Having stowed his baggage, the officer went in search of Cos. "I went to greet el senor Comandante General and at 12:00, by his order, I went to familiarize myself with the fortifications we were to defend," Sánchez-Navarro continued. "El capitan Videgaray served as guide." By midafternoon, the colonel had seen enough. "It was impossible to defend such an extended position with so few troops as were in the square and much less with troops in such a poor state as had arrived with me," he reported. "Besides there were no provisions nor hopes that any help might come."

Assuming the Texians had no way of knowing how poor the new *soldados* were, Cos resorted to a ruse. He placed a black flag of "no quarter" on the tower of San Fernando, while another bit the breeze over the Alamo. "Like a chameleon, General Cos had changed his colors again, and today a symbol of irreconcilable hatred . . . was displayed on the tower in the city," Ehrenberg wrote. "Now the black standard of death was hanging limp on the cupola of the tall tower. This wrinkled object was powerless, however, to intimidate the victorious besieging army." Meanwhile, the Mexican Federalist tricolor flag flew over the Texian camp.

Having delivered that message, Cos — reasonably secure for the first time due to his new reinforcements — took the initiative and attacked Burleson's camp at the Old Mill. He watched from the north wall of the Alamo as his Centralist troops boiled out of the Alamo, heading for the Texian rear. A squadron of cavalry cantered up the east bank of the river, splashed across at the upper ford, and approached the Texian camp from the north, while the infantry trotted to a position on the east bank directly across from the camp.

The Texians saw them coming. A gunner sighted a 6-pounder at the approaching enemy and waited for the best shot. Burleson "was prepared to give them a warm reception by opening a brisk fire of grape and canister upon their advance as soon as they approached within good cannon-shot distance," wrote William T. Austin. The mounted Centralists fired at the Texians, reined their horses, and retreated. "They were soon obliged to retire precipitately, by opening a six-pounder upon them," Burleson reported. A company under the command of Captain John M. Bradley crossed the San Antonio River and made sure the enemy was gone. "The enemy being surprised to find an encampment strong and protected by a park of artillery," Austin remarked, "declined making the intended attack, and suddenly drew off and retired within his walls." Cos' show of force had failed.

The Texians, having easily brushed back the threat to their camp and supplies, hunkered down. In Béxar, the embattled men in Zambrano Row continued to hold on, despite the close-ranged pounding by the Mexican 4-pounders in Fortín de Santa Ana. Their captured stone houses stood up well to the fire coming from just sixty yards to the west. That evening,

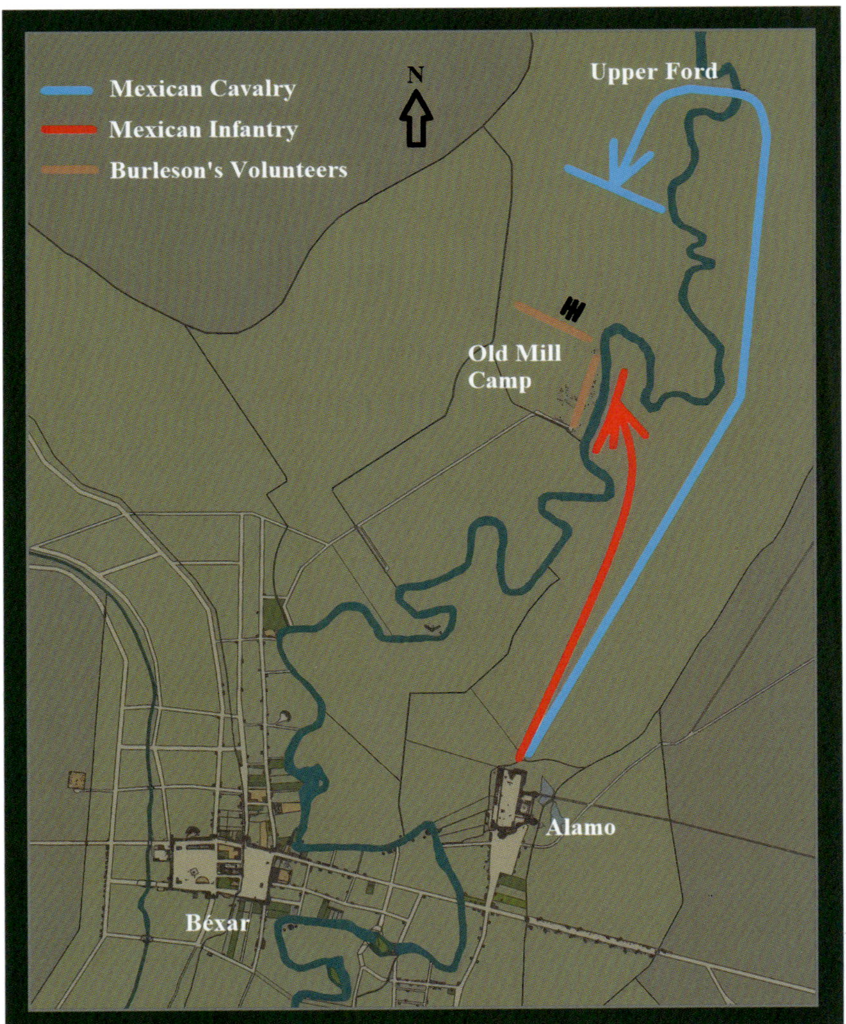

Cos' probable routes to attack Burleson's Old Mill camp.

confident that the position would hold, Johnson sent up four more companies under the command of Captains James G. Swisher, Thomas Alley, Haden Harrison Edwards, and Peter J. Duncan to prepare for the next move. Meanwhile, Burleson dispatched three companies from the Old Mill. These reserves, under Captains James Cheshire, M. B. Lewis, and William Sutherland, filled their places at the other captured houses. Despite the day's action, Johnson had lost only three men—a captain and two privates seriously wounded.

The next day might prove decisive, Johnson realized. So did his men. "Now there was nothing left for us to do but to take out one link in the chain of buildings that lined the big quadrangle, the city square," Ehrenberg wrote. "Doing that would put in our hands the magazines in the church that was situated in the middle of the square — and that would put the whole city in our hands." The move would be risky; the men were weary. Johnson called a council of his officers. They had seen the siege and battle to this point; would they now see it through and push the Centralists out of town?

Johnson turned to his very efficient quartermaster, Captain Cooke, and asked him if his New Orleans Greys could do the job. The officer turned to his men and "asked if there was any person who would go with him," wrote Mag Stiff. "The Grays all with exception of 3 said they would follow him to the devil." Captain William H. Patton and a handful of his Brazoria company volunteered as well. The next morning, these fifty Federalists would rush into the heart of Béxar to determine the outcome of the fight.

16

BREACHING PLAZA DE LAS ISLAS

That night, the rain stopped, the clouds parted, and the silvery light of a full moon bathed the battleground that was Béxar as the Texians made their next move. Captain William G. Cooke led his men into the pale light and toward their objective. The Texian officer scuttled down the trench to the De la Garza house. After gathering his detachment of forty-nine men and finalizing plans, Cooke led them across the alley and through the Menchaca house. From there, the raiders would leave cover, and danger would abound.

His guide, John W. Smith, led the war band toward their objective: the two Yturri houses fronting the Plaza de las Islas. "A tremendous fire was opened on us from every position occupied by the enemy," Cooke remembered. *Soldados* on rooftops and behind loopholes emptied their muskets as the shadowy figures rushed toward them, but without effect. Flashes of fire and clouds of smoke helped mask the Texian advance, and they made the back doors of their target without loss.

Not surprisingly, the Centralist *soldados* inside had barricaded and fortified the side of the houses facing the Texians. Remarkably, the guide had not anticipated this possibility, and the Texans began milling alongside its walls, trying to sort out their next move. Mag Stiff, watching panic set in, heard Captain Cooke yell, "Follow me boys!" The volunteers promptly obeyed. Cooke led his men sideways along this back wall of the Yturri house, his men ducking beneath the firing weapons of the *soldados* as they passed the muzzles of their muskets through the loopholes. "So near did they pass under the guns of the wall enclosing the yard of the house, and which had been pierced for musketry, that many of the men had their whiskers and hair burnt by the blaze of the guns," Colonel Johnson reported. The light artillery pieces in El Fortín de Santa Anna added their weight to the firefight.

Enveloped in noise, fire, and smoke, Cooke and his men made a thirty-five-yard sidestep north to the back of the home of Father Refugio de la Garza. "On arriving at the Priest's house we found the doorway barricaded up to the arch which was higher than our heads and left a space hardly sufficient to admit one man at a time," explained Cooke. "We climbed up, one at a time and fired off a few guns as we dropped down on the inside." The confusion of the attack and the sudden appearance of Texians spilling into the house drove the few Centralist defenders out the front door and into the plaza.

General Filisola later explained how the insurgents had carried the house so easily, attributing it to luck on the Texians' part and fatigue on his men's part. "This was because with the long vigils and the weariness that the officer and the troops had suffered from, drowsiness had overcome them, and they were sound asleep," he wrote. One of the *soldados* joined the insurgents, which had added to the chaos. "Fortunately, the officer as well as the four soldiers that were with him were able to save themselves and give the alarm to the other stations, getting them into action against the rebels."

Cooke and his raiders burst out onto the Plaza de las Islas to maintain their momentum. "We rushed upon the Square," he recalled, "where

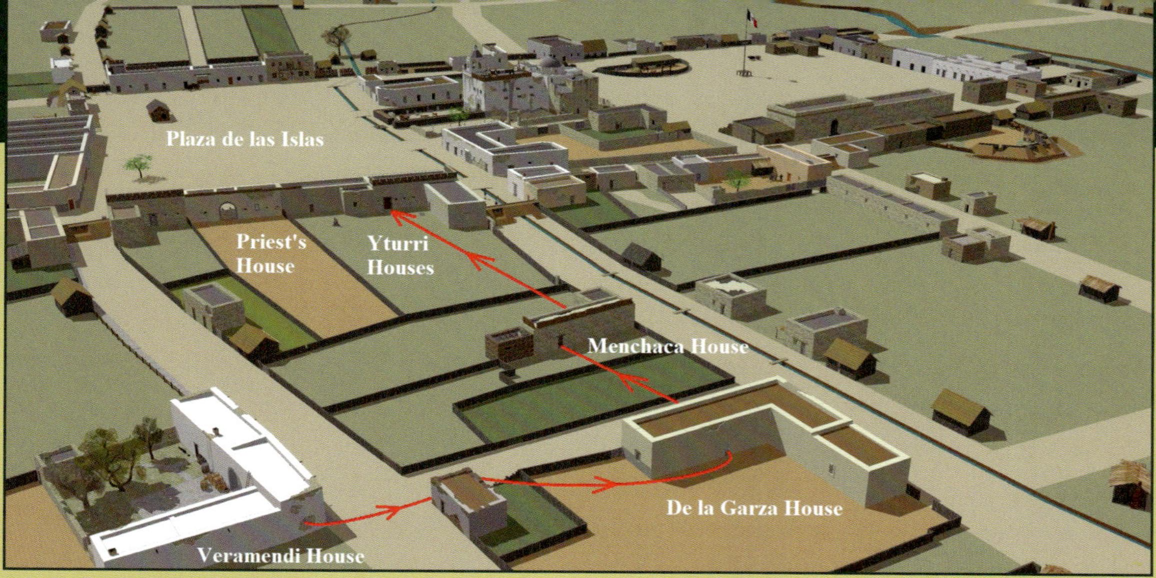

TOP: *Captain Cooke's route from the Veramendi house to the Yturri houses.*

BOTTOM: *The Priest's house and Yturri houses have direct access to the Plaza de las Islas.*

[there was a] large number of Soldiers collecting, but evidently in great confusion." In the moonlight, the attackers also spied a light cannon sitting conveniently outside the door, unattended. The piece had arrived with the Mexican relief column the day before and had yet to see action. Cooke ordered his men to seize the weapon. "This we took possession of and attempted to pull in the house, but by that time the fire from the enemy became so severe, we were compelled to retire to the house." A Centralist officer in the Morelos Battalion, Lieutenant Colonel Antonio Dionisio, rallied a squad of his men and charged the insurgents with fixed bayonets. The Texians fled back into the priest's house. John Belden of the New Orleans Greys spiked the cannon by driving a ramrod into the touchhole and then turned to gain cover as well. But as he entered the dwelling, a Mexican bullet blew through his eye socket and carried away part of his nose.

The Centralists now had Cooke and his men boxed in. The insurgents desperately fortified the building as best they could, filling the windows and door facing the plaza with logs, stones, or furniture. Across the plaza in the Erasmo Seguín house, Lieutenant Colonel José Juan Sánchez-Navarro was roused from a sound sleep by his aide, Captain Don Andres Videgaray. "You see, for two days I had not dismounted my horse. I slept so soundly that nearby cannon and rifle fire did not wake me," the officer explained. Once alert, he listened as his assistant breathlessly reported a disaster on the plaza. "We are lost," the captain told him. "I am going to take care of the official records because the enemy has taken the plaza."

Stunned, Sánchez-Navarro sprang into action. "I seized my sword, opened a window facing the plaza, and jumped out to join what appeared to be a patrol firing furiously as it withdrew," he reported. "I ordered them to halt and thereupon some other troops joined us. Having availed myself of rifle and cartridges, I began firing." Colonel Nicolás Condelle, commanding the Morelos Battalion, had stabilized the situation and made a report. The insurgents, he explained, were trapped. Sánchez-Navarro watched as Dionisio, sword in hand, steadied his troops as they poured volleys of bullets into the priest's house. "I will never forget the bravery of don Antonio," Sánchez-Navarro wrote. "This young man was gravely injured some days ago by a gunshot wound in the right shoulder and in that condition, he arose and remained at the front in danger all that sad night."

Condelle ordered his men to settle in for what would clearly be a bitter fight. Dionisio retrieved the abandoned cannon and fell back to the cover of the earthworks surrounding San Fernando Church. There Sánchez-Navarro ordered the men of the Morelos Battalion to serve this piece and a howitzer that also had arrived with the Centralist reinforcements and pound the enemy position. The troops "did this, so well," acknowledged General Filisola, "that the rebels did not ever dare to undertake a sally."

Sánchez-Navarro tried to get his inexperienced gunners to finish off the insurgents, but the eager infantrymen lacked the training to make well-placed shots. "The two field pieces did not have a full complement of men nor did I see at my side any to help me sustain them," the officer lamented. "I was in a tight spot and must become an artilleryman, corporal of cannon and commander of 2 field pieces."

Cooke's command, trapped like animals, grew desperate. Father De la Garza, trapped inside with his son and three daughters, was furious about the intrusion. When his son bolted for a window to make his escape, a soldier in the New Orleans Greys shot him. The enraged clergyman screamed at the insurgents that Mexican reinforcements had recently arrived "and that he had no doubt but we would be all killed," remembered Stiff.

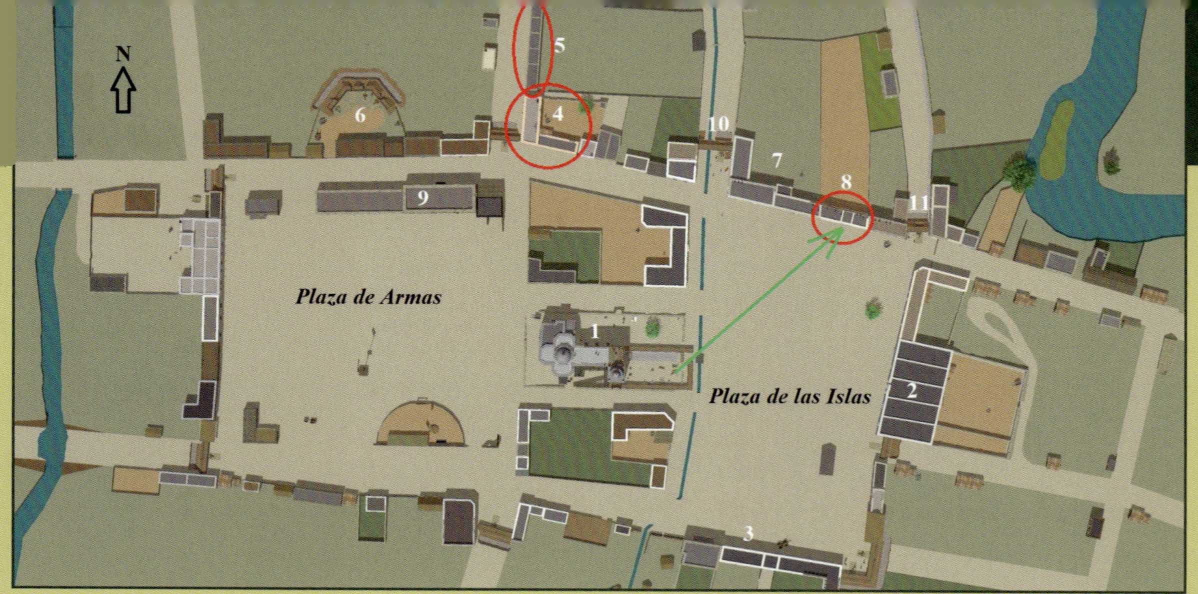

The Béxar plazas. (1) San Fernando Church, (2) Casas Reales (Cos' H.Q.), (3) House owned by Erasmo Seguín where Sánchez-Navarro slept, (4) Navarro house, (5) Zambrano Row, (6) three-cannon redoubt, (7) Yturri houses, (8) Priest's house, (9) Old Spanish Quartel, (10) Acéquia Street battery and barricade, and (11) Soledad Street battery and barricade. Red circles indicate buildings captured and occupied by Federalist troops. The green arrow shows the angle of cannon and howitzer fire at the Priest's house 100 yards away.

If the Centralists were to slay Cooke and his men, they would have to dig them out of their burrow. "We barricaded the doors, windows passages," Cooke wrote, "as well we could — which we accomplished, but very imperfectly, using our blankets, shirts, the library of the priest &c for that purpose." His soldiers began digging up the dirt floor to help barricade the doors and windows. "We also took the beds and trunks that were in the house to aid," Stiff wrote, "but as fast as we would put them up against the doors and windows they were shot out by the cannon of the enemy."

Cooke feared he had led his men into a slaughter pen. Solid shot blasted through door and windows, and it would only be a matter of time before the casualties would begin to pile up. "He then turned to the Company and asked them any which they would choose, retreat, Surrender, or die," remembered Stiff. "They all answered they would die or do."

Cooke and his little band settled in to endure the bombardment, hoping for some opportunity. If they could make it through until daylight, perhaps they could get control of the plaza out front with well-aimed rifle fire through windows and loopholes. With luck, perhaps they could even sally out and capture the Mexican cannon. Until then, they would have to endure. "The enemy continued their firing during the night without cessation which we answered from loopholes whenever opportunity presented to pick off a man," Cooke reported.

Behind the works at San Fernando Church, Sánchez-Navarro grew frustrated with his makeshift command. "In order to sustain the

BATTLEGROUND BÉXAR

position," he wrote, "they provided me with 10 men from Morelos and 80 replacements from those I had led here but as the aforesaid did not know even how to load [they were all conscripts] they did nothing more than add to the confusion." Sánchez-Navarro sent a dispatch to Condelle, who replaced the poorly trained troops with men from the presidial companies of Rio Grande, Agua Verde, and others. Where, these officers wondered, was General Cos, and why had he not taken charge of the situation?

He was at the Alamo.

The commander of the Centralist forces at Béxar knew he was facing a fragile situation. His gambit of taking the insurgent camp at the Old Mill had failed spectacularly. Fearing that his own forces were failing and that the Texians remained full of fight, he decided to contract his position and turn the former mission into a citadel. The Federalists, he believed, would find themselves incapable of storming the Alamo in the face of nearly 600 muskets and an array of cannon. Cos needed time, however, and Cooke's surprise attack had upset the schedule. "What had happened in the Béxar plaza then was very bad news for him when he was made aware of it," conceded General Filisola. "He foresaw the many difficulties that presented themselves in maintaining the town once the principal houses were occupied by the enemy, and no less for defending the Alamo at the same time and being able to procure the means of subsistence for the men and horses that were guarding both points." Cos did the best with what he had, but the arrival of Colonel Ugartechea and his unsupplied, unenthusiastic, and unrested reinforcements meant he did not have the food at hand to withstand a siege of the Alamo. The enemy, though, seemed well provisioned.

Cos and his officers faced hard choices. "The general's situation was indeed difficult and dangerous," continued Filisola. "This can be imagined if one considers that although, as reinforcements for him, there had arrived forty-seven infantrymen from Morelos, fourteen artillerymen, one hundred fifty cavalrymen from the presidio and four hundred replacements to take care of, there were in all six hundred consumers more for whom there were no supplies of any kind, and those that could be provided had to be brought from Laredo or Río Grande, that is at least sixty leagues distance from there." Up until their arrival, the Béxar garrison had been in high spirits and eager to hold on until help arrived. When they saw what kind of assistance they had received, the troops despaired — and they openly voiced their concerns. "They did not fail to manage to make known their dissatisfaction as soon as they realized that instead of supplies they had brought them men to take care of," Filisola wrote, "that would help to consume what there already was in the place."

The news from town troubled the Mexican general. At first light, the enemy would surely sweep the Plaza de las Islas with well-aimed rifle fire. Cos realized that he had lost the town. He ordered Condelle to pull out of the plazas and fall back to the Alamo.

The orders were simple. The sick and the wounded as well as arms, ammunition, and other gear should be withdrawn first, while the men of the Morelos Battalion covered the retreat. Once Condelle had collapsed his lines and fallen back, Cos would distribute his forces along the battered walls of the Alamo. "The best course to take in such circumstances seemed to be to put all the forces together in the Alamo and have part of the cavalry dismount so that they might aid the infantry in service to the garrison to support it," Filisola noted. "Also they should have the rest of the cavalry go out on the best horses to operate against the flanks and the rear of the enemy and to bring in supplies." The Centralists would make a last, hungry, and desperate stand at the Alamo.

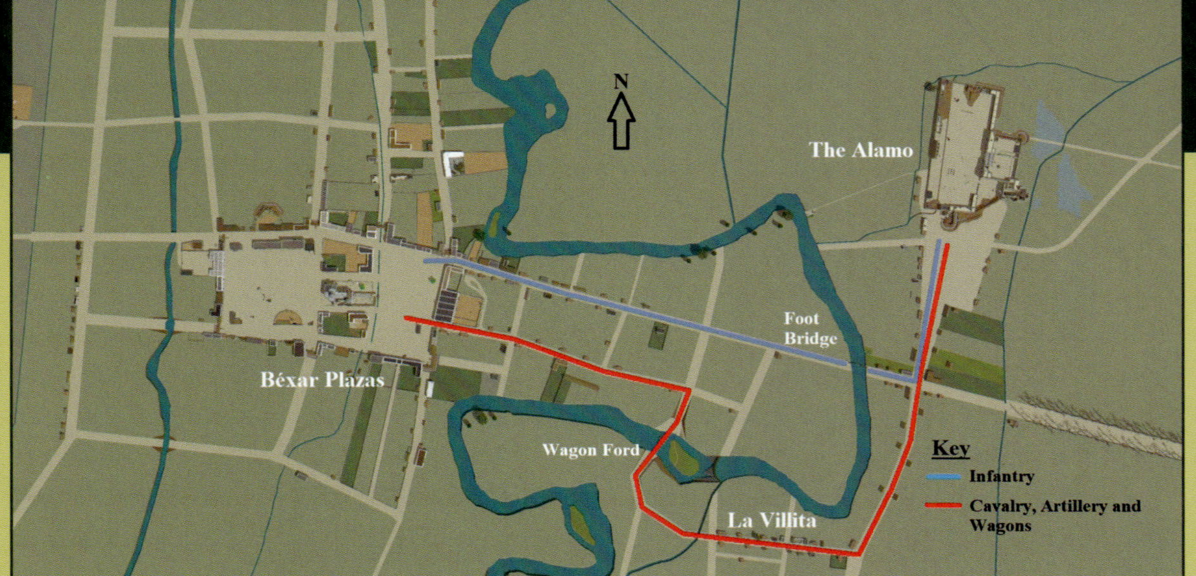

*The Centralist army's withdrawal
from the town plazas to the Alamo.*

Sánchez-Navarro received his orders. "The cavalry was ordered to saddle up and I was left with only the captain of the 1st Volunteer Company of Tamaulipas, don Manuel Lafuente, with something like 70 men of that company," he wrote. "Don Manuel acted with valor and confidence." The sounds of the retreating army dragging their cannon behind them filled the air. The infantry crossed the river by means of the footbridge at the end of Potrero Street; the cavalry dragged wagons and artillery across the low-water ford on the south side of the Potrero area, and then up the bank, through the small barrio of La Villita, and finally north on Mission Road to the Alamo gate. Sánchez-Navarro watched them go while he and his handful of *soldados* kept watch on the enemy from the earthworks of the San Fernando cemetery. He now had fewer than fifty men and a field piece

with very few rounds of ammunition left. The retreat "unsettled my men who were only pacified by my persuasions," he wrote, "and I think more with the constant presence of Condelle who repeatedly came to order me to defend the position at all costs. A thing which I was determined to do."

In the hours after midnight, the men of Captain Cooke's command trapped inside Father de la Garza's house noticed the lull in the Mexican fire. The bolder of their marksmen aimed through loopholes and barricades and harassed the enemy in the bright moonlight. *Soldados* moving across the plaza as well as Sánchez-Navarro's artillery crews in the San Fernando cemetery began to take hits. The Centralist cannon, under a steady whiz and snick of incoming bullets, fell silent. It mattered little: most of the ammunition had been shot away.

The threat from the Texian rifles was annoying, but the Centralists remained firm — until a runner brought crushing news. "At 4:00 A.M. precisely, rumor was heard that came near destroying us since it reported that El señor Comandante General [Cos] is dead and 4 captains have fled with their companies," reported Sánchez-Navarro. "Unfortunately, far from diminishing, such reports grew detailing that those that had fled." The story emerged that the forces that had failed in their attack on the Federalist camp the previous day had mutinied. Some 400 soldados and officers, the rumor told, had simply vanished after killing the commanding general of the Béxar forces.

There was other distressing gossip. The Texians had the troops on the plazas surrounded and were waiting for first light to finish them off, "all of which could well be believed for all the firing we heard in all directions from the point we occupied," wrote Sánchez-Navarro. The enemy rifles had fallen silent, as though preparing for a final push. The Mexican officer directed his men to continue their work against the insurgent positions ninety yards away, as much to disrupt their planning as to make them think twice about rushing their position. The anxious men believed they might have to make good on their promise to hold at all costs. "Don Condelle repeatedly said that we might have to die there," Sánchez-Navarro remembered, "but in no case were we to surrender the post."

The rising sun would determine the outcome. "We discovered that, now lacking the advantage of darkness, the enemy rifle fire was highly effective," noted Sánchez-Navarro. "In these circumstances upon firing the howitzer it jumped its mountings and I was making adjustments when [Lieutenant] Francisco Rada approached and said to me: 'El senor Comandante General commands you to stop what you are doing and come to him.' " Sánchez-Navarro refused the order. "I will not leave this place for el Comandante General is dead and I serve el Coronel Condelle, who commands this plaza," he replied. The messenger left and then returned with Colonel Condelle, who ordered Sánchez-Navarro to stand down and head to the Alamo — because Cos was in fact very much alive. Meanwhile, the colonel would maintain the positions around San Fernando Church.

Sánchez-Navarro's journey did little to give him hope, however. On the way to the Alamo, he learned the situation the army faced. His guide "told me that some soldiers had tried to kill the General and that it was true that the aforementioned officers had fled carrying with them lots of soldiers and that confusion and discouragement was general," he recalled. When he arrived at the post — his first visit to the Alamo — what he saw destroyed his confidence. "I saw about 50 horses that were eating the capes of the troops and even the trails [carriages] of the artillery," he wrote. "I also saw girls and women who had taken refuge there leaving their houses abandoned and open in Bexar; a few officials and squads of troops among whom I heard such things as 'We are lost' and 'What shall we do?' " Not only were there few supplies to be had, but the post had no reliable water. The compound itself was a morass, as men and animals had churned the soggy soil into a mire.

When Sánchez-Navarro reported to Cos, he saw the look of a man defeated. "Two companies of the Presidiales de Rio Grande with their officers, plus those at Agua Verde and some pikemen, with their captain, had deserted me," the general explained. "This occurrence had demoralized the other soldiers so much that almost all of them followed the example." Only 120 men of the battered Morelos Battalion and some dragoons remained. "Sánchez, by reason of cowardice and perfidy of many of our companions, all is lost," Cos continued. "How is the plaza? Has the enemy occupied it?" Sánchez-Navarro boasted that his seventy

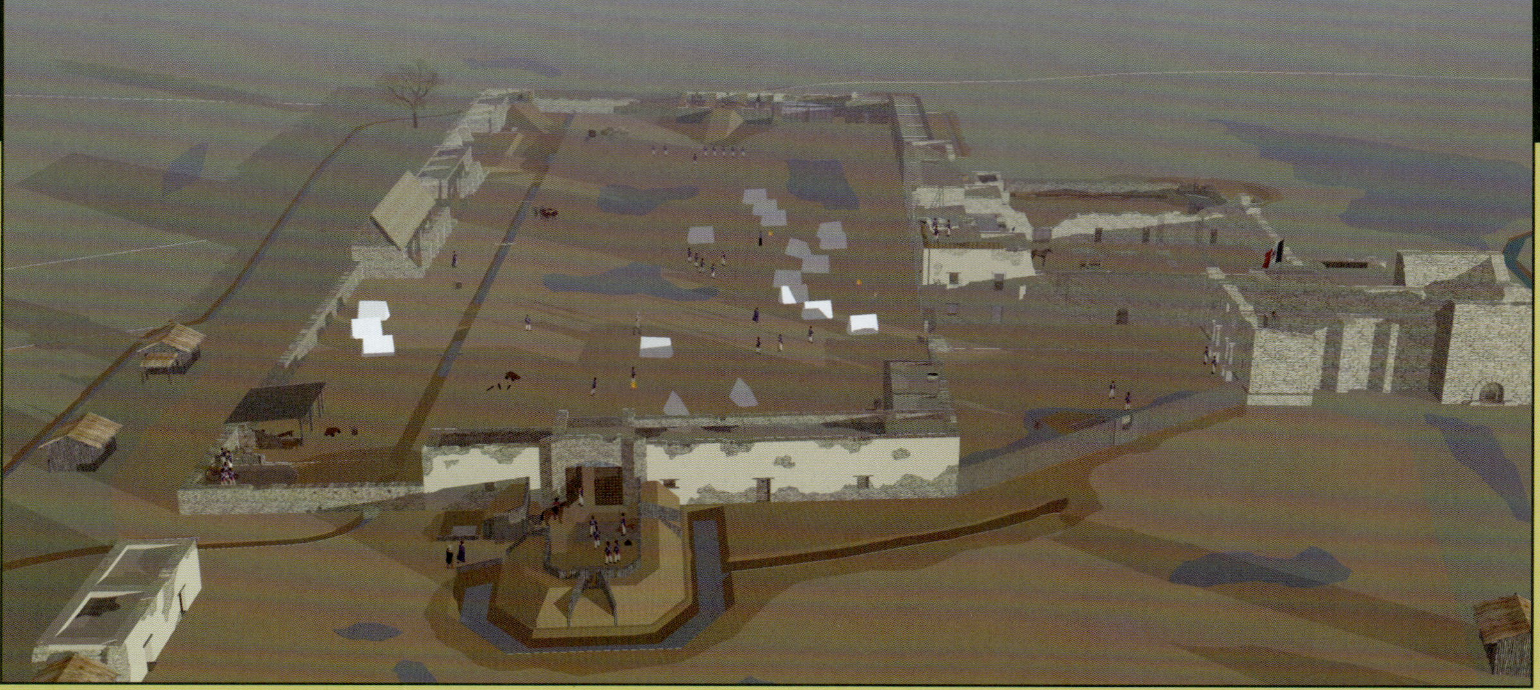

The Alamo compound at daybreak of December 9.

men remained true and would sell their lives dearly under Condelle's leadership. "Go save those brave men," Cos told Sánchez-Navarro. "I authorize you to approach the enemy and obtain the best terms possible."

The Centralists would surrender. "Save the dignity of our government, the honor of its arms," Cos directed, "and honor, life and property of chiefs, officials and troops that still remain with me even though I myself perish." Understanding the delicate nature of his mission, Sánchez-Navarro asked for some written authorization — some credentials — that would convince the Texians that he did, in fact, speak for the Centralist command. "The duty and authorization I give you suffices," shot back Cos — small reassurance for a man about to go face to face with the rebellious insurgents. The *jefe politico* of Béxar, Ramon Músquiz, and Lieutentant Rada would accompany him, along with a bugler.

The lieutenant colonel and his delegation headed back into town, the sound of gunfire still coming from the Plaza de las Islas. They crossed the Potrero Street footbridge and heard bugles and a crescendo of gunfire roll toward them. Fearing the final assault was taking place, the three men ran toward the fray. "I alerted my companions and we ran to arrive before the flag of Morelos, her brave chiefs and officials and the handful of valiant troops should perish," he wrote. The surrender delegates were relieved to discover that their comrades were in fact withdrawing, in good order, and were conducting a well-disciplined retreat.

The Mexican officers met, and tempers flared. "Sir, el Commandante General did not order you to abandon the plaza, only cease fire," Sánchez-Navarro protested. Condelle shot back: "Do you want the enemy to shoot us without it gaining any advantage? And where are you going?" Sánchez-Navarro then explained his mission. "You will not go," Condelle demanded, "for the Morelos Battalion has never surrendered." The other officers in the detachment threatened the surrender delegation; one officer, Lieutenant Juan Tello, pointed a musket at Sánchez-Navarro. "Gentlemen I am under command," Sánchez-Navarro explained. Then he wheeled toward Condelle. "As is known to you," Sánchez Navarro declared, "that against my will and only because you insisted, I left part of this troop and the two cannon that were trusted to me and now I am insulted?" The lieutenant colonel ended with a challenge. "If those who esteem themselves brave truly are, why are they abandoning the plaza? Let us return there and they will see if I am not the first to enter."

Condelle backed down. He called his troops to order and directed his officers to continue the withdrawal toward the Alamo. "Go, the responsibility will be . . ." he said, his voice trailing off as he and his men headed east.

The three-man peace delegation watched the *soldados* leave and then turned to face their fate. Passing up Calabozo Street, they entered the deserted Plaza de las Islas. Their bugler blew the parley call. "In an instant

the windows and loopholes in our quarters bristled with rifles each one trained on the party," Creed Taylor wrote. "We were frontiersmen who knew how to fight, but we knew little of military etiquette and ceremony. In other words, we did not understand the signal, and if someone had given the order to fire, the treaty negotiations might have been postponed for the time being, at least."

The surrender delegation understood their danger. "In place of a bugle we used a white flag, fearing at each step to be shot because we saw rifles in all directions," Sánchez-Navarro recalled. The change in approach worked. A few dozen Texians emerged from their wrecked positions and demanded to know what the four men wanted. Upon learning that Cos

Surrender flag over the Alamo.

wanted to surrender, the Texians hustled Sánchez-Navarro to meet with Colonel Johnson.

The Centralist representatives found themselves mobbed by the insurgent forces. "Soon we were surrounded by a group of colonists, among whom the best known was a certain Smith, a neighbor to Bexar and who asked us a thousand questions in some language which, because we did not understand, we could not answer," Sánchez-Navarro wrote, "and there followed undue demonstrations of anger." Father De la Garza intervened. "This worthy cleric has suffered a lot," Sánchez-Navarro continued, "and the only thing he has left is the house which I almost leveled last night. He remained with us at all times."

Using the priest as a translator, the negotiations continued. "I stated definitely that I was commissioned to speak solely with the commander of the besieging forces," Sánchez-Navarro explained. The Texians responded that Burleson would be along in a few hours. Meanwhile, "we were surrounded with crude bumpkins, proud and overbearing," the Centralist officer continued. "Whoever knows the character of North Americans may appreciate the position in which we found ourselves."

Eventually, Burleson arrived, and he and Col. Francis W. Johnson, Major Robert C. Morris, and James Swisher conducted negotiations. "I told him I proposed a cease fire so that women, children and wounded may not perish," Sánchez-Navarro explained. Fearing a ruse, the Texians demanded to know by what authority this request was made. "I said I did not have any and that our words and persons were in his power," the Centralist continued. The insurgent officers talked among themselves and then returned with their response. "You have only the right to be treated as prisoners of war. Three times we have sent spokesmen to your general, with a white flag, and you received them with cannon shots and yesterday you flew a black flag," they fumed "and now you come without any credentials and without evidence that you come by order of your general." Feeling squeezed, Sánchez-Navarro offered to send Lieutenant Rada back to the Alamo to procure the credentials he needed to complete the parley. "They agreed," he noted, "leaving el senor Músquiz and I as prisoners surrounded by armed and hostile men. The time passed slowly for us in such a position."

For the Federalist insurgents who had been fighting for days, the sudden change in the atmosphere seemed bewildering. "The white flag of submission was flying from the ruins of the Alamo," observed Ehrenberg. "The black one that had proclaimed death to us all was gone now from the tall church tower." Henry Dance was stunned. "Their war flag was gone and one in its place we took to be a white one." Other volunteers believed the silence that had fallen over the battlefield indicated a Federalist disaster, and a decisive Centralist victory, and made plans to abandon their hard-won positions and slip out of town. How could they be sure?

The surrender flag appearing over the Alamo convinced Burleson and his officers that Sánchez-Navarro and Músquiz were in earnest. "We were told that there was a parley flag flying from el Alamo and we were then treated with more consideration," Sánchez-Navarro wrote. "A little later Rada returned bringing an official letter." Burleson and his negotiators withdrew to another room to deliberate. They returned a short while later with a letter, in Spanish, agreeing that hostilities should end.

17

THE SURRENDER

The Centralists and the Federalist insurgents met. The council house — one of five old Spanish town government buildings called the Casas Reales (Royal Houses) and, until recently, Cos's headquarters — would serve for the surrender arbitration. Miguel Arciniega and John Cameron served as interpreters. General Cos designated adjutant José Juan Sánchez-Navarro, Lieutenant Francisco de Rada, and Don Ramon Músquiz, the Jefe Politico of Béxar, to act on his behalf. Colonel Burleson trusted Colonel F. W. Johnston, Major R. C. Morris, and Captain J. G. Swisher to represent his interests.

While these men hammered out a capitulation agreement, the Texians who had fought and bled over the last few days emerged from their battle-scarred houses and wandered the battlefield. Béxareños and many of the Centralist *soldados* did as well. "Our army quartered in the Square and were permitted to go where they pleased without their guns," noted Henry Dance. "We were soon amidst the multitude — this was very consoling to me as I had been confined to a gun better than 2 months."

Béxar had suffered. Dance was astonished, writing that "everything looked miserable — ornamental torn down — heaps of dirt and Stone — ashes from the burning of some wood breastworks and wood and grass covered houses burnt — holes through the wall with dead animals lying about — cannon balls & shot of every description thick on the ground with the plastering shot off the outside of the walls of the houses we were in — the Sides of houses winders doors and fences bore almost innumerable marks from the enemy's guns."

After wandering the streets fearlessly, the battle-weary soldiers experienced a catharsis. "We now belived all danger was over and commenced Rambling about hunting Something for ourselves and horses to eat," Dance wrote. "We found plenty honey some beef and corn and turtiers [tortillas] a bread made of boild corn ground on a stone by the weman — we also found some cordials & wine all of which was eagerly sized by our devouring apatites." Fed, tipsy, and content, "we then slept sound the Balance of the night," he continued.

In the council house, the negotiations continued to lurch along. "At the outset, the demands of the Mexican commissioners were exorbitant," noted Creed Taylor. "They wanted to be permitted to march out with flying colors." In fact, the Centralists demanded that the Federalist rebels fire a salute of honor as the enemy withdrew. Cos wanted to carry away all of his artillery, small arms, ammunition, and supplies as well, and he demanded that the insurgents give them rations for their journey to the Rio Grande. Once in Laredo, Cos declared, his men would be no longer bound by the terms of the surrender. "These and many other unreasonable demands were presented and as promptly rejected," Taylor continued.

Colonel Johnson railed at what he considered Centralist arrogance. "We are in position to dictate terms," he roared. "You are the real supplicants." If Cos refused to be reasonable, the fighting would spin up anew. "Powder is as cheap as provisions, and we have the powder," Johnson explained. "We know the conditions in your army. We are willing to deal justly with you. But we intend to see that our victory shall not be wholly barren."

The Casas Reales, directly across Plaza de las Islas from San Fernando Church, during the capitulation proceedings.

BATTLEGROUND BÉXAR

Capitulation Entered Into By General Martin Perfecto De Cos, Of The Permanent Troops, And General Edward Burleson, Of The Colonial Troops Of Texas.

Being desirous of preventing the further effusion of blood and the ravages of civil war, have agreed on the following stipulations:

1st. That General Cos and his officers retire with their arms and private property into the interior of the republic under parole of honor; and that they will not in any way oppose the reestablishment of the federal constitution of 1824.

2d. That the one hundred infantry lately arrived with the convicts, the remnant of the battalion of Morelos, and the cavalry, retire with the General, taking their arms, and ten rounds of cartridges for their muskets.

3d. That the General take the convicts brought by Colonel Ugartechea beyond the Rio Grande.

4th. That it is discretionary with the troops to follow their General, remain, or go to such point as they may deem proper; but in case they should all or any of them separate, they are to have their arms, etc.

5th. That all the public property, money, arms, and munitions of war, be inventoried and delivered to General Burleson.

6th. That all private property be restored to its proper owners.

7th. That three officers of each army be appointed to make out the inventory and see that the terms of capitulation be carried into effect.

8th. That three officers on the part of General Cos remain for the purpose of delivering over the said property, stores, etc.

9th. That General Cos with his force, for the present, occupy the Alamo, and General Burleson with his force occupy the town of Bexar, and that the soldiers of neither party pass to the other, armed.

10th. General Cos shall, within six days from the date hereof, remove his force from the garrison he now occupies.

11th. In addition to the arms before mentioned, General Cos shall be permitted to take with his force a 4-pounder and ten rounds of powder and ball.

12th. The officers appointed to make the inventory and delivery of the stores, etc., shall enter upon the duties to which they have been appointed forthwith.

13th. The citizens shall be protected in their persons and property.

14th. General Burleson will furnish General Cos with such provisions as can be obtained, necessary for his troops to the Rio Grande, at the ordinary price of the country.

15th. The sick and wounded of General Cos's army, together with a surgeon and attendants, are permitted to remain.

16th. No person, either citizen or soldier, to be molested on account of his political opinions hitherto expressed.

17th. That duplicates of this capitulation be made out in Castilian and English, and signed by the commissioners appointed, and ratified by the commanders of both armies.

18th. The prisoners of both armies, up to this day, shall be put at liberty.

continued on page 150 ▶

▶ continued from page 75

The commissioners, José Juan Sánchez, Adjutant-Inspector; Don Ramon Músquiz, and Lieutenant J. Francisco de Rada, and Interpreter Don Miguel Arciniega, appointed by the Commandant and Inspector, General Martin Perfecto de Cos, in connection with Colonel F. W. Johnston, Major R. C. Morris, and Captain J G. Swisher, and Interpreter John Cameron, appointed on the part of General Edward Burleson, after a long and serious discussion, adopted the eighteen preceding articles, reserving their ratification by the Generals of both armies.

In virtue of which, we have signed this instrument, in the city of Bexar, on the 11th of December, 1835.

José Juan Sánchez, F. W. Johnson, Ramon Músquiz, Robert C. Morris, J. Francisco de Rada, James G. Swisher, Miguel Arciñiega, Interpreter. John Cameron, Interpreter.

I consent to, and will observe, the above article. Martin Perfecto De Cos. Ratified and approved. Edward Burleson, Commander-in-Chief Volunteer Army.
A true copy.

Edward leson, Commander-in-Chief.

An inventory, showing the pieces of artillery, muskets, cannons, lances, and ammunition, was delivered by Juan Cortina, J. Francisco de Rada, and Francisco Herrera, and received by James Cheshire, William G. Cooke, and W. H. Patton.

F. W. Johnston, Col. Com'g.

The arguments continued until well past midnight. At 2 a.m., the parties agreed to terms and submitted the document to their commanders. "I acceded immediately," Burleson explained, "deeming the terms highly favorable, considering the strong position and large force of the enemy, which could not be less than thirteen hundred effective men." Cos signed as well. Béxar was a battleground no longer.

DECEMBER 11

Or was it? The Federalist rank and file believed they had a say. "No ashy faces now," wrote Henry Dance, "all a good humoured dirty long bearded set." The army assembled at 10 a.m., and Colonel Johnson informed the men that the fight was over, "addressing us in a very candid maner on the nature of the treaty and of our unfit condition to carry on war." The Federalist officers took charge of their men, insisting that each volunteer had the right to ratify or reject the Centralist surrender. If the men decided the battle would continue, there would be little their officers could do. Johnson and his men urged that the surrender be accepted. "The Return was made in a few minutes with a small majority <u>for</u> it," Dance remembered, "which caused some new troubles." One of the most outspoken opponents was Lieutenant William Ridgeway Carey. Wounded on the first day of the battle, he had boldly served the Texian artillery that had silenced the Centralist gun at the end of Acéquia Street. "A child's bargain," he grumbled. He was in the minority, though. Most of the men celebrated the victory. "Clear of enimys," crowed Dance, "we now had a splendid Spanish fandango."

18

THE FUTURE OF TEXAS

Béxar was a battleground no longer. On December 11, Colonel Francis W. Johnson penned his official battle report to Colonel Burleson. He concluded his brief litany of brave comrades, notable losses, and glories gained by stating: "The period put to our present war by the fall of San Antonio de Bexar, will, I trust, be attended with all the happy results to Texas which her warmest friends could desire."

On December 14, Burleson wrote to Henry Smith, the newly installed provisional governor of Texas, about the situation in Béxar. "General Cos left this morning for the mission of San José, and, to-morrow, commences his march to the Rio Grande," Burleson reported, "after complying with all that had been stipulated." The Texian military leader reported that more than 1,100 Centralist troops had evacuated the town, but many of them had peeled off the main column to make their own way to the Rio Grande.

There was also the butcher's bill to discuss. Dr. Samuel Stivers and Dr. Amos Pollard reported a total of two killed, two mortally wounded, and nineteen additional wounded in the ninety-eight hours of fighting. The Mexican army figures, though, remained unclear. While a few deaths occurred among the cavalry companies, most of the casualties were in the artillery company and the Morelos Battalion that tried valiantly to hold the plazas. Some believed Cos had lost more than 150 killed, wounded, and missing.

This task accomplished, the Federalist army of Texas — Stephen F. Austin's Army of the People — began to rattle apart. Having filed his reports, Burleson turned the command at Béxar over to Johnson. Within

To attempt to give you a faint idea of the intrepid conduct of the gallant citizens who formed the division under my command, during the whole period of the attack, would be a task of no common nature, and far above the power of my pen. All behaved with the bravery peculiar to freemen, and with a decision becoming the sacred cause of liberty.

The memory of Colonel Ben R. Milam, the leader of this daring and successful attack, deserves to be cherished by every patriotic bosom in Texas.

I feel indebted to the able assistance of Colonel Grant, (severely wounded the first day), Colonel W. T. Austin, Majors S. Morris and Moore, Adjutant Brister, Lieutenant Colonel Franks of the artillery, and every captain . . . who entered with either division, from the morning of the 5th, until the day of the capitulation.

Doctors Levy and Pollard also deserve my warmest praise, for their unremitted attention and assiduity.

Dr. John Cameron's conduct during the siege and treaty of capitulation, merits particular mention; the guides, Messrs. Erastus Smith, Hendrick Arnold and John W. Smith, performed important service; and I cannot conclude without expressing my thanks to the reserve under your command for such assistance as could be afforded me during our most critical movements.

The period put to our present war by the fall of San Antonio de Bexar, will, I trust, be attended with all the happy results to Texas which her warmest friends could desire.

Colonel Francis Johnson

weeks, hotspurs among the Texian leadership urged an advance against Matamoros, an impulse from the earliest days of the rebellion. By month's end, Johnson, Dr. James Grant, and most of the Federalist Army of Texas — the volunteers who had barely taken Béxar — had passed down the San Antonio River to rendezvous at Goliad with troops under Colonel James Fannin and Colonel James Bowie. From there, they would launch their campaign into the interior of Mexico. At the same time, Sam Houston continued his work as the commander of a new, regular army of Texas. His command was separate from the ragged troops who had captured Béxar. The confusion over who was in command, whether Johnson, Fannin, or Houston, and disagreements among the leaders of the Texas rebellion as to strategic direction resulted in a collapse of the insurgent government.

For the Spanish-speaking Texian Federalists in Plácido Benavides' and Juan Seguín's companies, the fight was over. They returned to their homes and ranchos, proud that they had taken this stand for their rights under the Federal Constitution of 1824. Yet three months later these same men, including many local Bexareños, would again be called upon to rally around a different standard: the flag of independence. For many, this was clearly more than they had bargained for. They remained loyal to Mexico — Federalist Mexico — and wanted no part in a breakaway republic, especially one dominated by Americans. This would create for many a division of loyalties, even within families.

Meanwhile, in Béxar, Colonel James C. Neill did the best he could with the remnant he had been left. He counted no more than 100 men to hold the town and the Alamo, and Grant and Johnson had taken most of the provisions and supplies. He focused his efforts on shoring up the battered walls of the Alamo until someone in authority could decide the future fate of Texas. By mid-January, Bowie and a handful of volunteers were headed to Béxar to retrieve Neill and abandon the town. Instead, impressed with Neill's efforts and the amount of artillery that remained on hand — "we could whip 10 to 1 with our artillery," claimed engineer Green Jameson — Bowie decided to keep the garrison in place. Neill had convinced him. "No other man in the army could have kept men at this post," Bowie reported to the Texian government, "under the neglect they have experienced."

What passed for the revolutionary government of Texas responded with reinforcements. William Barret Travis, who had figured so prominently in the early days of Béxar's siege, found himself a lieutenant colonel of regulars at the head of thirty or so mounted troops heading for the Alamo.

Of the hundreds of volunteers who had besieged Béxar and followed Ben Milam into the heart of the Centralist defenses, few remained just two months after the guns had fallen silent. Yet at least twenty-seven of the participants across the battleground of Béxar remained at the Alamo. This included the First Company, New Orleans Greys. One of its members, Lieutenant William Ridgeway Carey, was promoted to captain and placed in command of the Alamo's artillery company. The Siege and Battle of Béxar would never be accorded the historical niche attained by the last stand at the Alamo in 1836 or given the attention received by the vengeful victory at San Jacinto. It was, however, a superb example of the courage, determination, aggressiveness, tenacity, confusion, and luck that marked what became known as the Texas Revolution.

Subsequent events also shaped the way the events would be remembered. Names once celebrated in 1835 found themselves eclipsed just a few months later. Stephen Fuller Austin was the rebellion's greatest and earliest contributor and a talented war leader. Yet he is remembered more as a competent bureaucrat and diplomat today, and even then he

Colonel Neill's small command in San Antonio, in early January of 1836, was described by him in a letter to Governor Henry Smith on the 6th: "We have 104 men, and two distinct fortresses to garrison, and about 24 pieces of artillery … no Provisions or clothing in this garrison since Johnson and Grant left … [his men] not even sufficiently clad for Summer, many of them have but one blanket, and one Shirt."

Captain William Carey of the artillery company wrote to his siblings on January 12th that Colonel Neill's quarters were in the town, while he, Carey, commanded at the Alamo, but how many men were stationed there with him is not known.

There is no evidence that the Texians had already begun the dismantling any of General Cos's defense works constructed the previous fall. These included, as seen in the drawing, the palisade-and-earth wall that "enclosed" San Fernando Church, as well as the scaffold ramp built by the Mexicans to quickly access the roof of the church and haul cannon there. The precise location of this ramp is not known; its depiction here is purely hypothetical but certainly logical.

By January 18th, however, Captain Green B. Jameson wrote to Houston: "We have too few to garrison both places and will bring all our forces to the Alamo tomorrow as well as the cannons." If the cannon were hauled to the Alamo from the town on the 19th, all the men did not entirely abandon San Antonio, as subsequent events proved. But it is likely that the Texians finally did begin the process of tearing down Cos's fortifications around this time, and probably began transferring many of their timbers to the Alamo. Among the defence works in the fort that were probably constructed from the Mexican fortifications in the town was the interior wood-and-earth battery facing the Alamo's main gate.

It must be said that both Neill and Jameson complained that the private soldiers were reluctant — and most of the time even refused — to work, and that most of the labor was done by the officers. The men felt they had good cause for refusing to work in Neill's own words they were "almost naked" for lack of clothing, and they had received none of he promised payment for their service.

continued on page 154 ▶

was largely in the shadow of more popular personalities like Houston. Benjamin R. Milam, who had been a bold adventurer in the early days of the Spanish borderlands and Mexican Texas, faded from the scene until he is now barely remembered for uttering his famous challenge to assault Béxar before the army disintegrated. His death in battle placed him in the forefront of the Texian martyrs, but there would soon be many others.

Of all the participants, though, Colonel Frank Johnson is perhaps the most curious. He had been an early agitator for the rights of the American colonists in the face of Centralist demands and had been involved in some of the early dustups between Texians and government forces. He was the principal architect of the insurgent victory at Béxar. Then, wrapped up in the Matamoros fever of December 1835 and January 1836, he found himself eclipsed by the likes of Fannin and Houston. The men who remained loyal

▶ continued from page 153

The drawing shows a dawn roll call on the Main Plaza parade ground, and the motley crew the Texians must have appeared in early January: many men dressed in just shirts and trousers, a few lucky ones in greatcoats or blanket coats, some wrapped with blankets, and all possessing a variety of headgear, footwear, and weapons.

Description and art by Gary Zaboly. From Phil Collins, The Alamo and Beyond: A Collector's Journey (Kerrville, Texas: State House Press, 2012).

Description and art by Gary Zaboly

to him were largely annihilated in March 1836 at the Battle of San Patricio, although Johnson escaped. A commander without an army, he essentially quit the Texian cause. He spent the next few years attempting to remake his fortunes but instead went bankrupt and fled Texas, abandoning his family. His wife divorced him.

Yet like many Texans before and since, he made a comeback. He returned in 1847, remarried his wife, and settled in Ellis County. As secessionist agitation led to the American Civil War, Johnson left the state again, this time for Indianapolis, Indiana. After that conflict, Johnson returned to Texas and lived in Round Rock and Austin, devoting his time to researching and writing about the early days of Texas. He died in 1884.

In 1914, The American Historical Society published his collected works, *A History of Texas and Texans*, which remains a critical source for understanding the motivations and personalities of that tumultuous period.

BIBLIOGRAPHIC ESSAY

We certainly have become aware, over the decades, of all the publications out there about the Battle of the Alamo. Numerous books tell the story of the epic thirteen-day siege and last stand that took place in San Antonio, Texas, in 1836. Movies and television have portrayed William Barret Travis and Jim Bowie along with the nationally famous adventurer Davy Crockett as they led nearly 200 brave Anglo Americans and Tejanos (Texas Mexicans) in the attempt to hold off thousands of Mexican soldiers under the command of Centralist General Antonio López de Santa Anna.

Out of curiosity one day (and with a twinkle in my eye), I asked a well-known Texas historian how many "acts" there were in the Texas Revolution of 1835-36. His response was that there were two: Act I, he said, was the Siege and Fall of the Alamo, and Act II, the Texan victory at San Jacinto forty-six days later. I smiled and thanked him, leaving him perhaps with the feeling that I thought he was wrong.

Well, friends, the Texas Revolution was really a classic three-act play! The Alamo and San Jacinto were only Acts II and III. The first act several months earlier was a thirty-five-day siege followed by the four-day/four-night battle dubbed the Battle of Béxar (San Antonio).

Like so many other kids in the mid-1950s, I got hooked on the Battle of the Alamo from watching movies and TV shows that captured my imagination. As I grew older, Dad bought me several books on this very engaging — and true — story. I learned that the Alamo was more than just a fort in the middle of nowhere. It was at the edge of the town of San Antonio de Béxar (now part of modern downtown San Antonio). A 1955 children's book titled *The Story of the Alamo: Told in Exciting Pictures* by Frederic Ray opened with an illustration showing the main plaza of the Spanish Colonial town, and in the middle was its cool San Fernando Church. I was hooked, and I wanted to know more.

My first real book was Lon Tinkle's *13 Days to Glory: The Siege of the Alamo* (New York, McGraw-Hill Book Company, Inc., 1958). It presented this great Texas story as an exciting adventure — a good read, mostly read to me by my father. Three years later, Walter Lord's *A Time to Stand* (New York, Harper & Brothers, 1961) hit the bookshelves. As opposed to *13 Days to Glory*, this was a well-researched historical narrative that greatly increased my understanding of the facts, rather than just the oft-told "Texas creation myth." Without trying, it also succeeded in drawing my attention to the myraid errors in the very popular 1960 John Wayne movie *The Alamo*, which I had just seen thirteen times in six months.

My own development over the course of these two books and epic movie was unique. I began to gain an understanding of the real history of the Alamo rather than the myth, and this stimulated my desire to know even more. I became fascinated by the fact that there was actually a flowing river — and a large town — outside the fort's walls. This was a San Antonio very different from the Hollywood western movie-style village built for John Wayne's film, and I got to explore it in 1961 when Dad and Mother took me to San Antonio for the first time. Suddenly my passion was for more than just the Alamo.

The long-neglected Act I of the Texas War of Independence (October, November, and December 1835), with its five-week siege and four-day/four-night battle, is altogether as engaging in its goals, actions, setbacks, details, and intrigues as the rest of the story. The cast of characters is just as colorful as in the later months with many of the same performers, and the conclusion is quite dramatic. To my knowledge, the only book totally devoted to telling this story has been Alwyn Barr's fine 72-page jewel, *Texans in Revolt: The Battle of San Antonio, 1835* (Austin, Texas: University of Texas Press, 1990). While lacking in quotations from primary sources, the book thoroughly and accurately covers the events. It is the book that inspired me to tackle this one, and it was always by my side for guidance.

For the many quotes of battle participants in my book, I have depended primarily on a wonderful ten-volume set of reference books that I have owned since their publication: *Papers of the Texas Revolution 1835-1836* (Austin, Texas: Presidial Press, 1973), John H. Jenkins, general editor. If these had not been handy on my shelf, my book would never have been attempted.

Additional books in my library that I have used for various details include the following:

Richard Bruce Winders' excellent study *Sacrificed at the Alamo: Tragedy and Triumph in the Texas Revolution* (Abilene, Texas: State House Press, 2004) provided me with something I couldn't find anywhere else in my collection: a thorough explanation of the art of war and military techniques of nineteenth-century North America. Dr. Winders (past curator and historian at the Alamo for over twenty-three years) and I are old friends and collaborated as consultants for the Bexar County Parks Centennial Commission in late 2019 and early 2020.

Of all the actual 1835 participants quoted in my book, the most thorough eyewitness account of the final battle comes from Herman Ehrenberg, a German immigrant searching for adventure and excitement in Texas. His narrative, which he wrote after returning to Germany, is taken from *Inside the Texas Revolution: The Enigmatic Memoir of Herman Ehrenberg.* It was edited by Dr. James E. Crisp and translated from German by Louis E. Brister with the assistance of James C. Kearney (Austin: Texas State Historical Association, 2021). Many thanks to Crisp for making sections available to me before the book was published so I could weave Ehrenberg's material into the story.

Another key player in our story is Juan Nepomuceno Seguín. This popular Tejano resident of San Antonio de Béxar, like many other Tejanos and Anglo-American settlers of Texas, fought against President Santa Anna, who had just disbanded their Federal constitutional government and established a Centralist despotism in its place. Seguín's complete story is well told by Jesús F. de la Teja in *A Revolution Remembered: The Memoirs and Selected Correspondence of Juan N. Seguín* (Abilene, Texas: State House Press, 1991). Seguín is one of my favorite players and clearly demonstrates that this early stage of the war was not about Americans vs. Mexicans but rather Federalism vs. Centralism.

Various accounts from newspaper articles of the day quoting battle participants were of great enlightenment, reaching beyond the standard historical view. These are to be found in Gary S. Zaboly's *An Altar for Their Sons: The Alamo and the Texas Revolution in Contemporary Newspaper Accounts* (Buffalo Gap, Texas: State House Press, 2011). This book is an excellent source of previously unknown details and is highlighted by Zaboly's well-researched illustrations.

While my attention was focused on the last three months of 1835 and not on earlier events, it quickly became necessary to provide additional background material using these as well. Stephen L. Hardin's *Texian Illiad: A Military History of the Texas Revolution* (Austin, Texas: University of Texas Press, 1994) came to the rescue with nearly everything I needed. This superb and engaging history, along with more helpful illustrations by Gary Zaboly, provided all the basics. For additional details, I used Paul D. Lack's *The Texas Revolutionary Experience: A Political and Social History, 1835-1836* (College Station, Texas A&M University Press, 1992).

Biographical backgrounds were also needed for key players. Eugene C. Barker's *The Life of Stephen F. Austin: Founder of Texas, 1793-1836* (Austin, Texas State Historical Association, 1949) provided a solid foundation for this most important central figure, and Greg Cantrell's *Stephen F. Austin: Empresario of Texas* (New Haven and London: Yale University Press, 1999) written fifty years later brought much new information to the table.

Since Sam Houston also plays a part in this story, it became necessary to dig even deeper through my library. I succeeded in unearthing Donald Braider's *Solitary Star: A Biography of Sam Houston* (New York: G. P. Putnam's Sons, c. 1974); Marquis James's *The Raven: The Story of Sam Houston* (Indianapolis and New York: The Bobbs-Merrill Company, Inc., 1929); and Llerena B. Friend's *Sam Houston: The Great Designer* (Austin, University of Texas Press, 1969). I was also quite fascinated to discover what Houston's contemporaries had to say about him.

The four Spanish Franciscan missions downriver from San Antonio de Béxar, all now part of the San Antonio Missions National Historical Park, served as steppingstones for General Austin's "Federal Army of the People" as they approached the town in late October 1835 determined to oust Centralist General Martín Perfecto de Cos from the town plazas and the Alamo. Mission Espada, the farthest from town, was used as a campsite by James Bowie's division and later for Austin's main force. The first battle took place in a bend of the San Antonio River 600 yards northwest of Mission Concepción, and only two miles from town. Austin later used this mission as temporary headquarters. My source of information for all the missions was James E. Ivey's *Of Various Magnificence: The Architectural History of the San Antonio Missions in the Colonial Period and the Nineteenth Century* (Center for Cultural Sustainability, University of Texas Press at San Antonio in association with the National Park Service). I have always had a passion for these historic landmarks, spending many hours exploring and photographing them, and the details in Jake Ivey's dissertation provided a whole new level of understanding. I was able to apply this knowledge to the two virtual mission models I constructed and used for appropriate illustrations.

Austin's letters, located in *Papers of the Texas Revolution*, contain information on the artillery that was available to the Federalists, and at least one of these cannons (the 12-pounder gunade) is still on exhibit at the Alamo. For additional information, I depended on James V. Woodrick's *Cannons of the Texas Revolution* (self-published, 2015). This provided information about the artillery used by both armies during the Siege of Béxar, and particularly why the long-awaited 18-pounder, later used against Santa Anna in the Siege of the Alamo, never made it to Béxar in time to help the insurgents breach and capture the town plazas.

Illustrations for the book were "photographed" from several 3-D virtual computer models I have researched and constructed over the past fifteen years. These are of the Alamo, San Antonio de Béxar, Mission

Concepción, and Mission Espada as they would have appeared in 1835. The Sources for creating the accurate appearance of the town and buildings came from early paintings and drawings. One of the best was *A Seth Eastman Sketchbook, 1848-1849* published by the Marion Koogler McNay Art Institute with an introduction by Lois Burkhalter (Austin, Texas: University of Texas Press, 1961). James Patrick McGuire's book *Hermann Lungkwitz, Romantic Landscapist on the Texas Frontier* (Austin: University of Texas Press, 1983) provided paintings from 1856, including a view of the Alameda, a grove of cottonwood trees flanking the road that is now East Commerce Street. These trees were there during the Texas Revolution and are in my virtual model.

It goes without saying that scale models can be very educational. Texas artist-historian George Nelson has built one of San Antonio de Béxar as it was in 1835-36 that makes a viewer want to shrink himself down and walk the streets. This model tends to show up in different places over the years and has been on exhibit in San Antonio at the Witte Museum as well as in North Star Mall. Nelson's book *The Alamo: An Illustrated History* also has a two-page spread with his accurate aerial-view painting of Béxar and the Alamo looking from the southwest — a fine reference.

In addition, the following books were used for my research: Wallace Woolsey's *Memoirs for the History of the War in Texas*; J. R. Edmondson's *The Alamo Story: From Early History to Current Conflicts*; Jesús F. de la Teja's *San Antonio de Béxar: A Community on New Spain's Northern Frontier*; Craig H. Roell's *Remember Goliad*; Charles Ramsdell's *San Antonio: A Historical and Pictorial Guide*; Noah Smithwick's *The Evolution of a State or Recollections of Old Texas Days*; Richard Boyd Hauck's *Davy Crockett: A Handbook*; Archie P. McDonald's *Travis*; General Vicente Filisola's *The History of the War in Texas, Vol. 2*; Todd Henson's *The Alamo Reader: A Study in History*; Frank W. Johnson's *A History of Texas and Texans*; Phil Collins' *The Alamo and Beyond: A Collector's Journey*; Henderson Yoakum's *History of Texas*; and finally Bill Groneman's *Alamo Defenders — A Genealogy: The People and Their Words*.

It is becoming apparent that I could fill half the pages of this book with references to other books. I have indeed presented the best that I have found over the course of my life, and these have aided me in the preparation of yet another.

—*Richard L. Curilla*
May 12, 2022

ENDNOTES

CHAPTER 1

1 Lieutenant Francisco de Castañeda was in command of the Alamo de Parras presidial company permanently stationed in the Alamo. He owned the two northernmost stone houses attached to the inside of the west wall of the Alamo compound. Road mileages are based on research on 1835-36 routes.

2 The full name of the presidio (fort) was Nuestra Señora Santa María de Loreto de la Bahía del Espíritu Santo. Understandably, it was commonly known simply as Presídio La Bahía. A small Mexican village stood next to the fort and had just been renamed Goliad (Goliadh), an anagram of "Hidalgo" in honor of Father Miguel Hidalgo y Costilla, who had started the rebellion that ultimately liberated Mexico from Spain.

3 Don Miguel Barragán was a military hero during the days of the Mexican War for Independence and drifted away from his early Federalists leanings to become a reliable and trusted Centralist operator. While Santa Anna operated against insurrections in the country, he left Barragán in place as president, and he served from January 28, 1835 until illness forced him to leave office on February 27, 1836. He died three days later.

CHAPTER 2

1 A quire of paper is about 25 sheets, or about 1/20 of a ream.

2 Benjamin Fort Smith was a 39-year-old from Logan County, Kentucky. He fought in the Creek Indian War and served on General Andrew Jackson's staff during the Battle of New Orleans. He came to Texas in 1832 to import enslaved workers to the region.

3 Richard Bruce Winders' *Sacrificed at the Alamo: Tragedy and Triumph in the Texas Revolution* (Abilene, Texas: State House Press, 2004) provides an excellent understanding of frontier militia, their benefits, and their problems.

4 A beegum is a tall cylindrical hat and gets its name from the long straight trunk of a tree where honeybee nests could often be found.

CHAPTER 3

1 Tenoxtitlan was a Mexican fort constructed of logs in 1830 on the west bank of the Brazos River twelve miles above the ford of the San Antonio and Nacogdoches Road. By 1835, its Mexican garrison had moved out and it was occupied by Anglo-Americans, who had even set up a general store to trade manufactured goods for beaver pelts with the Indians.

2 Ezekiel Williams became judge for DeWitt's Colony (Gonzales) on April 21, 1834.

3 This camp was about 1.5 miles upstream from the present-day community of La Vernia.

CHAPTER 4

1 The three missions are, from south to north, San Francisco de la Espada, San Juan de Capistrano, and San José y San Miguel de Aguayo. A fourth, dangerously close to Béxar, is Mission Nuestra Señora de la Purísima Concepción de Acuña, or simply Mission Concepción. All four of these missions were secularized in 1824. A fifth mission, oldest of them all, was secularized in 1793. It was named San António de Valero but now commonly called the Álamo after a company of presidial soldiers stationed there from 1801 to 1824 who were from a town in Coahuila named Pueblo de San José y Santiago del Álamo de Parras. They began to call the mission El Álamo de Parras after their hometown in Coahuila. This name continued to be used by the locals, who sometimes shortened it to El Álamo.

2   Conclusions come from the thorough research of Richard Range. Also, there was no 18-pounder on the December 1835 capitulation inventory. The 18-pounder used at the Siege of the Alamo in 1836 arrived in San Antonio on December 12, 1835, three days after the capitulation. The 9-inch *pedrero*, on the other hand, was on the inventory. James V. Woodrick's *Cannons of the Texas Revolution* is a valuable resource as well.

3   Austin was drooling and may have been showing signs of the tuberculosis infection he picked up in prison, or he may have been suffering from nausea or from an upper respiratory infection.

CHAPTER 5

1   Starting from the gate of Mission Espada, it was 5.30 miles to the river ford south of Mission Concepción, 6.14 miles to Concepción, 8.50 miles to the river ford at La Villita and 8.75 miles to the S.E. corner of Plaza de las Islas (the central plaza) in Béxar.

2   More than likely this was Padre Refúgio de la Garza from San Fernando Church in town, who owned much of the land along the river southwest of the mission. Bowie and his late wife María Úrsula de Veramendi were married by Padre de la Garza in 1831. The sentinel in the bell tower was twenty-five-year-old Lieutenant Robert James Calder who in 1832 had come to Texas from Maryland with his grandfather and widowed mother.

3   The numbers given by the unit commander Lieutenant Colonel Mendoza are in his report of the battle. Primary sources variously call this a 4-pounder and a 6-pounder. The most reliable evidence calls it a 6-pounder.

4   Henry Wax Karnes was a native of Tennessee but grew to adulthood in Arkansas Territory where he learned the skills of a backwoodsman. He would prove brave and intrepid during the Texas Revolution and rose to the rank of captain in the Texian cavalry by the Battle of San Jacinto, April 21, 1836. He continued his service to the Republic of Texas until grievously wounded by a Comanche in an 1839 battle and falling to yellow fever the next year.

5   Maverick's hearing "9 rounds of artillery" corresponds precisely with Bowie's report of the battle.

6   Bowie apparently wrote his official report, from which all his above quotes have been taken, several days after the battle.

7   The Mexican infantry (seventy men) was led by Lieutenant Colonel José María Mendoza. The cavalry (209 men) was led by Captain Rafael de Ugartechea. Two companies of light-horse presidial soldiers stationed in the Alamo (sixty men) were led by Lieutenant Francisco de Castañeda. Austin no doubt believed that it was Colonel Domingo Ugartechea, who apparently remained in town with General Cos.

8   It is not clear whether the Federalist army camped at the mission or along the river where Bowie and Fannin originally camped, although Austin apparently used the mission as his headquarters several times during the rest of the siege.

CHAPTER 6

1   The 18-pounder was awaiting large wheels to support its weight so it could be pulled over the roads to Bexar. The expected vessel on the coast and additional "accessions" in Natchitoches, suggested 300 reinforcements were on their way rather than 145.

2   A look forward in history reveals that Royall ultimately succeeded in locating or making appropriate wheels to transport the 18-pounder, but not in time to meet Austin's needs. On January 16, 1836, a man named John W. Little was paid $35 for "bringing wheels of 18 pdr. from Matagorda to Bexar." While the 18-pounder tube (barrel) arrived in Béxar on December 12, 1835, after Cos surrendered, the wheels did not arrive until January 16, 1836, and the cannon was probably mounted in the Alamo two days later.

CHAPTER 7

1 Dr. John Sutherland, who was in Béxar between the Battle of Béxar and the Siege of the Alamo, stated in his memoirs: "When Col Almonte arrived on the 23rd February, he Started a flag to Col Travis, which was met by one from Travis, carried by Maj. Morris & Capt. Martin, the flags met on the footbridge leading from the city to the Alamo (there was no wagon bridge then)."

2 The depiction of a two-story wing on the northwest corner of San Fernando Church in my virtual model rather than the one-story wing in all early photos is the result of the research of colleague Brad Ponder. The pre-photography drawings of the church clearly show this feature as depicted, and the failing parts of the church architecture were rebuilt in the time between the revolution and the first photograph.

CHAPTER 8

1 Cos does not have an 18-pounder. It is possible that, since Sam Maverick has been sneaking messages out to Austin, Maverick's earlier mistake in relation to the size of the cannon rushed past him to the Alamo is responsible for this error. Maverick said it was an 18-pounder, but it was most likely the 12-pound *pedrero* that Cos had used three days before to fire on Austin's cannoneers. Perhaps this is Austin's source for his comment.

CHAPTER 10

1 In Austin's order of November 21, he says the distance from the planned Dirt Battery to "the walls of the fortifications" is only 300 yards. Primary accounts clearly state that the site of the Dirt Battery was on the west side of the river. Assuming that the battery was in the cul-de-sac below the Garza Mill — the closest possible point to the Alamo across the river — its actual distance would have been at least 450 yards. If Austin meant the fortified town plazas, it would have been 800 yards. Even the northern part of town (the nearest to the battery) was 500 yards away. It must be remembered that Austin would not have had a map or the opportunity to pace off the actual distance.

2 Erastus (Deaf) Smith (1787-1837) was born in New York State and lived for a time in Natchez, Mississippi Territory; he lost his hearing due to a childhood illness. He settled in San Antonio in 1821, where he married a Mexican widow the following year. Upon trying to enter San Antonio to visit his family in 1835, he was rudely denied entry by a Mexican sentry and thereupon joined Stephen F. Austin's besieging army. Smith was extraordinarily active during all phases of the Texas Revolution. As he composed his memoir in 1842, Ehrenberg was aware of Smith's service as commander of a company of Texas Rangers that defeated a Mexican force at Laredo, on the Rio Grande, in February 1837. Smith died nine months later after resigning from the service.

CHAPTER 13

1 Thanks to Clinton M. M. McKenzie of the Department of Archaeology, University of Texas at San Antonio, for researching and pinning down the location of the Cadena house.

2 Ehrenberg here echoes a line from the "band of brothers" address by William Shakespeare's King Henry V, from *The Life of King Henry the Fifth,* Act IV, Scene iii: "The fewer men, the greater share of honour."

CHAPTER 14

1 The existence and location of this lime kiln are revealed in the field notes and plat of a land survey made by Francois Giraud for William Elliott on September 18, 1848, located in the San Antonio Archives, Civil Engineer Survey Book 1, pp. 32-33. The lot was being purchased from José Antonio de la Garza, and the kiln was used as the benchmark for the survey. Lime kilns were numerous in Spanish Colonial San Antonio due to the continual need for lime in construction.

2 The large double doors of the Veramendi Palace entrance have for many years been on exhibit in the Alamo in San Antonio.

[3]   Primary accounts from participants in the 1835-36 war refer to the two westernmost houses on the north side of Plaza de las Islas as the Yturri houses, and yet current research by the University of Texas at San Antonio as presented in its archaeological report reveals that Manuel Yturri purchased these two houses from Francisco de Arocha on March 6, 1838, so it is assumed that Yturri lived in them before he purchased the lots.

[4]   All information on Cos's artillery count and caliber is based on the thorough research of Richard Range and James Woodrick presented in James V. Woodrick's *Cannons of the Texas Revolution*. It is unknown how many of Cos' cannon were in the Alamo and how many in town at any specific time. Some primary accounts refer to two guns being at each street barricade, but research better supports the presence of only one cannon at each of the Soledad and Acéquia street batteries.

[5]   With permission of the Spanish governor, Garza became the first person to coin money in Texas. On one side of the coin were his initials, "JAG," and the date 1818; on the other side was a single star, perhaps the first use of the "Lone Star" in association with Texas.

[6]   In Gary Zaboly's, *An Altar for Their Sons: The Alamo and the Texas Revolution in Contemporary Newspaper Accounts* (Buffalo Gap, Texas: State House Press, 2011), singer Phil Collins, who has a large collection of 1835-36 artifacts, explains the background of the East India Brown Bess musket, one of his prized artifacts:

"During those wars [the Napoleonic Wars], a staggering 2.8 million of these Brown Bess muskets were produced for the British government. They obviously thought they were going to be busy not only building the empire but also enforcing it. When the wars ended in 1815, there was a considerable surplus, so in 1823 when the Republic of Mexico needed replacements for its poor weapons, a contract was agreed upon to purchase the surplus firearms for Mexico. The predominant weapon was the East India Brown Bess and many of [these] muskets were among those sold, finally ending up in Texas and used at the Alamo, Goliad, and San Jacinto. This sale from England to Mexico continued until 1835."

CHAPTER 15

[1]   Wilhelm Langenheim (1816-74) was indeed a Braunschweiger (in English, from the city of Brunswick, in today's Lower Saxony, near Hanover). After coming to the United States in 1830, he settled in Texas in 1833 with other emigrants from Ireland and Germany in the Power and Hewetson Colony, which came to include the settlement at Refugio. In 1835, Langenheim joined with the Texan forces besieging San Antonio, where he served as an artilleryman. He was captured in 1836 along with other men serving with Frank W. Johnson on the prospective Matamoros Expedition. He ended up imprisoned in that city until released by the Mexicans in 1837. An amateur geologist and chemist, he later became a prominent photographer with a studio in Philadelphia, where he died in 1874.

INDEX